D1522718

Siege in Lucasville

Gary Williams

ROOFTOP
publishing

Rooftop Publishing™
1663 Liberty Drive, Suite 200
Bloomington, IN 47403
Phone: 1-800-839-8640

First published by Rooftop 09/15/06

ISBN: 1-60008-005-7

Library of Congress Control Number: 2006930144

Printed in the United States of America
Bloomington, Indiana

This book is printed on acid-free paper.

All photographs provided by the Ohio State Highway Patrol, Lt. Howard W. Hudson, III and used by permission of the Hamilton County, Ohio Prosecutor's Office, Mark Piepmier, Special SOCF Prosecutor.

The author has endeavored to write as fair and accurate a book as he could. The events recounted in this book took place during a confusing and difficult period. Memories of some of the participants vary and witnesses' accounts may differ. Any slights of people, agencies, or organizations are unintentional and the author cannot be held liable for errors, inaccuracies, omissions, or other inconsistencies.

Acknowledgments

This work has been a compilation of years' worth of memories, documents, and reports. Dozens of public employees have contributed significantly to the research and documentation contained in this book, and I am indebted to each of them.

A special thank you to the following: Rodney McIntosh, Nancy Frye, Arthur Tate, Anthony Brigano, Helen Thompson, Phil Millhouse, Lt. John Wood, Captain Troy Lynch, and Richard Jesko. To Cliff Crooks, my mentor of several years, who believed in this project and me when I didn't believe in myself, thank you will never be enough.

My heartfelt appreciation to Matthew Patton and Kevin King at both AuthorHouse and Rooftop Publishing for their constant inspiration and gentle persuasion in keeping this project moving forward.

A special and sincere thank you to all of the hundreds of present and former staff of the Southern Ohio Correctional Facility in Lucasville, Ohio, for their encouragement and sacrifice. To the family of Correction Officer Robert "Bobby" Vallandingham, nothing we say here will ease the pain of your loss. Only time and the grace and mercy of a loving God can accomplish that. Please take comfort in knowing that your ultimate sacrifice is not forgotten and serves as a source of strength and encouragement for all Ohio correctional personnel.

Acknowledging the work and sacrifice of others would not be complete without the special mention of the leadership of the Ohio Civil Service Employees Association (OCSEA), Local 11, of the

American Federation of State, County, and Municipal Employees (AFSCME). AFSCME President Gerald McEntee, OCSEA President Ronald Alexander, and SOCF Chief Steward Nate Miller have sought to keep the memory of April 11-22, 1993, alive. Corrections Assembly President Tim Shafer's tireless work on the front lines to keep the interest of public officials focused and to properly fund our correctional facilities and the officers who staff them through the AFSCME-funded Corrections United is critical to all who work inside correctional facilities. His near decade of selfless advocacy on the behalf of correctional employees has helped lead the way to many of the correctional reforms over this period of time. All of us owe him a great deal of gratitude for his sacrifices on our behalf.

The most sincere and heartfelt thank you to Mr. Larry Dotson, whose sacrifice is beyond measure. It has been my honor and privilege to put his message on paper. He is one of the most gracious and genuine individuals I have had the honor to know and serve. To have had the added privilege of working side by side with him for a period of nine years at the Corrections Training Academy is a time that I will not forget.

Contents

Foreword

I've been a corrections professional and employee of the Ohio Department of Rehabilitation and Correction (ODRC) for nearly thirty years. Most of my career has been spent at the Central Office level, managing programs that support the work of front-line employees and their supervisors.

On reflection, I've seen it all in my thirty years or so in the corrections profession, and much of it has been a seesaw of change. There's been one new corrections model after another; a progression of laws that reflect incredible shifts in cultural attitudes about the field of corrections; a phenomenal growth in local, community corrections programs and in the political power they yield; at least one massive prison building program; the birth of highly specialized prisons; privatization of correctional services born from the reengineering government movement; unionization of line staff; one rollercoaster budget cycle after another; and, recently, several prison closings and the resulting layoffs of employees, conducted at the order of the governor to correct budget shortfalls.

During my years in the profession, I've lived through two tragedies, and both impacted me in ways I'm still discovering. The first involved the brutal murder of Parole Officer Robert White, who was shot in the head with his own handgun while working alone on the streets of Cleveland. Officer White's death has driven nearly every decision I've made in my career about the type of resources necessary for parole officers to safely perform their duties.

The second tragedy was the vicious and brutal Easter prison riot that occurred in April 1993 at the maximum-security Southern Ohio Correctional Facility, located in Lucasville, Ohio. Like my colleagues, I spent eleven agonizing days watching TV, listening to the radio, and combing through newspapers trying to get any information I could about the riot and the hostages held by the inmates at Lucasville.

During those horrible days, I also spent considerable time roaming the halls at work talking to friends, some of them in fairly high positions, trying desperately to separate fact from fiction. Of course, I also sought out friends to try and make sense out of a totally senseless act.

I actually thought at the time that my friends would have facts about what was happening at Lucasville and that they'd be willing to share them. I never expected all the facts. I know that when any large governmental agency experiences a major crisis on the scale of the riot at Lucasville, the agency hunkers down and, good or bad, facts become controlled commodities.

Looking back on those eleven days, I would have appreciated any fact. Like my colleagues, I was hoping that firsthand reports from the scene at Lucasville would yield some sign of hope to dispel the nonstop, horrifying rumors about the hostages and inmates that dominated our conversations.

Facts were simply hard to come by for the average ODRC employee during the eleven-day endurance test at Lucasville. The bits and pieces of information we did receive were hard to piece together into any sort of a coherent reality.

As a result, my personal experiences of the riot are a blur of themes and feelings. The themes I recall include the dread I felt about the fate of the hostages, the vicious murder of Correctional Officer Robert "Bobby" Vallandingham, the on again off again negotiations with the inmates, the surreal surrender, and the discovery of the cells inside the devastated prison after the riot where "death squad" inmates murdered their own kind.

Most of us at Central Office didn't know the hostages. We didn't have to know them. They were us. There's no other way to say it, and you have to work in corrections to understand the feeling of family that permeates the business. We worried about the hostages who were hurt, the hostages who were released, and the hostages who were held until the bitter end.

We cried for Correctional Officer Robert Vallandingham and his family when we learned that he'd been killed by inmates. The rumor mill ran rampant about his murder. While the media was spinning their own version of the facts about the killing, we agreed that Robert Vallandingham was killed by the inmates in cold blood to leverage their position during negotiations.

We cheered and then cursed and cheered and cursed again as negotiations with the inmates went up and down. It's been thirteen years since the riot occurred, but I can still hear the voice of inmate negotiator George Skatzes on the radio. I distinctly remember the anger I felt listening to his demands and taunts.

I felt conflicted as I watched the drawn-out, Kabuki-like theatre of the inmate surrender on television. A part of me felt numb, sad, and empty, and a part of me felt happy and relieved to have it finally over.

We all suspected that inmates would run wild inside the prison during the riot and kill other inmates. After all, a riot is like the act of rape. It's about control, submission, and a kind of violence that's unleashed with a fury that's just impossible for the average person to comprehend. My friends and I knew that the riot at Lucasville was no exception, and the worst was confirmed when stories about "death squad" killings circulated shortly after the surrender.

Like my friends and colleagues, I had more questions when the riot ended than when the riot began. What actually caused it? Of all the prisons in Ohio, how could the maximum-security Southern Ohio Correctional Facility be so vulnerable? What were the dynamics that forged the alliances that held different inmate gangs together to sustain an eleven-day riot? What inmates were in charge during the riot, and how did they maintain their power?

How is it that the inmates seemed to anticipate our riot response strategies? Who were the outside negotiators, and why did an attorney from Cleveland play such a prominent role in the negotiated surrender? Why didn't our tactical teams or the Ohio State Highway Patrol or the Ohio National Guard get the approval from the governor to storm the prison to regain control and release the hostages? How were inmates killed by the "death squads"? Who ordered the killings and who carried them out?

The danger of working in corrections was brought home to all ODRC employees in a dramatic fashion during those eleven agonizing days. As a result, in the aftermath of the riot, all ODRC employees expected some answers, any answers, to our questions.

Maybe it's my own experience, but instead of answers, I remember relative silence intermingled with the spin of news releases and official statements mourning the loss of life and decrying the brutality and destruction at the prison. This was followed by reports that weren't readily available to the average employee, legislative hearings, a criminal investigation that focused on the inmates responsible for the takeover and killings, and lawsuits filed by victims, inmates, and others.

For most ODRC employees, the riot resulted in additional levels of bureaucracy, more policies, stricter controls, the shuffling and reshuffling of administrators, increased staffing in prisons, a new specialized level of staff members assigned the job of monitoring inmate gang members, and one interminable training session after another. It was tough to connect the dots to get any real answers to the questions that haunted us.

After their recovery, several of the hostages spoke to employees in training sessions I attended. They used rather broad terms to describe the riot and their personal hostage experiences. They chose their words carefully, and their presentations usually focused on safety preparedness and the mechanics of surviving an event that really amounts to kidnapping and torture.

We treated the hostages with great respect, deference, and kindness. We listened to them carefully and thought we knew what they'd seen and experienced. We thought we knew how they felt. We thought we knew the pain they were feeling. Of course, we couldn't begin to know what they experienced or what they felt.

In the years since the riot, the structural damage at Southern Ohio Correctional Facility has been repaired and a state-of-the-art "super max" prison has been built in Youngstown to house ODRC's most predatory and dangerous inmates.

Lawsuits brought by the hostages, inmates, and inmate families were settled. Employees have come and gone, and many of the principals who made command decisions before, during, and after the riot have retired or moved on to other careers.

Sadly, for many ODRC employees, the eleven-day riot has been relegated to stories and remembrances told by experienced staff members and student discussions in training classes. Robert Vallandingham's ultimate sacrifice is remembered each year when his name and the names of other employees who lost their lives in service to ODRC are read at the annual ODRC memorial service.

Of course, the inmates convicted for crimes committed during the riot, including Robert Vallandingham's murderers, are still incarcerated, most at the "super max" prison in Youngstown. They spend their time doing time and contesting their convictions, which, ironically, is what most of them were doing before they unleashed the 1993 riot.

The answers to my questions were finally answered in 2003, ten years after the riot, when I received the manuscript for *Siege in Lucasville*. I read it through in one sitting, and then read it again. I was struck by Gary Williams' attention to detail, his meticulous background research, and, of course, the riveting and factual account of the riot, told through the eyes of one of the hostages, Larry Dotson.

Larry was the only hostage I knew personally. I met him after the riot when he was assigned to ODRC's training academy as a training officer. I knew Larry as a kind, soft-spoken, God-fearing family man who carried his personal burden of the riot on his broad shoulders with quiet dignity and self-deprecating humor.

While I was full of questions about the riot, I could never bring myself to ask Larry about his experiences. I knew he spent a considerable amount of time telling students at the academy about the riot, and I didn't want to take advantage of our relationship by asking him questions to satisfy my needs. Instead, Larry and I often talked about the values important to him, values associated with family, the loyalty of friendship, the need for a strong faith, living life to the fullest, and the belief that everything happens for a reason.

The depth of information in the original *Siege in Lucasville*, projected against the backdrop of Larry's experiences during those horrific eleven days, finally answered most of my questions about the riot. This edition goes a step further and gives life to the old saying that "every good story teaches a good lesson," because this edition of *Siege in Lucasville* is a great story that teaches a multitude of lessons.

This book is a compilation of available source documents brought together in a comprehensive case study of what happened at Lucasville and why it happened. The multi-layered problems of a large and often cumbersome bureaucracy are laid bare for analysis. As a result, this edition is a must-have for academicians who dissect and evaluate organizational behaviors and, especially, organizational decision making.

The ebb and flow of daily life and mundane routine in prison was literally turned upside down for eleven days in 1993, resulting in the needless murder of a correctional officer, untold trauma to ODRC employee hostages and their families, and the vengeful slaughter of nine inmates by other inmates. For employees relatively new to corrections or anyone contemplating a career in corrections, this story contains one training lesson after another, focusing on the many risks inherent to a corrections job.

Experienced correctional employees, who have devoted some years to their profession, will also benefit from the lessons in this book. For them, *Siege in Lucasville* is a pragmatic survival manual. Larry Dotson's painstaking descriptions of how he acted and coped during his ordeal are invaluable to corrections professionals who ask themselves, "What would I do if this happened to me?"

Prison administrators and managers would do well to heed the lessons in this book that are clearly aimed at them. There's much to be learned about identifying and managing inmate gang members, safeguarding employees who work within the security perimeter of a prison, recognizing and acting on the red flags that could signal an impending riot, understanding the limitations of decision-making that resides in what is essentially a highly charged political situation, balancing use of force and negotiations during a riot or other disorder, and dealing with the aftermath of what is ultimately a life-changing event for an organization, its employees, and employees' families.

Corrections, law enforcement, and other criminal justice and social science students will greatly benefit from this edition of *Siege in Lucasville*. The book contains much more information than the first edition. It remains, however, a textbook study of gangs, life inside a maximum-security prison, and how prison riots form, unfold, explode, and are managed as critical incidents.

Everyone, including the reader with only a casual interest in the events that took place in Lucasville thirteen years ago, can learn something else from this book. At its core, this is an emotional and magnificent story of the triumph of the human spirit, exemplified in the survivor's message of hostage Larry Dotson.

The lessons I've taken from the story told in this and previous editions of *Siege in Lucasville* have taught me a great deal about the precarious balance of safety inside a prison. More important, I've learned a great lesson, through the depth of information provided by Gary Williams and the experiences of Larry Dotson, about the resilience of my fellow professionals and colleagues who work every day inside prisons to keep the community safe. Only time will tell if these lessons are learned by others.

—Cliff W. Crooks

Introduction

Nothing will strike more fear in a correctional staff member's heart than the term *prison riot*. For the 15,000-plus staff members of the Ohio Department of Rehabilitation and Correction (DRC) and the 650-plus staff members assigned to the Southern Ohio Correctional Facility (SOCF), that fear became a stark reality at 2:50 p.m. on April 11, 1993.

As we look back on the nation's longest and third bloodiest prison riot, many lessons have been learned. Unfortunately, many also have not. Every correctional facility or agency believes they are prepared for a major disturbance. In fact, Ohio believed that it was prepared. Then director of the Ohio Department of Rehabilitation and Correction, Dr. Reginald Wilkinson, wrote:

> *Ohio was not unprepared for a riot in 1993. We had in place Disturbance Control Teams, Hostage Negotiation Teams, Sniper Teams, Public Information Teams, and the like. However, our state of readiness perhaps was dwarfed by the unprecedented growth in our inmate population, staff, and number of facilities. Our readiness had been untested for many years at a time.*

In the corrections profession, it is a given that criminals sentenced to prison will remain criminals after arriving in prison and that criminal conduct occurs in prisons on a regular basis. Prison administrators, therefore, have an affirmative duty to be properly and reasonably prepared for all such eventualities and must accept the liability when the inevitable occurs.

The inevitable occurred on April 11, 1993. The cost was measured in terms of lives, facilities, and dollars. However, the real cost cannot be calculated, because it has not yet been fully paid—and it never will be. The lives of hundreds of people were changed in the "blink of an eye" forever on that fateful Easter Sunday in the small southern Ohio town of Lucasville.

For the thirteen staff hostages, their "crime" was being in the right place at the wrong time, or in some cases, the wrong place at the wrong time. Their lives have been changed forever—as have the lives of their families.

For the family of Correction Officer Robert "Bobby" Vallandingham, murdered at the hands of rioting inmates on day five of the riot, nothing can fill the void of a lost loving husband, father, son, and brother. The riot at the Southern Ohio Correctional Facility that began on April 11, 1993, raises several questions:

Could the nation's longest and third deadliest prison riot have been prevented? Were there warning signs? Did the DRC do anything that increased the likelihood of the riot? Did prison administrators and other SOCF staff know there was impending danger of an inmate uprising? Did the SOCF prison administrators make the appropriate notifications and necessary requests? Did those who were entrusted with the authority to act on those requests fail to do so? Did lower-level personnel take the political, economic, and career "hit" for higher-level administrators?

The pages that follow will attempt to answer those questions. Some will disagree with our assessments, findings, and conclusions. We understand. Over three dozen resources were consulted, including official reports from the Ohio State Highway Patrol, Ohio Department of Rehabilitation and Correction, Governor's Media Task Force, Ohio Civil Service Employees Association, Correctional Institution Inspection Committee, and numerous Hamilton County Common Pleas Court and Ohio Supreme Court documents, depositions, and transcripts, as well as media reports from all across Ohio.

We believe the overwhelming majority of Ohio Department of Rehabilitation and Correction as well as Southern Ohio Correctional

Facility staff will concur with our findings, while drawing their own conclusions.

For those who live and work in the "ivory tower," they, no doubt, will disagree. We understand. We also understand that life-and-death decisions are made based on the numbers on a balance sheet and plausible deniability. While we do understand, we respectfully disagree.

This is the story of one hostage—the story of one who survived the eleven days of Lucasville "in the belly of the beast"; the story of one who paid, and continues to pay, the price for the decisions of others whose only price has been that of maintaining their "political cover." Correction administrators at the highest levels have been frequent guests at law enforcement and corrections conferences, symposiums, and meetings. Some have been elected to national office of some of the largest law enforcement associations in the world, enhancing their next career.

For those who paid the real price of the Lucasville riot, such opportunities have not been forthcoming and their story has not been told. For and to those brave individuals and families, this work is written and dedicated.

Part 1:
Pre-Riot

Chapter 1: History

Introduction

April 11th marks the anniversary of the riot at the maximum-security prison known as the Southern Ohio Correctional Facility (SOCF) in Lucasville, Ohio. It was on that date that inmates returned from recreation on Easter Sunday, 1993, assaulted the entry officer, took his keys, and thus began the longest and third deadliest prison riot in United States history.

The aftermath of the eleven-day siege was busy with the physical restoration of the prison, investigations, trials of the inmates involved, re-vamping long-standing policy and procedure, hiring and training new staff, and inevitable rounds of finger pointing. During the course of the riot, eight inmates were murdered at the hands of other inmates, the L-corridor of the prison was totally destroyed by rioting inmates, and $41 million was spent bringing the prison and the department to a "new normal" method of operation.

There was the usual post-incident internal and external "political" posturing, media attention, and creation of media celebrities. As a result, Columbus WBNS television reporter Bob Orr was whisked away to Washington to take a position with the CBS national affiliate. In fact, Lucasville and its aftermath created opportunities for several individuals. Some Department of Rehabilitation and Correction (DRC) administrators subsequently left the department and now are serving as highly paid consultants to federal and state agencies. Others have been frequent speakers on the lecture circuit; some have used their prominent positions in DRC to become office-holders in national correctional organizations and serve on national boards and commissions; and still others have had their careers enhanced through promotional opportunities as a result of the riot. With rare exceptions, this has not been true for the Lucasville hostages.

Much has been written about the inmate rioters, their respective trials and re-trials, the perceived causes and precipitating factors, as well as the numerous policy and procedure changes throughout the department. Study after study, report after report, task force after task force detailed the riot and the cost to the Ohio taxpayer.

Building Lucasville

To better understand the Easter 1993 riot at the SOCF, we must take a serious look at the facility itself. SOCF, or Lucasville, as it is known within the DRC, grew out of the creation of the independent department. Until 1972, the DRC was a part of the Ohio Department of Mental Hygiene.

However, when Ohio House Bill 494 was enacted, the DRC became an independent agency. Its first director was Bennett Cooper, who essentially created the agency and laid the groundwork for the unprecedented growth the department has endured over the past thirty years.

One of the first of many "first things to do" was to complete the replacement of the ancient Ohio Penitentiary on Spring Street in Columbus, Ohio. Construction had begun on the Southern Ohio Correctional Facility on June 28, 1968, in the town of Lucasville just off of State Route 782, known locally as Minford-Lucasville Road, in Scioto County at the southernmost part of Ohio. Lucasville is located 110 miles east of Cincinnati and eleven miles north of Portsmouth. The construction of the state's newest prison was a welcomed addition to the always-struggling rural economy. The architect for the facility was George S. Voinovich, brother of future Ohio governor George V. Voinovich.

At a cost of $32.5 million, it was to be a state-of-the-art maximum-security penal facility and the pride of the department, as well as one of the most technologically advanced facilities in the nation.

Prison Design

Its design-rated capacity was 1,640 cells. It was designed and built on the "telephone pole" concept. There was a main center corridor that extended the length of the facility. Corridors extended off the main corridor, hence the telephone pole concept.

SOCF had three main residential areas designated J-block, K-block, and L-block. L-block was entered by passing through two large gates to a main corridor with a large gymnasium at the end. Between the second gate and the gym, cellblock ranges ran off the main corridor. There were eight such ranges in K- and L-blocks, numbered one through eight.

Each cellblock range contained eighty cells, with twenty cells located on a lower left-hand level, twenty cells on a lower right-hand level, twenty cells on an upper left-hand level, and twenty cells on an upper right-hand level. At the front of each cellblock range was a console that consisted of two panels with electric switches to open and close all of the doors to the cells and showers. The console area would accommodate two to three people and was designed to give a view of the entire cellblock area. From the console, the operator could see the area in front of each cell door but not necessarily into each cell.

Utilizing this design concept, the SOCF had twenty-two acres under one roof and sat on 1,900 acres encompassing seventeen separate buildings. It also contained a revolutionary new concept known as "safe havens," which were designed to be a safe zone for staff in the event of a major disturbance. Safe havens were located in the rear of each cellblock and were accessed by heavy-duty steel doors that were secured with five-inch solid-brass Folger-Adams keys. These safe wells had direct telephone contact with the main Control Center 1, which was one of three control centers, and also had outside access, allowing those in the safe well to be evacuated from the outside in the event of an emergency.

Amidst much ceremony and fanfare, the Southern Ohio Correctional Facility opened its doors in September 1972 and received its first busload of inmates from the Old Penitentiary with William J. Whealon as its first warden. Whealon had been appointed in September 1971 to oversee the construction. The SOCF's mission was:

> To efficiently provide a safe, secure environment for inmates, employees, and the community, and to promote the incarcerated offenders positive adjustment, behavior and ability to return to a lower security facility.

Southern Ohio Values

Like most major employers in a small, local economy, the SOCF became a major part of the region. In this small town of 1,500, almost everyone worked at the facility, had a relative who worked there, or knew someone who did.

The workforce at the SOCF opened the facility with the same rural values that governed their lives. Indeed, the SOCF provided over 600 jobs—good-paying jobs—with full benefits. The town of Lucasville and the entire southern Ohio region embraced not only the facility, but also all of those who worked there.

Despite all of the technological advances, equipment, and training, the SOCF became the deadliest prison in Ohio. It would only take a few months after its celebrated opening for this deadly history to begin.

Violence and Murder

On July 24, 1973, inmate Wayne Raney took Officer Randy Gardner, Officer Gary Underwood, and Lt. Roger Crabtree hostage in K-block cell three. Underwood had begun his corrections career in 1972 at the Ohio Penitentiary. He transferred to SOCF on March 4, 1973. During the crisis, Raney ordered Underwood into inmate clothing. A staff member who misidentified Underwood as the inmate accidentally shot Underwood. Underwood died at the age of twenty-four on July 24, 1973—after a mere four months of employment at SOCF. Officer Gardner and Lt. Roger Crabtree were released.

In April 1976, prisoners staged a three-day hunger strike protesting conditions at SOCF. Ninety-five percent of the prisoners boycotted meals. In July 1977, two inmates filed suit against the state for "cruel and unusual punishment" and overcrowding. The prison, designed with single cells, had begun housing two prisoners per cell to alleviate a rapidly growing inmate population. A joint legislative committee, the Correctional Institution Inspection Committee, was established with the primary responsibility of oversight and making recommendations regarding Ohio prisons.

In March of 1978, a federal judge ordered state officials to cut back twenty-five prisoners per month to lessen overcrowding. In June of 1978, the United States Supreme Court ruled that double-celling prisoners was not unconstitutional, which led to a short hunger strike by inmates.

On February 2, 1984, inmate William Bradley murdered sixty-three-year-old industry shop foreman Eric Bowling with a piece of steel pipe in an unprovoked attack in the SOCF shop area. Bradley was remanded to DRC on March 12, 1984, from Cuyahoga County for murder. Interestingly enough, Bradley was a former death-row inmate who was released from death row in 1972 when the liberal U.S. Supreme Court found the death penalty to be unconstitutional. Bradley was sentenced to death for Eric Bowling's murder under Ohio's most recent death penalty law and is currently on death row at the Mansfield Correctional Institution.

On November 24, 1984, with Terry Morris now serving as warden, Adult Basic Education teacher Beverly J. (Shoemaker) Taylor began her career at SOCF. Her inmate clerk, Eddie Vaughn, murdered thirty-two-year-old Mrs. Taylor on June 7, 1990. Vaughn was convicted of her murder and is now serving life. Vaughn was in Lucasville convicted of aggravated arson and triple aggravated murder from Summit County. He was described as "big as George Foreman and four times as strong." These murders strengthened and galvanized the Lucasville community. Frequent and vocal cries of lax security were denied by Warden Terry Morris, but the murder of Beverly J. Taylor was a "watershed" event for the SOCF.

Political Posturing

In the decade leading up to April 1993, few public policy issues had received more attention than prison overcrowding in Ohio. In 1984, Governor Celeste appointed a twenty-four-member Governor's Committee on Prison Crowding that was chaired by Ohio State University Professor Simon Dinitz. The committee's responsibility was to examine prison conditions and make appropriate recommendations. In 1989, Governor Celeste, under Chairman Bennett Cooper, established a new Governor's Committee on Prison and Jail Crowding.

In 1990, State Representative Patrick A. Sweeney chaired a Select Committee established by Ohio House of Representatives Speaker Vern Riffe to investigate conditions at the SOCF.

However, by 1990, the Correction Institution Inspection Committee (CIIC) had submitted only two reports to the state legislature (1979 and 1981) and had reduced itself to the role of an inmate advocacy group. During the nine years prior to the riot of 1993, two Governor's Committees, a Governor's Task Force, and legislative committees had studied the problems of not only the SOCF, but also of all Ohio prisons.

Ohio ranked ninth in the nation in overall assaults on staff and second in the number of assaults requiring medical attention. According to data available at the time, an average of almost five employees could expect to be assaulted by an inmate at the SOCF each and every week of the year. In fact, the 1990 House Select Committee that investigated conditions at the SOCF found that it was a

> *loosely run and operated organization lacking in the necessary attention to detail one would expect from a maximum security facility ... as a result SOCF is not operating as a maximum security facility.*

During that time, the overcrowding soared from 142.2 percent to 186.9 percent.

Hung Out to Dry

In light of the history of the SOCF, stinging legislative reports, and the findings of numerous commissions, task forces, and committees, in early October 1990, then DRC director George Wilson announced "Operation Shakedown" and appointed Arthur Tate as the new warden at the SOCF. Former warden Terry Morris was reassigned as the warden of the Chillicothe Correctional Institution (CCI).

Arthur "Art" Tate was well liked and respected throughout the department, not only by the administration, but by line staff as well.

He held a B.S. in sociology and an M.S. in corrections from Xavier University in Cincinnati. He stood over six feet tall and weighed in at over 250 pounds. It was his job and challenge to bring the SOCF up to nationally accepted standards and operate as a maximum-security institution.

Warden Tate was quoted as saying:

> *I am not so sure that a guy should expect to get a college degree in the state's maximum-security prison. I think he should want to work his way out of this prison. This place should be tightly run. People should not get comfortable here.*

Operation Shakedown was designed as a way to more effectively manage the facility. Ten critical areas were identified for modification or complete overhaul. Those areas were:

Inmate Population: A ceiling population of 1,609 was established for the safe and effective management of SOCF. However, on April 11, 1993, the population was 1,820 with 804 inmates double-celled. Inter-institutional transfers and institutional populations were controlled by the Central Office, Bureau of Classification.

Movement and Control: All movement of inmates was to be under strict staff control to conform to Level 4 supervision standards. Corridor hall traffic was modified to establish clear inmate and staff traffic patterns. It also established limits, such as only one cellblock at a time in the corridor for inmates going to and from recreation or the yard. As had become the practice, on the day of the disturbance, inmates were permitted to enter the recreation yard using no particular system to comply with the movement restrictions.

Inmate Work Assignments: All sensitive inmate work assignments were required to be evaluated and inmates removed from some of the areas and replaced by civilian staff. On the date of the disturbance, some inmates were still unofficially involved in some work areas and assignments that gave them access to restricted information.

Ohio Penal Industries: The Sheet Metal Shop was labeled by Warden Tate as a "weapons factory for shanks." It was closed and moved to another institution.

Inmate Programs: Certain programs for Maximum Security Level 4 inmates had restricted access. Restricted access was also initiated for certain work programs. As a general rule, this was being followed with few exceptions on the day of the disturbance.

Recreation: It was recommended that Maximum Security Level 4 inmates be segregated from other inmates with lower security levels and that they receive fewer hours of recreation to create an incentive to achieve a lower security level. However, on the date of the disturbance, the following cellblocks were together for outside recreation: L2 Close Security; L6 Maximum Security; L7 Close Security; and K6 Maximum Security.

Institution Shakedown: All areas of the SOCF were scheduled for evacuation and shakedown for weapons. While this was accomplished, it became very obvious that by the day of the disturbance, the inmates had replenished their stock.

Employee Staffing: Thirty additional correction officers were assigned to the areas recommended by previous audit teams and Warden Tate. In addition to the officer positions, ten food service, five recreation, seven maintenance, five secretarial, one health and safety, one account clerk, and one locksmith were hired.

Security Hardware: Recommended was the purchase and installation of security-enhancing devices. Additional metal detectors and mirrors were installed in various designated areas. The recommendation for a number of cameras and monitors had not been approved for purchase by the Central Office.

Inmate Housing: It was recommended that the SOCF be designated as a single-cell institution. However, due to the Central Office's re-designation of Mansfield Correctional Institution (MANCI) from Maximum Security to Close Security, a large number of inmates were shuffled back and forth between MANCI and SOCF. The National Institute of Corrections' Policy Statement for managing maximum-security inmates called for using single "inside cells" for enhanced security. At the time of the disturbance, there were 548 Maximum Security Level 4 inmates double-celled in "outside cells" at SOCF.

The population level at the SOCF at the time of the disturbance did not permit maximum-security inmates to be single-celled as was nationally recommended and was the case after Operation Shakedown when the population was reduced to 1,600. The institution security designations, inter-institutional transfers, and inmate population were controlled by the Central Office, Bureau of Classification.

Almost immediately after Tate's arrival, five death-row inmates, John Byrd, J.D. Scott, Eric Swafford, Richard Cooey, and William Zuern, held officer William Dunn hostage, and after the inmates listened to their demands on radio, broadcast by a local station, they surrendered. The officer was released unharmed. Nineteen ninety-two marked a near fourteen-fold increase in inmate assaults against Ohio prison staff requiring medical attention over the previous two years. Shortly after becoming warden, Tate said:

> *Lucasville had never functioned as a real maximum-security prison. This place is full of a lot of good, professional people. It's no one's particular fault. It is something that happened over a period of years ... when it is mealtime, these guys just pile out of the cellblocks and into the halls. A lot of the violence is occurring in the hallways ... there are more than twenty acres under this roof, and long corridors. An inmate has a right to feel that he can walk down a hall without fearing he will be stabbed with a shank.*

Despite a 265 percent increase in prison staff assaults, all too often, the official mentality was that inmate assaults were an occupational hazard. At a time when the prison population was growing at an exponential rate, the staff of SOCF and all of Ohio's prisons were expected to "do more with less" long before Governor George V. Voinovich made these words his political motto in the 1990s.

One of the new thirty correction officers hired was Larry Dotson, who hired in on February 6, 1991. Dotson was making corrections a second career after serving twenty years in the United States Air Force in a military police unit. Working at the SOCF afforded Larry the opportunity to return to his southern Ohio and northern Kentucky roots. With only two years of institutional seniority, his normal assignment was "relief" on second shift. Relief officers were assigned as needed to cover other officers who were on their respective days off, vacation, or other types of leave.

Dotson says:

> *I was happy to be working at SOCF. Corrections was what I knew best because of my military background. It gave me and my wife, Emma, a chance to return to southern Ohio, a place that I grew up and where my family lived. We were glad to be home.*

Dotson, along with all security staff, had been trained, since the prison opened in 1972, that during a time of life-threatening emergency to enter the safe haven and call for help on the telephone and wait until help arrived. Gaining access was a practiced and repeated subject of officer training. For twenty-one years, staff had been ingrained with the training and philosophy of the safe havens. In addition, each shift was responsible for visually inspecting the safe haven. The storage of equipment or supplies there was strictly prohibited.

Prison officials, trainers, and security staff had no way of knowing that, for some reason, the steel reinforcement in the walls had been omitted during the construction of the safe havens. The safe havens, as a result, were only two concrete blocks thick with no steel reinforcement and, therefore, took rioting inmates only about ten minutes of pounding with forty-five-pound universal weight bars to break through the walls. Interestingly enough, the only reinforced walls were the inmates' cell walls. This omission led to numerous hostages and serious physical and psychological pain and injury.

Despite all of Tate's efforts, his problems were compounded when the DRC Central Office's Bureau of Classification transferred 209 dangerous, maximum-security prisoners from the Mansfield Correctional Institution to SOCF, in exchange for 250 Lucasville prisoners who presented a lesser security risk. This move was made in response to the inmate killing of Correction Officer Thomas Davis in Mansfield. The number of mentally ill inmates increased dramatically. More than 300 prisoners under treatment for mental illness were sharing a total of nineteen hours of psychiatric services a week.

Bureau of Classification

The Central Office's Bureau of Classification, in the year prior to the riot, arbitrarily denied 75 percent of all inmate re-classifications forwarded by the SOCF staff. Most of these denials cited absolutely no reason. The Bureau of Classification, located on the first floor of the DRC Central Office, was then and continues to be known as the "Dead Warden's Spot." This is the bureau to which all top-level administrators and wardens who publicly embarrass the director or demonstrate such a level of performance as to leave no doubt about their incompetence were reassigned.

Few personnel were actually hired for this bureau; most "landed there" because there was no place else to put them. The DRC rarely fires any of its demonstrably incompetent top-level staff. Instead, positions, titles, and assignments are created for them to keep them employed. Most do several months' to a few years' "sentence" in classification until they are deemed worthy for a real assignment elsewhere, the public "firestorm" that resulted in their reassignment blows over, or they suddenly retire. Former director Reginald Wilkinson would endeavor to find positions within the department for individuals who had reached pay ranges 13-14.

Worst of the Worst

At the beginning of 1993, Ohio ranked as the most understaffed prison system in the nation, according to information provided annually by the Criminal Justice Institute in New York. Despite the recent addition of the previously noted staff, as late as March 11, 1993, Warden Tate expressed concern to the Central Office about staffing levels. His concerns obviously fell on deaf ears.

As a result of several liberal federal and United States Supreme Court decisions, Sunni Muslims were permitted to use the prison chapel as an unsupervised meeting site. Muslims were regularly permitted to meet in the chapel and posted their own inmate "guards" to prevent being monitored or overheard by prison staff.

There were over 250 inmates who had been identified as having gang affiliations, with the Sunni Muslims being the largest. Tensions were also very high because there was a tremendous influx of young white and black inmates.

The older inmates referred to these people as the "crack generation." Inmate violence had also increased between the older and younger inmates. The SOCF was under a consent decree that required that random cell assignments be made. Essentially it meant that inmates were racially mixed in single cells, many times over the objections of the inmates themselves. In most states, cell assignments were made based on security status. Only Ohio and Alaska made a policy of interracial celling. During the January through March 1993 period, ten staff had been assaulted by inmates in different incidents at SOCF.

Trouble from Within

Tate also was hampered by a few high-ranking administrators who did not appear to belong in a maximum-security environment. Tate was at odds with at least two of his deputy wardens and several unit managers and captains. While on paper the deputy wardens reported to the warden, in fact, all deputy wardens were then and continue to be appointed by the director and in reality reported to him, providing him a direct "back channel communication pipeline," thereby circumventing the warden in many cases.

Deputy wardens more interested in "making points" with the director than administering a maximum-security prison hampered administrative efforts. This was certainly the case at the SOCF. Tate was unable to replace several of his administrative staff that he distrusted. It appeared to me that Tate distrusted Deputy Warden of Administration David See and Deputy Warden of Operations Roger Roddy, as well as several of his unit managers and captains.

According to the Disturbance Cause Committee, comprised of high-ranking DRC officials, on page three of their findings issued June 10, 1993, "serious problems exist regarding interpersonal communication between staff and inmates at this facility. This disruptive relationship is both racial and cultural in its origin ... two employees were physically observed to have lightning bolt tattoos, a sign associated with the Aryan Brotherhood ... The security of the institution is further diminished by inmate clerks performing sensitive responsibilities..."

The Disturbance Cause Committee report continued on page ten, "It was observed during staff interviews that two employees had lightning bolts tattooed on their body. During these interviews, it was reported by three employees, one who had a lightning bolt tattoo, that one additional employee had a lightning bolt tattoo."

Larry Dotson and Michael Hensley told the author that in fact four officers, Jeff Ratcliff, Brad Wederbrook, David Rogers, and Ronald Malone, had lightning bolt tattoos. Former hostage and key post-riot prosecution witness Michael Hensley, who worked with each of these four officers on second shift, stated that Malone "had lightning bolt tattoos on his neck and a similar Aryan tattoo on his lower arm." According to Hensley, Ratcliff, Rogers, and Wederbrook all received their tattoos after partying at a bar they frequented in Jackson, Ohio. The tattoos were located on the underside of the upper arm, and he testified in open court numerous times to these facts.

David Rogers, in a letter to the author received in early December 2005, adamantly denied that his tattoo signified any connection with the Aryan Brotherhood. Rogers wrote, "I do have a similar tattoo that I acquired while in a drunken state at a party back in 1991 or 1992 … I have never created a serious problem for the safety and security of the institution."

Nevertheless, the Disturbance Cause Committee, on page ten concluded, "Aryan Brotherhood members tattoo lightning bolts on their body to signify their affiliation. An officer hostage reportedly has a lightning bolt tattoo. This officer said during a news release that inmate Aryan Brotherhood members protected and prayed with him and another officer hostage."

Larry Dotson personally observed Brad Wederbrook wearing one of these tattoos. Both Dotson and Hensley were reticent to work with these officers because of the tattoos and what it could mean if a disturbance broke out. Dotson personally confronted Wederbrook about his tattoo, to which Wederbrook responded, "We got drunk one weekend and we all got tattoos."

Clearly indicating that the lightning bolt tattoos created a threat to the safety and security of the institution, according to Michael Hensley, Deputy Warden Roger Roddy spoke to the four officers and instructed them to keep the tattoos covered. However, according to both Larry Dotson and Hensley, each of the four officers "showed the tattoos to both staff and inmates." Subsequent to the riot, the DRC adopted policy 401-06, currently known as 31-SEM-06, which states,

It is the policy of the Department of Rehabilitation and Correction that personnel of the Department present a professional and dignified image, commensurate with their responsibilities, in order to instill public confidence and establish respect from those offenders under the supervision of the Department.

(A)(1) Any body marking which is inflammatory or known as a gang insignia such as, but not limited to, swastikas and double lightning bolts, are not to be displayed at work by any employee or independent contractor. Such body markings are strictly prohibited.

Inmates housed at or sent to Lucasville had been identified as the most violent, disruptive, and manipulative in the Ohio prison system. Most of the inmates were serving extended sentences, with the typical SOCF inmate serving an average of fifteen years. There was very little that could be done in terms of punishment beyond what they were already serving to encourage compliant behavior.

Set Up to Fail

On March 22, 1993, Warden Tate, recognizing the physical limitations of the facility, sent a strongly worded and detailed memo to South Regional Director Eric Dahlberg. It stated, in relevant part:

Over the past several months I have expressed my concerns relative to the need for a maximum-security unit at this facility which is suitable to house those prisoners who are high security risks requiring maximum levels of supervision as well as a physical structure designed to effectively house them ...

I have serious concerns regarding our ability, from a design standpoint, to effectively house and manage these individuals safely. SOCF is now 23 years old and is no longer "state-of-the-art" regarding its ability to securely house certain categories of high security inmates ... I want to reiterate that in my opinion, I cannot stress enough our need for a unit of this nature...

The memo speaks for itself.

To compound the problem, approximately six weeks before Easter, an active case of tuberculosis (TB) had been detected, and, as a result, the Central Office mandated that all inmates had to be tested for TB. On March 4, 1993, Dr. Marsha Smith, SOCF medical director, informed Deputy Warden David See of "one reported case of active tuberculosis" and the need for staff and inmate testing.

On March 10, 1993, Dr. Smith sent a memo to all inmates informing them of the mandated TB testing procedure. At some point, Dr. Smith became aware of the vehement refusal of Muslim inmates to submit to TB skin testing and communicated in writing to Dr. Larry Mendel, DRC medical director from the Central Office. In his written response on April 5, 1993, he stated in relevant part:

> *Thank you for making me aware of the concerns about TB skin testing expressed by some of the Muslim inmates at your facility. Fortunately, these issues have been raised before ... It is the department's position that no inmate be permitted to refuse a TB skin test ... we must insist on patient cooperation and notification that force will be used if needed.*

Radical Muslim inmates at several other institutions refused testing on alleged religious grounds but subsequently submitted after opinions from state and national Islamic organizations determined that TB skin testing did not violate their religious beliefs.

This, however, was not good enough for SOCF inmate Sunni Muslim leader Carlos Sanders. On April 5, 1993, Warden Arthur Tate and Chaplain Warren Lewis held a meeting with inmate Carlos Sanders, who objected to DRC-ordered TB skin testing. Warden Tate reiterated his position to test all inmates regardless of their objections. The meeting was rumored to be quite confrontational.

On April 7, 1993, Warden Tate received a copy of a January letter from the director of the Islamic Center of Greater Toledo indicating "that Islam does not prohibit any medical test or inoculation," as well as a February letter from the Islamic Council of Ohio stating, "Islam does not prohibit TB skin test or inoculation or medical test." The wardens of several other Ohio prisons, in order to calm previous Muslim concerns, utilized these same two letters. But, this was not good enough for Muslim Carlos Sanders.

On the same date, Warden Tate notified Eric Dahlberg in writing at the Central Office. The memo, in relevant part, stated:

> *Over the past several weeks we have endeavored to test the entire SOCF inmate population for TB. I am advised that of our total population (1820), nearly 200 individuals have refused to be tested. I have further learned that the majority of these inmates profess to be Sunni Muslim who follow an Imam in South Africa. On April 5, 1993, I met with several inmate "leaders" of this group and discussed our intentions to proceed with testing and that everyone would be required to comply. This information was not well received by the inmates ... I thought you should be aware of this situation in light of the large numbers of inmates who initially refused the test ...*

No assistance or guidance came from Eric Dahlberg or Central Office despite the fact that they were aware of a letter from Mujlisul Ulema of South Africa dated December 9, 1992. It was this Muslim imam whom SOCF inmates professed to follow. Imam Ulema's letter stated, in relevant part:

> *The Shariah's Ruling on Tuberculin Testing*
> *Having perused the explanation of tuberculin testing on prisoners, we hereby issue the following ruling in terms of Islamic law:*
> *(1) The substance injected into the body contains alcohol which is not permissible for Muslims.*
> *(2) Mandatory testing is against the free will of a human being and is an infringement of his right and not permissible.*
> *(3) The very concept of introducing poisonous substances into the human body for mere testing purposes is un-Islamic and not permissible.*
> *(4) Islam teaches that disease will be acquired only by the Will of Almighty Allah.*
> *(5) Islam rejects the concept of a disease being contagious.*
> *In view of Islamic beliefs, we exhort the Prisons Department to exempt Muslims from this mandatory test.*

A memorandum dated April 8, 1993, from Warden Arthur Tate to inmate Carlos Sanders reiterated his intention to skin test all inmates:

> *Reference is made to your attached kite as well as our conversation of 4/5/93. I believe you realize that I have the utmost respect for both you personally and for your religious beliefs.*
>
> *Your position relative to TB testing is, however, one that is not rational nor will it be accepted by me. Your options have been explained and I expect full compliance to my orders for all SOCF inmates to be tested. There will be no deviations to this order.*
>
> *I trust you, as well as others who feel as you do, will comply with this policy. You are in no position to dictate to me how you perceive this should occur. I am certainly hoping that there will be minimal difficulties associated with this process. If there are further questions, please advise.*

On Our Own

Warden Tate was neither stupid nor inept. He knew his inmate population, the Muslims, and Carlos Sanders. He communicated with the DRC Central Office and the Ohio State Highway Patrol, informing them of potential trouble with TB testing. On Good Friday, April 9, 1993, Warden Tate met with his executive staff, Food Service Manager Briton Hughes, and the medical administrator. He informed them of the impending three-day lockdown that was to begin on Monday at 1:00 p.m. to enforce the mandatory TB testing. As a result, inmates would be fed in their cells, thus necessitating the assistance of Food Service Manager Hughes, who normally did not participate in executive staff meetings.

Tate, fully aware of his communications to Central Office and the lack of assistance from them, informed his executive staff that he had requested the local post of the Ohio State Highway Patrol to have thirty riot-equipped troopers on standby Monday as he was anticipating trouble. He also planned to send extra security teams into K and L cellblocks. All in attendance were required to maintain strict secrecy about the lockdown and the plans discussed in the meeting because of the very high risk of trouble.

Incompetence from Within

However, at the conclusion of the meeting, Food Service Manager Hughes returned to his office and promptly instructed his inmate clerk "Foots" Foreman to order 3,500 brown lunch bags and twenty cases of mustard for Monday. The inmate clerk may not have been as naive as Food Service Manager Hughes assumed him to be. The inmate most likely reported this information to Carlos Sanders and other would-be riot leaders.

Later that same day, Chaplain Warren Lewis had a confrontation with inmate Carlos Sanders in the prison chapel. During this incident, inmate Sanders and other Muslims who were meeting in the chapel became physically intimidating toward the chaplain by surrounding him so that he was forced to shove his way past them in order to leave the chapel.

Despite this incident and being in the April 5, 1993, meeting with Warden Tate, Chaplain Lewis did not report this incident. It was believed that the reason inmate Sanders was so confrontational was because the inmates believed that the chaplain had overheard them planning the riot.

Chaplain Lewis was required by policy to report such an incident but failed to do so until April 26, 1993, nearly a week *after* the riot. His failure to report was incredulous because he was well aware of the confrontational attitude and posture that Sanders had taken with the warden. A report by Chaplain Lewis would have resulted in Carlos Sanders being segregated in the SOCF disciplinary block and out of L-corridor, denying the Muslims their leader.

In fact, inmate Sanders earlier that same day had assaulted Officer Nate Thompson in L-block by dropping a broom from the upper tier and striking Officer Thompson on the head. Officer Thompson wrote a conduct report called a "ticket" and placed it under Unit Manager Oscar McGraw's office door for processing as required. It remained there until the riot.

Riot in the Making

On April 10, 1993, following his two "good days" (Thursday and Friday) off, at approximately 1:50 p.m., Larry Dotson began the walk to his second-shift assignment. He was assigned to the institution's Control Center 1 with fellow officer John Woodward. Control Center 1 was one of three control centers that served as the main communication and security control centers of the prison.

This was the first day that the recreation yard would open since winter began. Jason Robb, a "captain" in the Aryan Brotherhood, held a meeting with one of his "lieutenants," Roger Snodgrass, and told him, "Be on your toes tomorrow, because something is going to happen." Robb did not elaborate.

Dotson recalls:

> *Tensions were high during the next eight hours. There were rumors that the Ohio State Highway Patrol had been notified to be prepared for potential trouble over the weekend at SOCF. What tipped the inmates off about the lockdown was that an inmate clerk who worked in the dining hall had been instructed to place an order for 3,500 brown bags because the inmates were going to be fed in their cells.*

Following his contentious meeting with Warden Tate, it was learned, inmate Sunni Muslim leader Carlos Sanders had been meeting with other inmate gang leaders on the recreation yard track and inside L-corridor to devise a strategy to prevent the TB testing the following Monday by staging a riot. If Sanders and the inmates were to avoid being tested for TB, and he was to salvage his prison image and reputation in his confrontation with Warden Tate, it was evident that the Muslim inmates would have to take action before Monday. Easter Sunday became the logical choice because after the meetings on Thursday, it gave the inmates two days to plan their strategy.

Nothing Coming

It was also rumored among staff that Warden Tate had requested approval up the chain of command for increased staffing over the holiday weekend. The normal channel of communication for such requests would have been through Richard "TJ" Turjanica, the southern regional security administrator. Turjanica would have then sought approval from Eric Dahlberg, the southern regional administrator. No additional staffing was produced. Dotson recalls:

Another rumor that was causing tension among the staff was it was reported that inmate Carlos Sanders had met with Warden Tate on either Thursday or Friday and Sanders told the warden that the Muslims would not allow themselves to be TB tested. It was rumored that Warden Tate told Sanders, "You do what you gotta do, and we'll do what we gotta do." I had a lot of respect for Warden Tate, and still do, but that had everyone on pins and needles.

However, rumors were frequent inside the prison, and there was no sign of trouble for the remainder of the 2:00 p.m. to 10:00 p.m. shift. The absence of accurate information encouraged the rumor mill, which increased tension and anxiety among the staff. In this case, the rumors were true.

Dotson thought to himself, *Another welcomed routine weekend second shift.* He remembers:

We were always hearing rumors, most of which were later found to be false. However, after you have been working inside for a while, you begin to get a feel for what is normal and when something is just not right ... things were not right, and a lot of people sensed it, and I believe that some people in a position to know knew it wasn't right.

At approximately 9:50 p.m., the third-shift officers relieved Officers Dotson and Woodward. Both Larry and John began to work their way down the concrete block hallway to the institution's entry foyer and out the front door for the thirty-yard walk to the facility's small entry building that housed the all-too-familiar time clock. At exactly 10:00 p.m., Larry punched his beige time card and returned the card to its normal slot.

He slowly walked the fifty-plus yards to his 1992 Pontiac Sunbird, parked in its usual parking place in the second-shift officers' parking lot. He felt a big sense of relief that this shift was over. One weekend shift under his belt and one to go.

Larry turned left onto State Route 728, which ran directly in front of the prison and drove the twenty miles home where his wife of twenty-six years, Emma, and his daughter, Kimberly, and son, Joe, awaited his arrival. The major news story on the radio was the fiery climax to the standoff in Waco, Texas.

It is ironic that some of the personnel and equipment being utilized in Waco, Texas, would be brought to the SOCF in a matter of days to assist in freeing Larry Dotson and his fellow officers.

Like nearly all corrections employees, Larry did not share his concerns or talk much about his job at the SOCF with his wife and family. Larry comments:

> *It's not something you really talk about, because if your family knew what it was really like, they would worry constantly. The potential was always there, especially in a maximum-security prison like SOCF. At the time we had the worst of the worst. When other prisons couldn't handle an inmate, they were sent to us.*

The statistics clearly demonstrated that from its opening in September 1972 until April 10, 1993, Lucasville was the deadliest prison in Ohio with thirty-eight inmates and five staff members murdered. In less than eleven days, those numbers would increase dramatically.

Chapter 2:
Riot Gangs & Their Leadership

In April 1993, 13.7 percent of the inmate population had previously been identified as having gang affiliations. The gangs that had been recognized at the SOCF were the Aryan Brotherhood, Black Gangster Disciples, Sunni Muslim, Original Gangsters, Vice Lords, Dynamite Devils, Imperial Gangsters, Crips, Black Supremacist, and White Supremacist. However, there were three main prison gangs that operated with any strength and organization at the SOCF and were directly involved in the riot. We will focus our attention on the following:

(1)   Aryan Brotherhood
(2)   Sunni Muslim
(3)   Black Gangster Disciples

Aryan Brotherhood
This gang originated at the San Quentin Prison in California with inmate David Snow. It was designed as a paramilitary organization with a highly organized command structure that included a president, vice president(s), captains at each prison, lieutenants appointed for each block (housing unit), sergeants, sergeants at arms, soldiers, enforcers, and probates.

Originally, it was established to protect white prison inmates from assault and rape from black and Hispanic gang members. It masked its gang activity under the cloak of religion, utilizing the cover of the Odinist religion to hide the illicit business practices.

While most gangs recruit to increase their membership, the Aryan Brotherhood only recruits those who will further its cause. Therefore, membership in the Aryan Brotherhood is by invitation only. Before gaining membership, a "recruit" or "probate" must prove his dedication by carrying out a significant act of violence against a person targeted by the Aryan Brotherhood. This act is known as "making your bones." Membership is for life.

The only way out of the Aryan Brotherhood is by death. Members released from prison are expected to support members who are still incarcerated. They live by the philosophy of *BLOOD IN, BLOOD OUT.*

The Aryan Brotherhood is very aware of the operations of the prison. They will place members in key locations of the prison to gather information or make weapons and tools for future altercations. They are known for planning for the future. An Aryan Brotherhood member is always a white supremacist, but not all white supremacists are members of the Aryan Brotherhood.

In the highly respected reference *Gangs and Their Tattoos: Identifying Gangbangers on the Street and in Prison*, author Bill Valentine identifies the eleven rules of the Aryan Brotherhood:

(1) After reading these rules and you decide you would like to be in the Brotherhood and you are voted in and accepted, there is only one way out; that is death.
(2) Once you enter into the AB, do not try to backslide in any way! You are not being given a free ride through this prison.
(3) After you are sworn into the AB, you will be advised of the social structure of the AB and will be expected to recognize it and abide by its decisions and orders.
(4) The AB is exactly what it says, "A Brotherhood." When you see a brother involved in any sort of trouble or hassle, you go to his side. You may not be on the best of terms with the man, but he is your brother and will be treated as such. So back him! He is going to do the same for you when you need him!

(5) A brother can sometimes be wrong, but in front of a non-brother, he's right! Afterwards when you are alone, his being wrong can be dealt with. But never in front of a non-brother!

(6) You will not bullshit or play games with a brother in front of non-brothers. Always show respect to a brother and let everyone around you know that the respect is there!

(7) We take care of our own! We don't have time for the games that non-brothers are involved in! You will protect your brother, his property, and the interest of the AB as if it were your own! Your brothers will be doing the same for you.

(8) If you are told to do something, there is a reason for you being told to do it, so do it!

(9) You are in the AB for life! If you hit the streets and come back, you're still in it! You must be willing to do for a brother what you want him to be willing to do for you. No matter where you are.

(10) After a certain length of time, it will be necessary to make a donation to a bank account in case any brother is placed in the adjustment center (maximum security detention). A brother is to be taken care of to the fullest of the AB's capacity! The donations will be reasonable.

(11) The purpose of the Aryan Brotherhood is to bring back the respect that is long overdue in coming to this prison and to the White Race! At all costs! We will strive to maintain that respect!

The origins of the Aryan Brotherhood in the Ohio prison system came from the Marion Correctional Institution and the inmate program called Seven Steps. It was a front for gang activity headed by Gary Collmar, #180-553, from Summit County, serving a lengthy sentence for aggravated robbery. Collmar was the "director" and screened all applicants to enter the group. Collmar ended up at the SOCF.

In November 1992, Collmar left the SOCF and was transferred to the Mansfield Correctional Institution. Prior to his departure, Collmar ordered that Paul Johnson (a.k.a. "Tramp") would be the new "director." Captains for the new organization would be Jason Robb, George Skatzes, and Jesse Bocook.

Jason Robb, #131-789, from Montgomery County, was in the SOCF serving a seven-to-twenty-five-year sentence for voluntary manslaughter. George Skatzes, #173-501, from Logan County, was serving a life sentence for aggravated murder. Jesse Bocook, #195-537, from Muskingum County, was serving a four-to-fifteen-year sentence for burglary.

Bylaws for the SOCF chapter were drawn up and included:

(1) No member would ever cell with a black,
(2) No contact or cooperation with any Corrections Officers,
(3) No CO's or police could ever be members of the Aryan Brotherhood,
(4) No homosexual activity,
(5) No dealing with blacks unless you make a profit,
(6) No dealing with blacks if the blacks make a profit,
(7) If you went to another institution, you had a right to start a new chapter, but the Lucasville chapter would be your parent chapter,
(8) In times of "war", you must follow orders. If you did not follow orders, the unwritten penalty was death.

In March of 1993, Jason Robb was elected as "director." At this time, there were about twenty members, including Roger Snodgrass, who was promoted to sergeant. Most of the AB violence was directed toward the Black Gangster Disciples.

Black Gangster Disciples

David Barksdale, leader of the Gonzanto Disciples, and Larry Hoover, leader of the Black Gangster Disciple Nation (BGND), formed Black Gangster Disciples (BGD), originally part of the BGDN on the south side of Chicago in the late 1960s. David Barksdale became the leader of BGDN, and Hoover became his second in command.

Barksdale died in 1972, and Hoover took over the leadership position. After Barksdale's death, Jerome Freeman, who was loyal to Barksdale and never wanted the two groups to unite in the first place, established a parallel leadership position to Hoover. The Black Gangster Disciples have recruited extensively, and as a result, they are one of the country's largest criminal organizations and are considered one of the most notorious.

In the SOCF, the BGDs united with allied gangs under the guise of the Brothers of the Struggle (BOS) and operated under the Folk Nation. The leader, known as the "king," was Anthony Lavelle. The "king" received a percentage of the profits from all of the gang's illegal activities. Consistent with their illegal street businesses, the gang was into large-scale drug trafficking, murder, and white-collar crime.

Currently, there are in excess of 800 known members. Their bylaws are:

(1) All members shall abide by the code of secrecy and silence.

(2) Every member should believe in respect and no disrespect to every member and nonmember.

(3) No member shall take any property from any other member or non-standing member.

(4) No member shall take any addictive drug.

(5) No member shall break and enter any building, which may cause institutionalization.

(6) All confrontations with any other members or non-standing members will be reported through the proper chain of command whether major or minor.

(7) No member will argue with any officers or guards.

(8) No member shall gamble unless all merchandise is up front.

(9) All members must pay dues.

(10) All members are requested to have personal hygiene.

(11) All members are required to exercise daily.

(12) All members are required to aid and assist when asked to.

(13) All members must participate in all meetings and gatherings.

(14) No member shall participate in homosexuality.

(15) All members are required to be on the money.

(16) All members are required to uphold all laws set forth.

The BGDs were small in number at the SOCF in 1993 with its prominent leaders being Anthony Lavelle, #153-099, out of Scioto County, serving a seven-to-twenty-five-year sentence for attempted aggravated murder, and Aaron Jefferson (AJ), #230-397, serving a sentence for aggravated murder.

Muslims (Sunni)

By far, the largest gang at the SOCF, consisting of about forty to fifty inmates, was the Muslims led by Carlos "Hasan" Sanders. Other prominent members included Leroy Elmore, #191-839, serving a sentence for murder; Stanley Cummings, #230-002, from Cuyahoga County, serving a sentence of ten to twenty-five for aggravated robbery; James Were (a.k.a. Namir Abdul Mateen), #173-245, from Lucas County, serving a seven-to-twenty-five-year sentence for aggravated robbery; James Bell, #179-394, from Hamilton County, serving a life sentence for aggravated murder; and Cecil Allen, Jr., #197-506. Carlos Sanders, #130-559, was serving a life sentence for aggravated murder from Hamilton County.

Sanders and his followers also used the cloak of religion as a cover for their gang activity and, because of this constitutionally protected cover, were granted numerous privileges that eluded other gangs. Most of the Muslim leadership had adopted Muslim names, held services, dressed in Muslim garb, and practiced modified dietary habits. However, Muslim leaders from Ohio and around the nation were quick to disassociate themselves with the "extremist" beliefs of Sanders and his followers.

All evidence clearly showed that it was Sanders who planned and directed the riot after his high-profile confrontation with SOCF Warden Arthur Tate regarding TB skin testing. Sanders claimed such testing violated his religious beliefs, because the test allegedly contained alcohol. This was patently untrue and was supported by both state and national Islamic organizations.

This was a power play by Sanders to justify his position as Sunni Muslim leader and to save face inside the institution. Sanders was feared by many of the other inmates at the SOCF. He had a history of violence against both inmates and staff, and constantly kept a store of weapons on hand for use at a moment's notice. He would deal with anyone who could provide him with the weapons he needed.

Sanders' reputation at the SOCF was such that riot preparations were cleared through him, and other rival gang leaders consulted with him.

Sanders' high profile before, during, and after the riot resulted in his death sentence for the murder of Corrections Officer Robert Vallandingham. Sanders also ordered, and was convicted of, the killing of several other inmates.

Approximately two weeks before the riot, Anthony Lavelle, Carlos Sanders, and Jason Robb had several meetings to settle gang differences. On April 11, 1993, Captain Jesse Bocook met twice with Carlos Sanders. Bocook warned his fellow Aryans to stay away from the "police." While the Aryans did not plan the riot, they were certainly aware of when, where, and how it was going to take place.

Most of the Aryans stayed on the recreation yard until approximately forty-five minutes after the riot had begun. Most of the Aryans became involved when several white inmates came staggering out onto the recreation yard from L-corridor stating, "They are killing everything white in there."

The Aryans armed themselves with weapons and entered L-corridor and found mass chaos. Several Muslims were guarding the doors but said nothing to the Aryans, who soon found out that it was not a racial riot. For the first two days of the riot, the Aryans made their "headquarters" in the L-corridor gymnasium and then moved to L-2, where they remained for the duration of the riot. It was clear to both the Aryans and the Black Gangster Disciples that the Muslims were in charge of the riot. It soon became quite clear to the DRC as well.

Overall, gang activity was poorly monitored at best. Post-riot investigations revealed the following:

- While 13.78 percent of the SOCF population had been identified as being members of a gang, investigating committee members identified an additional thirty inmates who had not been previously identified by either the gang coordinator or the institutional investigator.
- There was a Muslim constitution written by and/or possessed by Muslim inmates. The constitution cited activities that clearly suggest that the Sunni Muslim group at the SOCF was not for religious purposes, but rather functioned similarly to a gang versus any DRC-approved group. The constitution of the group operated outside of the guidelines of the DRC and SOCF policies and procedures.
- Recreation staff and inmates verified that unauthorized Muslim "worship" or meetings took place in the yard and gym outside of their normally scheduled religious service. These unauthorized meetings were similar to the unauthorized meetings of the Aryan Brotherhood.
- The SOCF gang coordinator did make his gang information accessible to any staff member interested, upon request. However, there was no formal system to communicate gang information from line staff to the captain or investigator.
- The institutional investigator did not have a formal system for establishing gang-related official investigations.

Part 2:
Riot Duration

Chapter 3:
Anatomy of a Prison Riot

April 11, 1993

Easter Sunday in southern Ohio began as a brisk spring day. Larry was up early to attend church services with the family. Following the service, he and his family returned home and ate lunch, and he began to prepare to return to the SOCF for another quiet and routine shift.

He left home at his usual 12:30 p.m. for the 2:00 p.m. shift. Weekends off for corrections officers were reserved for those with a large amount of shift seniority. That was something that Larry Dotson did not have, as he hired in at the SOCF on February 6, 1991. In fact, his seniority dictated not only his days off, which were called "good days," but his shift as well. His seniority gave him second shift with Thursdays and Fridays off. Warden Tate was looking forward to spending Easter Sunday with his son in London, Ohio.

Meanwhile at the SOCF, recreation began at 12:30 p.m. Inmates from L-2, L-6, L-7, and K-6 were permitted on the yard along with sixty other specially "passed" inmates.

Late morning, Officer Robert "Bobby" Vallandingham, who was not scheduled to work on this day, received a telephone call from the SOCF requesting that he come in to work for second shift. He agreed and told his wife, Peggy, "Something is going down today." On this day, the SOCF housed 1,820 prisoners—including 357 murderers,

279 rapists, and 388 armed robbers. Dotson and his fellow second-shift officers had no way of knowing that earlier in the day final preparations were completed on the event that would change their lives forever and end the life of Officer Bobby Vallandingham. White Supremacist leader and "captain" of the Aryan Brotherhood Jesse Bocook and Muslim leader Carlos "Hasan" Sanders had met twice on the recreation yard. The Aryans had been told by Bocook "to stay away from the police, some sort of [expletive] is going to go down." Early in the afternoon, the word had spread among the white inmates that the Muslims were planning to riot and the whites were to be aware of what was happening, in case it turned into a racial war.

Muslim inmates had been purchasing large quantities of weapons called "shanks" from inmate John Fryman, who had the reputation of being able to make a weapon out of anything that could hold an edge and not bend. Because of his dealings with black inmates, Fryman was despised by the Aryan Brotherhood.

Bailing Out

At 1:50 p.m., reporting for his shift "roll call" briefing, Larry was originally assigned to the institution's hospital unit known as the infirmary; however, seven of his fellow officers had called in "sick" on this weekend holiday. If Easter Sunday had been a recognized paid holiday, there would have been an excess of staff because all would have wanted to collect what amounted to time and a half for a holiday worked. Being just another day, albeit a religious holiday, numerous staff routinely called in sick.

The officers calling in sick were David McGuire, Michael Lehn, Rick Malone, Paul Goshorn, Darren Mustard, Nedra Chapman, and Romulus Hurst. To cover for Romulus Hurst, Larry was reassigned to cellblock L-3, one of the three huge corridors that housed eight cellblocks. His partner was Conrad Nagle, a likeable, no-nonsense ex-marine with whom Larry had worked numerous shifts. Due to seven officers off sick, Vallandingham was called in to work overtime. Dotson recalls:

> *In the back of our minds, we knew of the rumors, and while we didn't talk about it, the thoughts were there. You could feel the tension in the air. Ten officers had been assaulted over the*

past couple of months. We knew something wasn't right; we just didn't know what.

Unfortunately, Dotson and his colleagues in L-corridor would not have to wait long to find out. Dotson and Nagle made their way down the long L-corridor. Nagle commented, "It's going to be a quiet night … no rec [short for recreation], no cell clean-ups … a quiet Sunday night at SOCF." Larry replied laughing, "Sounds like a plan."

"Routine" Beginning

They arrived at L-3 at approximately 1:55 p.m., and the cellblock door was unlocked for them by the upper corridor officer, James Bolden, who had just relieved his first-shift counterpart. Nagle and Dotson received a brief report from the two first-shift officers—quiet, normal, routine weekend holiday shift. Just what both wanted to hear. So far, so good. That would change very shortly.

The first-shift officers departed at 1:58 p.m., and the L-3 cellblock door was locked and secured by Officer Bolden. Larry and his partner began their normal beginning-of-shift routine. Being the relief officer, Larry was considered "extra" and therefore would respond to any emergency or "man-down alarms" throughout the institution and would do the "gopher" work for this shift assigned to L-3.

At 2:05 p.m., Larry and his partner began their walk-through inspection of the cellblock and conducted their normal second-shift count of the inmates. All was in order; most all inmates were accounted for and in their respective cells because L-3 was not scheduled for recreation. It appeared Conrad Nagle would be correct, "a quiet night at SOCF." With the rumors that had been circulating, both were more than happy to have most of their 105 inmates securely locked in their cells, while the remaining inmates were on the recreation yard.

Coworkers assigned to the remaining cellblocks in L-corridor included Officers Robert Schroeder and Bobby Vallandingham in L-1, Jeff Ratcliff in L-2, Howard Fraley and Larry Buffington in L-4, Darrold Clark and Mike Hensley in L-5, Johnnie George and Mark Milliken in L-6, and Tony Demons and Lloyd Truesdell in L-7. L-8 was closed for repairs and security upgrades.

On the recreation yard, Activities Therapist Bryan Sparks and Officers John Neff, Michael Stump, Rodney Pennington, and Mark Milliken were monitoring inmates.

Plan A

At 2:10 p.m., the Muslim-planned riot was scheduled to begin. Carlos "Hasan" Sanders entered through the gymnasium metal detector and made his way to L-2 with a number of Muslim inmates to retrieve the large cache of weapons that they had stored. When he had retrieved the large number of weapons and returned to the metal detector, the riot was to begin. However, Sanders ended up being locked in L-2, so the plan did not work. As a result, many of the Muslims went back out onto the recreation yard and ganged up over toward the K-corridor side of the yard near the boxing ring.

Plan B

It was believed that several of the inmates communicated with Sanders to devise a new riot plan through an open window. At some point between 2:10 p.m. and 3:00 p.m., Aryan "Captain" Bocook talked with the Muslim leaders one more time and was informed that the riot would begin at 3:00 p.m. when the yard was closed.

The Aryans were reluctant and stayed back and together, believing that, according to Snodgrass, "the Muslims may be going to do something, and they were afraid that in fact that it was going to be some sort of assault on the white guys."

At 2:50 p.m., the loudspeaker announced, "Attention on the yard, attention on the yard. The yard is closed. I repeat, the yard is closed. All inmates return to your lock." The loudspeaker ordered recreation closed and all inmates off the yard. Inmates quickly began making their way toward the gymnasium door and the recreation metal detector. This activity was observed by Officer Milliken to be unusual because the inmates usually moved slowly to extend their recreation period. Stationed at the metal detector was Officer Michael Stump, and standing next to him was Officer George Horsley.

Officer Horsley was the lower corridor officer and, by policy, possessed all of the large brass Folger-Adams keys to the corridor's seven cellblocks and both the L-side and K-side gymnasium doors. Coming in off of the recreation yard were more than 100 inmates from

L-6, another 180 inmates from L-2 and L-7, as well as approximately 100 inmates from K-6 and the sixty inmates on special recreation pass. The announcement closing the yard was repeated over the public address system at 3:00 p.m.

Riot Inception

At 3:03 p.m., as the inmates backed up at the metal detector and began the slow process of "clearing" the metal detector, Muslim inmates led by Carlos Sanders brutally attacked both Officers Stump and Horsley, taking their keys, handcuffs, and side-handled police batons called PR-24s. Inmate James Were began beating Officer Michael Stump with a baseball bat.

The special radios carried by correctional staff, known as "man-down alarms" were automatically set off by the attack, thereby notifying Control Center 1 of the emergency. Officer Bolden witnessed the attack but called the alarm in as a fight rather than an inmate attack on staff, which would have brought more of a response.

Shift Commander Lt. Wayne Taylor and Lt. Gary Brown responded at 3:06 p.m. and were attacked immediately upon entering L-corridor. A second alarm was announced, and Officer Dotson tossed his keys to his partner while giving him a concerned look. "We seemed to exchange mutual looks of concern, sort of an 'Oh no, this is it' kind of look." Dotson ran to the cellblock door. Looking out the window, he saw "mass chaos ... inmates running in the corridor swinging PR-24s, baseball bats, weight bars, and mop wringers."

Dotson saw Officer John Kemper respond from C-corridor, running into L-6, and what seemed like a few seconds later, he saw Officer Johnnie George run out of L-6 with two inmates "all over him." Seconds later, upper corridor officer James Bolden opened the L-3 cellblock door, and Larry bolted into the corridor and was immediately confronted with the unbelievable and chaotic scene of staff members being beaten by a mass of rioting inmates. Dotson thought to himself, *This just can't be happening.*

Lloyd Truesdell and Rodney Pennington responded from the recreation yard and were brutally assaulted in L-corridor seconds after entering from the gymnasium. Officer Mark Milliken heard the man-down alarm, but during his two years at the SOCF he had responded to numerous alarms. Unaware of the true nature of the situation in L-corridor, he chose to remain on his post and allow other officers to handle the alarm.

Many white inmates remained on the yard, and Officer Milliken was observing them. However, when he reached the gymnasium door that led into L-corridor, he saw Officer George Horsley badly beaten, bleeding, and staggering out of the gymnasium door. He assisted Officer Horsley to a nearby weight bench and again tried to enter the gymnasium door. As he opened the door, he was struck on the arm with a PR-24. The inmate who hit him, Robert Jenkins, yelled, "We're taking this [expletive] place over!" Milliken immediately slammed the door closed to protect himself and Officer Horsley.

Officer Kenny Daniels responded from the Control Center 3 metal detector, and Sgt. Darrell Shepherd responded from J-block, where he was making his security rounds. Larry immediately drew his PR-24 from his belt ring with a powerful wide sweeping motion known as a "power draw" and prepared for the worst; and the worst was well on its way. As he looked down the long narrow L-corridor hallway toward the gymnasium, all he could see was a wave of rioting inmates bearing down on him carrying weight bars, baseball bats, PR-24s, and other weapons fashioned from tables, chairs, brooms, and mop wringers. Dotson painfully recalls, "The corridor was a literal wall of hundreds of inmates, and they were rolling over anyone and anything that got in their way." Dotson continues:

There is just no describing the savagery of a prison riot. I had seen videos of the Attica, New York and the Sante Fe, New Mexico riots during training, but until I saw that wall of inmates coming at me, I would have never believed it. It is something I will never forget.

He suddenly remembered that he had seen Officer Kemper run into L-6 and only Officer Johnnie George run out; he was sure that Officer Kemper was still in L-6. Dotson recalls:

I saw John go in but didn't remember seeing him come out. I'm a career military man; we don't leave anyone behind. I went in after John. I don't regret what I did; John would have done the same for me. That's just the way it works.

Meanwhile, the officers assigned to the other cellblocks retreated to the locked stairwells known as safe havens located at the far end of the cellblocks, seeking safety as they were trained to do.

The Aryans moved from the K-corridor side of the yard to the basketball court. Hearing the riot inside, they remained afraid that the Muslims would begin attacking the white inmates because the Muslims outnumbered the Aryans nearly two to one.

Officer Milliken looked into the gymnasium through the door window and saw inmate Jenkins run up the steep access ramp deeper into L-corridor. Milliken then re-entered the door and immediately saw Officer Michael Stump lying in a pool of blood at the base of the ramp just outside the gymnasium. Milliken then cautiously worked his way up the ramp and saw Officer Darrold Clark banging on the L-5 cellblock door, yelling to be let out. However, Officer Milliken had no keys and was unable to do so. He yelled to Officer Clark. He saw Sgt. Darrell Shepherd trying to defend himself from inmates James Bell and Anthony Byrd, who were beating him with a PR-24. Sgt. Shepherd yelled to Officer Milliken, who was then being beaten by inmate Robert Jenkins, "Let's get out of here; we've lost it!" Sgt. Shepherd announced over the radio that L-corridor had been lost. Milliken retreated the same route he had entered. He stopped to assist Officer Michael Stump out the gymnasium door and across the recreation yard to the base of one of the armed security towers. Witnesses reported that Officer Stump had been held with a knife to his throat and one hand in a handcuff. He began swinging the loose end of the handcuff as a weapon to escape. Sgt. Shepherd made it back to the Control Center 3 crash gate alive but badly injured.

The Taking of Hostages

Officer Robert Vallandingham, unable to make it to the safe haven, locked himself in his cellblock restroom. Inmates saw Officer Vallandingham enter the bathroom, and eyewitnesses testified that several inmates were ramming the steel door with a large steel desk in order to gain access to the restroom. Inmates verbally guaranteed Vallandingham of his personal safety if he exited the restroom. Fearing serious physical harm or even death, the officer exited the restroom and was beaten and taken hostage, and was then handcuffed by riot leader Carlos Sanders and led away.

Officer Schroeder was also beaten and taken hostage. The officers assigned to the facility's remaining corridors K and J began locking down all of their inmates to keep the riot from overtaking their cellblocks. One officer from each K and J corridor cellblock responded to L-corridor. Officers assigned to K-corridor called for emergency stretchers as they watched injured officers cross the recreation yard.

By that time, the inmates had opened L-3, L-4, L-5, L-7, and L-8 and had broken through a window and gained access to L-2. Officers Michael Hensley and Darrold Clark called Control Center 1 from their safe haven. Officer Clark had the forethought to secure his handcuffs to the safe-well hand railing to prevent them from being used against him. He watched out the safe-well door as rioting inmates destroyed the cellblocks' control panels.

Larry recalls:

> *I had seen John Kemper run into L-6 being chased by inmates. I followed John by only a few seconds, and when I entered the cellblock, I looked off to my left toward the ice machine and saw John lying in a pool of blood not moving. I saw that armed inmates had surrounded me, and I started swinging my PR like a baseball bat. About that time, someone knocked my feet out from underneath me with what I think was a broom handle, and down I went. I clearly remember being hit in the face with a mop wringer, and it was lights out.*

Officer Charlie Miller, assigned to Special Duty Pack Up, responded from another part of the institution and attempted to rescue Officer Dotson in L-6, who was being beaten by Leroy Elmore, Carlos Sanders, Edward Joulious, and others. Officer Miller, in a heroic attempt to rescue Officer Dotson, had a hold of Dotson at one time, but the inmates had a hold of Miller, trying to drag him deeper into the cellblock. Miller lost his grip on Dotson when the inmates began pulling the two officers apart. After hitting one or two of the inmates and breaking free, Miller staggered and fell backwards out of the cellblock door into the hallway. Severely beaten and with a three-inch gaping laceration on his head, Miller was forced to withdraw. After being initially treated in the SOCF infirmary, he was transferred to the Southern Ohio Medical Center for further treatment. Officer

Miller ignored medical advice and returned to the SOCF to rejoin his fellow officers.

Officer James Bolden was later found standing uninjured near the Control Center 3 metal detector with his keys and radio intact, quite a distance from his assigned post. It remains a mystery how the upper corridor officer could have unsecured the upper cellblock doors, assisted staff, and escaped getting caught up in the riot and being injured. All staff assigned to L-corridor, recreation, and the L-corridor cellblocks were beaten or taken hostage—except Officer James Bolden, who escaped without injury. Shaking his head, Dotson relates:

> *I just don't see how he could have escaped uninjured. Make no mistake; I'm glad he did. I wouldn't wish what happened to us to happen to anyone, but the only way I can see of making it out totally uninjured was that after he let me out into the corridor he ran for the crash gate. There is no other explanation for it. It's been ten years, and I haven't heard of or thought of one yet.*

Officer David Porter, overcome with fear, was found sitting outside Control Center 3. He had not entered L-corridor. Meanwhile, Officer Conrad Nagle, still in L-3, was surrounded by ten to twenty inmates, knocked to the ground, handcuffed, and his keys taken. He was taken to the recreation room and thrown to the ground. Two inmates began beating him with his own PR-24. He was hit in the head at least three times before he lost consciousness. Upon regaining consciousness, he was taken back to the shower area with other staff hostages. Officers Buffington and Fraley made it to the safe well in L-4 and believed they would be safe. Officer Buffington called Control Center 1 for help, but no one answered the phone.

Lt. Brown and Lt. Taylor, both bludgeoned by inmates Johnny Roper and Cecil Allen, Jr., fought their way out of L-corridor and back to Control Center 3. Lt. Wayne Taylor announced over his radio that L-corridor had been lost and ordered Control Center 1 to close and secure the security crash gate separating L-corridor from the rest of the institution. After running from L-6 with inmates close behind,

Officer Johnnie George was badly beaten but managed to make it to the Control Center 3 crash gate just before it closed. Dotson says:

> *I've spoken with Wayne, and I know how painful it was for him to give the order to close that gate and leave us in there, but we all know that it was something he had to do or we would have lost the entire institution and ended up with dozens of hostages and who knows how many dead. Knowing you did the right thing is small comfort when your men are being savagely beaten. He did what he had to do, and I would have done the same thing if I had been in his position. To me, Lt. Wayne Taylor is one of the real heroes of the riot. There is no telling how many lives and serious injuries he saved that day.*

The Importance of Leadership

Dotson is correct. The closing of this one crash gate prevented the rioting inmates from obtaining control of Control Center 3, which would have given them access to both K-block and J-block, which housed the state's death row inmates as well as the entire prison facility, granting riot leaders access to over 1,800 accomplices and numerous additional staff hostages.

Officers in K-corridor began building a barricade at the K-corridor door to the recreation yard, using chairs, tables, and other objects. The goal was to prevent inmates from entering the adjacent K-corridor, because they knew that the inmates had obtained the keys to the K-corridor gymnasium entrance from their attack on Officer Horsley. Officers Darrold Clark and Michael Hensley again called from their L-5 safe haven.

Held Hostage

As he began to regain his mental bearings, Larry Dotson was placed in the L-6 shower cell—alone. With his glasses long since shattered and lost, he remembered looking out of the shower cell and watching an inmate "working the cellblock console like he knew what he was doing," despite the inmate having his face covered with what appeared to be a pillowcase. Dotson believed that the inmate operating the console panel was Timothy Grinnell—he couldn't be sure. Right then, that was one of the least of his concerns. He looked down and saw the entire front of his uniform soaked with blood—his blood.

> *I remember seeing the water in the shower running, so I took out my handkerchief and tried to wash off my face. It was then I realized that I was badly injured. I also remembered ... looking out at that inmate working the console and thinking that this just can't be happening to me, and then suddenly it hit me that this was real. This was a defining moment for me. I now realized that we were in serious trouble.*

At 3:20 p.m., Officer Jeff Ratcliff jammed paper into the keyhole of the L-2 corridor door in an effort to stop the inmates from entering and then ran for the rear stairwell and safe haven. With him was long-term inmate and forty-one-year-old Vietnam veteran Earl Elder, #167-095, who accompanied him into the safe haven. Elder was a talented paint artist and not the least bit interested in participating in the riot. Rioting inmates broke through the concrete walls with their weight bars. As they pulled inmate Elder through the wall, beating him, they said, "Since you want to be with the police, we'll treat you like the police." He was later taken to a cell and locked up. Officer Ratcliff was beaten and taken hostage. White inmates who had made it out of the riot-laden L-corridor straggled out to the yard yelling to the other Aryans that "they are killing everything in there that's white." The Aryan members took up makeshift weapons and expected to find a race war upon entering L-corridor; however, they were not attacked. The black inmates guarding the doors were not derogatory or belligerent. In fact, several other members of the Aryan leadership, including George Skatzes, were actively participating in the riot by destroying property and burning files and records.

Officer Michael Hensley again called for help from the rear of L-5 along with Officer Darrold Clark. He made telephone contact with Control Center 1 on four separate occasions. No one, however, was sent to get them out.

At 3:23 p.m., Control Center 1 notified the Portsmouth Post 73 of the Ohio Highway State Patrol (OSP) that the SOCF was in a full riot. OSP Post 73 notified Jackson Post 40, Chillicothe Post 71, Athens

Post 5, Gallipolis Post 27, and OSP Central Command of the Signal 40 (major disturbance) at the SOCF. All units were ordered to report to the SOCF.

Although seriously injured, Shift Commander Lt. Wayne Taylor inspected the K-side barricades and cellblocks and then ordered all staff out of K-corridor. Officers also dropped the fire door at the K-side gymnasium. Weapons from the armory were issued to officers, and they were sent to secure the perimeter fence. Lt. Gary Brown ordered the electrical fuses pulled for the K-side crash gates, meaning the inmates would have to operate them manually.

Officer Ratcliff made his fifth call to Control Center 1 at 3:30 p.m., and despite his physical injuries, Sgt. Darrell Shepherd courageously led a team of three officers to the rear of the L-5 safe haven to rescue Officers Darrold Clark and Michael Hensley, but they heard a large number of inmates breaking through the safe-well walls—they were too late! Inmates Darnell Alexander, Thomas Blackmon, and Orson Wells broke through the safe-well wall to get Officers Hensley and Clark, who had been calling for help for one hour. Inmate Thomas Blackmon shoved garments through the safe-well door's broken window and ignited them in an attempt to force Hensley and Clark from the safe well. The Ohio State Highway Patrol began to secure the institution's outer perimeter.

The inmates moved Officer Conrad Nagle from one holding cell to another. During the move, an inmate stabbed him in the back of the shoulder, and he was again assaulted, suffering extensive head wounds.

Officer Ratcliff called the control center but had trouble getting the telephone to work. After six attempts over the period of an hour, he finally made contact. No rescue team was sent.

Failure to Communicate

At 3:37 p.m., Officer Baker, assigned to Control Center 1, used the rotary telephone line to call for Warden Arthur Tate, Deputy Warden Roger Roddy, Major Roger Crabtree, and Duty Officer Oscar McGraw on their respective institutional pagers. Precious minutes were lost, however, because Officer Baker had not been trained and therefore did not realize that a touch-tone telephone was required to activate institutional pagers.

Warden Tate, visiting family, was notified of the riot by family members who had heard news of the situation at SOCF over the radio. Tate made several attempts to telephone the institution without success. He immediately left to return to SOCF, continuing attempts to reach the institution by telephone.

Officer Howard Fraley called the control center from the L-4 safe well seeking assistance. No one answered the telephone. He tried to call again, and someone answered but then hung up. By this time, inmates had broken through the door window and sprayed Officers Fraley and Buffington with a fire extinguisher. Twenty minutes after they entered the safe well, the two officers were severely beaten and taken hostage.

Assembling the Hostages

Carlos Sanders ordered that all staff hostages be taken to the L-6 shower area and protected for the time being. At 3:45 p.m., fellow hostages Robert Schroeder, Robert Vallandingham, Conrad Nagle, Tony Demons, Mike Hensley, and Darrold Clark were brought in and locked in the shower cell across from Dotson ... minutes later, the inmate rioters placed him with his fellow hostages.

That was the only time that all of the staff hostages were together. In the shower cell were two inmate "guards" armed with PR-24s and handcuffs shouting obscenities and ordering them to "sit down and keep your mouths shut." All hostages were now housed in the L-6 shower cell together, where they were handcuffed or blindfolded or otherwise restrained—and in shock.

Inmates must have obtained a copy of the prison *Hostage Negotiation Manual* and *Disturbance Control Manual* from Unit Manager Oscar McGraw's locked office. Inmate riot leaders Carlos Sanders, who represented the Muslims, and George Skatzes, one of four "captains" in the Aryan Brotherhood, took Officer Mike Hensley to the Unit 3 offices and ordered him to call Control Center 1 and give the following demands:

(1) News media notified,
(2) SOCF staff off of the roof, and
(3) Ability to talk to the governor.

The officers were ordered out of their uniforms and placed in inmate clothing. This was something the officers did not want to do. It was giving up their identity as officers, something the officers were trained to resist. However, in this riot situation, they simply had no choice. The inmates put them into inmate clothing to disguise their identity as staff members if an armed assault occurred by other prison staff. Dotson remembers:

> When they forced us out of our uniforms and into inmate clothing, this went against everything we had been instructed to do, but we did not have any other option. All of us had been beaten severely; all of us were in shock and had severe head injuries. We were in absolutely no position to refuse—at least refuse and live. It's one thing to say what you would do in that situation; it's another to be living it.

Inmate Rick Hurst, who had provided some first-aid treatment to Dotson, assisted him in changing out of his uniform into inmate clothing and stated to him, "You're gonna be okay." Hurst did not identify himself, but Larry recognized the voice.

Abdication of Leadership

Acting Duty Officer and Unit Manager Oscar McGraw requested a police escort through Portsmouth to reach the institution. It was provided by Portsmouth Police Department at 3:48 p.m. However, upon his arrival at the institution, McGraw abandoned his duty officer responsibilities of incident command and drew a weapon and reported to one of the perimeter towers. He was later recorded asking several times for a "green light" to shoot inmates that he had sighted in the scope of his rifle.

At 4:00 p.m., Deputy Warden of Administration David See arrived at the SOCF as well as the institution's Tactical Response Teams (TRT). OSP Post 73 notified the Scioto County sheriff, Jerry Sutterfield, and requested all available units to the SOCF, and the institutional command center was established.

At 4:15 p.m., SOCF Deputy Warden David See notified Central Office Duty Officer Sharron Kornegay and requested to speak to the director. He also interviewed Shift Commander Lt. Wayne Taylor, who was in the institution's infirmary being readied for emergency transport to the Southern Ohio Medical Center via Life Flight. Finally, at 4:30 p.m., a full ninety minutes after the riot began, Deputy Warden David See ordered all tower officers to draw their weapons, and the SOCF Command Center spoke with Assistant Director Thomas Stickrath.

After returning Officer Mike Hensley to the L-6 shower cell at 4:37 p.m., all of the hostages were taken to the "dayroom" between cellblocks L-3 and L-4. The inmates had set up their own makeshift infirmary staffed with four inmate medics and the basic first-aid kits that were located in each of the cellblocks and unit offices. Dotson recalls:

> *I was very surprised at how much this inmate knew about first aid. Certainly our injuries were more than he could handle, but I was grateful for what he was able to do. In that situation, we were thankful for any care we received.*

At the same time, two inmates climbed out onto the L-corridor roof and surrendered. Larry Dotson, along with several other officers, was severely wounded. His injuries were numerous and included a shattered right cheekbone, crushed right hand, a broken right ring finger, three broken right ribs, left knee contusions, lower back contusions, and numerous deep head and facial lacerations.

Limited and superficial attempts were made to dress the lacerations above his eyes by the inmate medic, because: (1) the inmate medic had limited medical training, and (2) only limited and basic first-aid supplies were available. While in the makeshift infirmary, Dotson had an opportunity to talk with two of his fellow hostages, Kenny Daniels and Bobby Vallandingham.

> *I really only had the chance to talk with Bobby then … he was telling me how much pain he was in and the extent of his injuries. He said that he thought he had several broken ribs and a broken shoulder and a lot of other cuts and injuries. He told me that he did not think that he was going to make it out of there alive. I told him to "hang in there; we can do this." I tried to give him as much encouragement as I could, but he made me promise to tell his wife and family that he loved them*

49

and was thinking of them. The inmates did not let us talk long. I made that promise to him, and I kept it.

Despite having a severely shattered right arm, a broken nose, and head injuries and awaiting a Life Flight helicopter, Lt. Taylor refused to leave until a complete report was given to SOCF Deputy Warden David See in the institution's infirmary, where Taylor was being treated by the SOCF medical staff. After being transferred to and treated at the Southern Ohio Medical Center, he returned to work in efforts to retrieve his men.

At 4:45 p.m., Aryan leader George Skatzes began yelling at the officers on the secure side of the Control Room 3 crash gate, telling them that he had one of the officers badly injured. Skatzes said he would take the officer to the safe haven at the rear of cellblock L-8, where staff could retrieve him. When the inmates arrived at L-8, they knocked a large hole in the wall with the weight bars and placed the injured officer through the hole of the safe haven. They watched as a SOCF tactical team retrieved Officer Howard Fraley, who had severe head injuries from the beating he received at the hands of the rioting inmates. He was treated in the infirmary before being transferred to the Southern Ohio Medical Center.

At 5:00 p.m., Deputy Warden David See paged Director Reginald Wilkinson and spoke with Chillicothe Correctional Institution (CCI) Warden Terry Morris and Ross Correctional Institution (RCI) Warden Ronald Edwards and requested that their respective institutional tactical teams be sent to the SOCF.

By 5:10 p.m., OSP Colonel Thomas Rice had been notified and was responding to the SOCF, and other OSP posts were also sending all available off-duty units to the SOCF.

At 5:14 p.m., Deputy Warden David See talked with Director Wilkinson and opened a direct communication line to the DRC Central Office, and the Central Office Command Center was established. Major Roger Crabtree telephoned each of the safe wells but got no answer.

At 5:45 p.m., Maintenance Superintendent Bill Seth arrived and provided incident commanders with detailed blueprints and drawings of the SOCF. OSP Post 73 notified the Ohio Department of Transportation of the need to block State Route 728 on both sides of the SOCF beginning at 6:00 p.m.

Ten staff hostages had been confirmed: Officers John Kemper, Robert Schroeder, Robert Vallandingham, Kenneth Daniels, Conrad Nagle, Tony Demons, Darrold Clark, Michael Hensley, Jeff Ratcliff, and Richard Buffington. Officer Larry Dotson was known to be on duty at the time of the riot, but his exact whereabouts remained unconfirmed.

Warden Tate Assumes Command

Institutional Warden Arthur Tate, Jr. arrived at 6:00 p.m. and assumed command of the incident. Until Tate's arrival, no real command and control had been established by SOCF administrators. At the same time, the Ohio Emergency Operations Center was activated at the Beightler Armory in Columbus, Ohio, with Michael Dawson in command. The Ohio Emergency Operations Center is the statewide incident command center established to monitor and assist in any incident that could have statewide implications or require the use of multiple state resources.

OSP Plane #1 was en route to the SOCF at 6:31 p.m. and stated that there were two news helicopters following them. The news helicopters were advised to stay at 1,000 feet above the facility.

The SOCF riot had now gained the attention of the national and international media. In fact, several hundred media representatives came from as far away as Japan and Europe. More than a dozen satellite trucks would eventually descend on the SOCF.

Large numbers of both rioting and non-rioting inmates were still on the SOCF recreation yard. The Ohio State Highway Patrol had 100–120 armed troopers surrounding the prison by 7:00 p.m. and declared the outer perimeter secure. DRC Southern Regional Security Administrator Richard "TJ" Turjanica arrived at the institution. Turjanica, a thirty-plus-year career employee of the prison system, was highly regarded among staff, having risen from the ranks of correctional officer. It was strongly rumored that he was soon relieved of his official position of regional security administrator by Regional Director Eric Dahlberg and relegated to the task of taking pictures.

The bodies of inmate John Fryman, who prior to the riot was housed in L-6 cell 55 A, and Officer John Kemper were placed on the yard by rioting inmates, who believed them both to be dead as a result of their injuries. Inmate John L. Fryman, #199-058, from Butler County, was at the SOCF serving fifteen to twenty-five years for aggravated robbery. Fryman was covered by a large, blood-soaked American flag.

Officer Kemper and inmate Fryman were retrieved by SOCF Special Response Team (SRT) members at 8:00 p.m. and subsequently taken by a Life Flight helicopter to Scioto County Medical Center, where they were later transferred via Life Flight to Grant Hospital, the nearest Level I Trauma Center in Columbus. K-corridor was secured with thirty-two correction officers, two supervisors, and a shotgun-equipped tactical team.

At approximately the same time, hostage Officer George Horsley was escorted out of the gymnasium by inmates because of his injuries. He was secured by staff and taken to the institution's infirmary. He was provided emergency treatment and then debriefed by Jon Pence from CCI to gain some intelligence information on what was occurring inside L-corridor. Trying to contain the riot from spreading to other areas, and with K- and J-corridors secured, inmate counts were being conducted every hour by prison staff.

Hostage Family Notification

Attempts to reach the hostages' families continued throughout the afternoon and evening. Attempts to reach Larry Dotson's wife, Emma, were unsuccessful as she had gone to her mother's following Easter Sunday church services. After hearing of the riot on the radio, she telephoned SOCF and was put through to Chaplain Warren Lewis. He informed her that Larry was inside working and that they hoped that he had made it to a safe haven and was safe, but they were not sure as they had not had any reliable confirmation on his location.

She was instructed to go to the Valley High School directly across from the SOCF, where arrangements had been made by DRC officials to utilize the newly constructed but yet-to-open high school as a safe area for the hostages' families as well as the support personnel needed for the families.

Emma Dotson called her brother, a local minister, to take her and their daughter, Kimberly, to the school. Dotson's son, Joe, was working at a local restaurant and was picked up and taken to the school by Kimberly's fiancé. Upon the Dotson family's arrival at the school, they were immediately taken into the music room for a briefing.

The families were told that they had talked with each of the hostages or otherwise had confirmation on everyone's safety—except one. DRC and SOCF officials declined to identify for whom they had no confirmation. Based on her previous conversation with Chaplain Lewis, she knew it was her husband, Larry, although she did not relay this information to her children or other family members.

Tactical Team Assembled

There was a tactical team consisting of thirty-two heavily armed officers, medical staff, and OSP troopers assembled at 8:33 p.m. to retrieve the remaining hostages. At this same time, Muslim leader Carlos Sanders was meeting with a group of inmates at the horseshoe pit on the recreation yard.

Riot at Scioto County Jail

With news reports covering the riot at SOCF, and in an apparent show of support for the riot, the inmates at the Scioto County Jail also began rioting. Having already committed all available troops to the SOCF riot, Sheriff Sutterfield declared a state of emergency in Scioto County. According to Dotson:

> *That was naturally something that we weren't aware of. In fact, I just recently learned of it. I am sure that it was directly related to the riot ... like a riot in support of the SOCF riot.*

Officer Nagle Released

At 9:15 p.m., the inmates released Dotson's L-3 partner, Officer Conrad Nagle, and the bodies of five murdered inmates. Officer Nagle was released because the inmates believed that his head injuries were life threatening and significantly worse than Dotson's. In fact, just the opposite was true. When informed that he was being released, Officer Nagle courageously informed his inmate captors that Officer Dotson's injuries were much more severe. The inmates disagreed and released Nagle. He was subsequently transferred to Southern Ohio Medical Center and treated for his injuries.

Inmate Demands

Finally, at 9:30 p.m., inmate riot leaders released a list of nineteen demands. One hundred fifty OSP troopers and fifty SOCF correction officers were on the institution's perimeter. The Ohio National Guard had 250 troops from the 216th Engineering Battalion on alert.

The nineteen initial demands communicated to Director Wilkinson were:

(1) No repercussions against inmate leaders. Access to media/Cleveland *Plain Dealer* and TV, and access to Muslim imam, Catholic priest, and Protestant pastor.

(2) No selection of supposed leaders.

(3) Medical personnel for injured; no radios, no weapons, ID of possession.

(4) Don't have to pay for damages.

(5) Snipers removed.

(6) Abolish Unit Management/Security status.

(7) No forced integrated celling.

(8) No close inmates at SOCF.

(9) Unsubstianted records and/or RIB used or Parole Board be stopped. Including class III's.

(10) Reduce overcrowding in Ohio.

(11) No petty harassment (i.e., walking in groups by lines, ill-fitting uniforms, shirt in pants, hair-cut policies, medical treatment, phone calls to families, less idle time.

(12) Upgrade educational programs and make accessible [sic] to all inmates.

(13) Food improved.

(14) Do not destroy inmate personal property.

(15) Mail.

(16) Review records for released transfer.

(17) Inmate committee with staff, Ideal programming, outside help statewide group.

(18) Re-work education department.

(19) Dismissal of Warden Tate.

Officer Schroeder and "Snitches" Released

At 11:02 p.m., Correction Officer Robert Schroeder was released along with the body of inmate Walker, who was thought to be dead as a result of beatings at the hands of other inmates. The SOCF TRT removed the bodies of inmates Albert Staiano, #178-153; William Svette, #183-955; Darrell Depina; Franklin Farrell, #172-407; and Bruce Vitale, #159-865, from the yard.

These inmates were believed to be "snitches" and collaborators with the institutional administration and were therefore brutally murdered at the hands of what was to become known as the "death squad" led by inmate Keith LaMar. The work of the inmate death squad is graphically detailed in chapter four. DRC Director Reginald Wilkinson ordered a department-wide lockdown of all state prisons and told wardens to use their discretion in dealing with their respective inmate populations.

First Hostage Contact

SOCF Hostage Negotiation Team members spoke with Officers Michael Hensley and Tony Demons at 11:46 p.m., who, under duress, declared that all hostages were alive and being treated well. Dotson says:

> *There is no doubt they were under duress, but I could understand how it could be perceived that we were being well treated. Setting aside that we were hostages, we were given medical care for our injuries and were being given food and water. After what we had just been through, it could be seen as well treated.*

Murder at Midnight

Just before midnight, Aryan leader George Skatzes summoned Aryan Lt. Roger Snodgrass and instructed him to bring a shank. Skatzes took Snodgrass to the cell that held inmate Earl Elder, who had previously been pulled through the wall with Officer Jeff Ratcliff.

Skatzes instructed Snodgrass to kill Elder to "earn your bones." (The term "earn your bones" means to kill someone who was targeted by the Aryan Brotherhood in order to be worthy of membership.)

The cell door opened, and Snodgrass entered the cell and stated to Elder, "Have you made peace with your maker? I hope so, because you're about to meet him." Snodgrass beat and stabbed Elder to death. A subsequent twenty-five-page autopsy report from the Franklin County Coroner's Office described the wounds to Earl Elder to include but not be limited to:

> *Multiple stab wounds (163), multiple blunt force injuries; bilateral hemothoraces; skull fractures; bilateral subdural hematomas; subarachnoid hemorrhage; cerebral contusions; perforating stab wound to the lower lobe of the right lung; perforating stab wound to the upper lobe of the left lung; perforating stab wound to the lower lobe of the left lung; perforating stab wound to the superior vena cava; and a perforating stab wound to the right atria of the heart.*

Elder's body was placed on the recreation yard and recovered by DRC forces. Larry Dotson had come to the end of his first of three days in the "custody" of the Aryan Brotherhood and first of eleven days as a hostage in what would go on to become the longest and third deadliest prison riot in United States history. He adds:

> *By this time, I believed that I would probably be okay so my thoughts went out to my family, Emma, Joe, and Kimberly. I was praying for strength, for both them and me. I was reassured that I knew where real strength came from, and I was going to lean on Him because this was something that was bigger than me, but I also knew that whatever the problem, it wasn't bigger than Him. To a believer, there is no greater assurance. In a situation like I found myself, He is the only one who was bigger than the entire situation that was happening.*

Questions

As we look back on the first day's events, one must ask the question, did any of the seven officers who called in sick on this day know something that the other sixty-eight staff did not know? When asked, they all denied any knowledge of the riot or having been warned.

When informed that his fellow officer Bobby Vallandingham was called in on overtime, in all likelihood to cover for the seven call-ins, Dotson, in a moment of reflection, and with a tear in his eye, just looked toward the floor and said nothing.

Chapter 4:
Inmate "Death Squad"

The mass chaos of the first day of the riot provided what was believed to be the perfect cover for the deliberate and brutal execution of five inmates who were known as "snitches." Snitches were inmates who were believed to be collaborating with or otherwise funneling information to prison authorities.

At the same time rioting inmates were rounding up all of the staff hostages, another inmate group gathered up all of the snitches and secured them in cells of the L-6 cellblock. Still early in the riot, the L-corridor had been divided into inmate jurisdictions. The Muslim inmates had their headquarters in L-6 and were led by Carlos Sanders, Leroy Elmore, Stanley Cummings, James Were, James Bell, and Stacey Gordon. The Aryan Brotherhood, during the first two days of the riot, were headquartered in the gymnasium, but then relocated to L-2. The Black Gangster Disciples, a prison gang led by Anthony Lavelle, set up their respective headquarters in L-1.

One of the inmates on the recreation yard was Keith LaMar, #210-958. He was serving an eighteen-years-to-life sentence for a previous 1989 murder conviction from Cuyahoga. He was not a Muslim and had nothing to do with the planning of the riot or the takeover of L-corridor.

However, concerned about his personal property inside the L-corridor, he and a couple of associates, Derrick Cannon from Hamilton County, #221-663, serving a twenty-years-to-life sentence for aggravated murder, and Louis Jones entered the L-corridor and soon became caught up in the riotous rampage. After completing their "contribution" to the riot, LaMar and his two associates attempted to re-join the other inmates out on the recreation yard and escape injury, death, and hopefully prosecution. Dotson relates:

> *I was not that familiar with LaMar. Working relief, I rarely was in the same place for several days … I mean, I knew of him but wasn't all that familiar with him. However, I was fully aware that if he was one of our inmates that he was one of our department's worst; that is why he was at Lucasville.*

During their time in L-corridor, the Muslims had blocked both entrance and exit from the corridor. Things were not going as planned. LaMar stated to his two companions, "Ain't no need in us staying in here getting caught up in something we're not a part of. Let's kill all the snitches and get out to the yard."

Keith LaMar approached one of the Muslim riot leaders named Cecil Allen from Hamilton County, #197-506, serving a ten-to-twenty-five-year sentence for aggravated robbery, and offered a deal: "If we kill all the snitches, could we be let out on to the yard so we don't be a part of this?" After conferring with several other Muslim leaders, including Carlos Sanders, Allen came back and confirmed the deal. Kill all the snitches.

In a hurry to get the job done and get back out on the recreation yard, LaMar and his two associates began recruiting other rioting inmates to join their "death squad." They recruited Hiawatha Frezzell (a.k.a. "Pittsburg") from Franklin County, #195-593, serving a six-to-twenty-five-year sentence for aggravated burglary, and Eric Scales (a.k.a. "Tiger") from Scioto County, #223-096, serving a twenty-years-to-life sentence for aggravated murder. LaMar also recruited Derrick Mathews from Cuyahoga County, #142-546, serving a five-to-twenty-five-year sentence for aggravated robbery; Rasheem Matthews from Cuyahoga County, #223-185, serving a fifteen-years-to-life sentence for murder; Albert Young (a.k.a. "Da-Da"), #138-939; and Gregory Curry from Scioto County, #213-159, serving a twenty-years-to-life sentence for aggravated murder.

Having no real weapons, the members of the makeshift death squad fashioned weapons from baseball bats, shovels, and the now frequently used universal weight bars obtained from cellblock L-2. Wishing to be unidentified, they wore masks made of towels, T-shirts, and other clothing items. They were now masked, armed, and ready. They returned to the L-6 cellblock, where all of the believed snitches were being kept.

Inmate Timothy Grinnell, #218-140, who arrived at the SOCF in 1990 and was serving a twenty-years-to-life sentence for aggravated murder out of Franklin County, operated the control console that controlled access to the individual cellblock cells.

Inmate-on-Inmate Murder

Their first victim was located on the upper tier of the cellblock and was inmate Andre Stockton from Hamilton County, #154-686, who was serving a seven-to-twenty-five-year sentence for aggravated arson. Dragging him kicking and screaming from his cell, LaMar and the other death squad members beat him with their shovels and bats. Having beaten Stockton, and believing him to be dead, they moved on to their next victims, who were located in adjoining cells. Stockton survived his beating, and he was later placed on the recreation yard as other inmates believed him to be dead.

The adjoining cell was occupied by inmates Ellis Walker from Summit County, #150-973, serving a seven-to-twenty-five-year sentence for kidnapping, and Darrell Dupina from Medina County, #174-877, serving a seven-to-twenty-five-year sentence for kidnapping. Refusing orders by LaMar to exit their cell, both were dragged from their cell and beaten repeatedly. Dupina died as a result of his beating.

The next victim was inmate Bruce Vitale from Hamilton County, #159-865, serving a five-to-fifteen-year sentence for felonious assault, who tried to save himself by crawling under his steel bed. He was not successful. He died in the same brutal manner as the others.

The death squad then approached the cell of Thomas Taylor, #199-001, who arrived at the SOCF in 1987, serving a five-to-twenty-five-year sentence for aggravated robbery out of Lorain County. LaMar was told that Taylor was under Muslim protection. LaMar didn't believe the protection claim, but unwilling to chance Muslim repercussion, he agreed to spare Taylor if he killed the inmate in the next cell—Albert Staiano from Trumbull County, #178-153, serving a ten-to-twenty-five-year sentence on a charge of kidnapping. Taylor agreed. Using a ball bat, Taylor beat Staiano until the baseball bat broke. With Staiano still alive, Taylor then grabbed a fire extinguisher and finished his murderous rage.

The death squad's last victim proved to be the most difficult. Inmate William Svette, #183-955, was an elderly inmate who got around with the aid of a walker. The defiant Svette began taunting LaMar and his companions with racial slurs and obscenities. After opening Svette's cell, they beat him until they believed he was dead. Amazingly, he survived that beating, as well as another. William Svette died following his third beating.

Dotson heard nothing during the time of the executions or about them until after the riot was over.

> *I don't remember hearing anything about what was going on with the so-called snitches. There was so much noise and chaos throughout L-corridor, and with our head and other injuries, it was difficult to remember things, especially right after our beating. The fact that they were moving us so often because they were afraid of an assault by the department ... we had little time to really get a mental grip on what was happening at times.*

The hostages were moved constantly because the inmates were convinced that there would be an immediate assault on L-corridor by corrections officials, the Ohio Highway Patrol, and the Ohio National Guard that had been requested by Corrections Director Reginald Wilkinson. An assault was planned if negotiations failed. However, negotiations succeeded. Dotson thankfully adds:

> *I am glad that they did not assault, because we were constantly being told in very plain language that they would kill us if an assault came, and I have no doubt about that. Each of us had an inmate assigned to us that was ordered to kill us if the assault came in. The inmate assigned to me said that he had nothing against me so he would kill me quick. I remember*

he said, "I can't do you like that; you've always been straight with me, Mr. D. I'll make it quick and painless."

Running for Cover

After completing their murders, LaMar returned to the recreation yard and blended in with the other 300 inmates. He and the other inmates were secured by SOCF staff and placed in holding cells for processing. The inmates on the yard were believed to be inmates who were either no longer willing to participate in the riot or non-participants from the riot's inception. LaMar believed he was home free.

Having completed his side of the deal with the murdering Muslims inside, he had rid the institution of all the "snitches" and escaped back onto the recreation yard; he was processed by SOCF and other DRC officials as a non-participant.

He was placed in a cell in K-2 with nine other inmates: death squad members Eric Scales and Hiawatha Frezzell; Dennis Weaver, #143-185, from Cuyahoga County, serving a seven-to-twenty-five-year sentence for aggravated murder; William "Geno" Washington, #261-831, from Hamilton County, serving a life sentence for aggravated robbery, rape, and murder; Jeffrey Mack, #136-648, from Cuyahoga County, serving a seven-to-twenty-five-year sentence for rape; Michael Childers, #329-975, from Jackson County, serving a six-to-fifteen-year sentence for felonious assault; Ricky Rutheford, #231-322, from Scioto County, serving a five-to-twenty-five-year sentence for involuntary manslaughter; William Bowling; and John Malveaux, serving a four-to-fifteen-year sentence for robbery out of Hamilton County. Those ten inmates remained in the cell without a problem for the remainder of the day.

The next day, tensions began to rise. LaMar and Scales began harassing Weaver, accusing him of being a snitch, and told him, "All snitches should be killed." Weaver denied being a snitch and urged his fellow cellmates to protest what he perceived as mistreatment of the inmates who were not involved in the riot. LaMar became enraged and yelled, "Shut up, snitch," punched Weaver in the face, and forced him to a corner of the cell. Scales and Mack also joined in on the attack on Weaver. Later, LaMar ordered that Weaver, Malveaux, Bowling, and Childers be tied up.

Later that day, LaMar announced to his cellmates, "I want Mr. Weaver dead. I want that snitch dead right now." LaMar then accused Bowling of being a snitch and threatened to kill Bowling if Bowling did not kill Weaver. LaMar untied Bowling, handed him some string, and watched Bowling choke Weaver. LaMar also threatened Rutheford, who then aided Bowling in the assault by holding Weaver's feet.

LaMar became impatient with Bowling's progress and told Childers, "If you want to live, if you ain't no snitch, then you help kill him." LaMar then untied Childers, who complied with LaMar's order by choking Weaver, using the ropes with which LaMar had tied Childers' wrists. When Childers began hitting and kicking Weaver, LaMar told him to "just strangle him" because LaMar wanted "to make it look like he hung himself." LaMar aided Childers by stuffing toilet paper and pieces of plastic down Weaver's throat in an effort to silence him. Weaver eventually died while Childers was choking him.

After Weaver died, LaMar instructed Bowling and Malveaux to move the body to a corner of the cell. He also ordered them to tie a string from a cell mattress around Weaver's neck "and hook it to the coat hook to make it look like a suicide." Before corrections officers removed Weaver's body, LaMar instructed everyone in the cell to tell them that Weaver had killed himself.

Subsequently, the grand jury indicted LaMar on nine counts of aggravated murder for his role in the deaths of Depina, Staiano, Svette, and Weaver. Five of the aggravated murder counts alleged that LaMar killed each of the victims with prior calculation and design, facts that are clearly related in investigative and court records.

The remaining counts charged LaMar with murdering Depina, Staiano, and Svette while committing or attempting to commit kidnapping. In addition, the grand jury charged LaMar with four death-penalty specifications attached to the first eight counts of the indictment.

Naturally, at trial, LaMar testified on his own behalf and denied any involvement in any of the murders. Keith LaMar was convicted of murdering five prison inmates during the riot. The trial court sentenced him to death for four of these murders.

The Ohio Supreme Court upheld both the conviction and the sentence. LaMar sits on Ohio's death row while his appeals are filed by the Ohio-taxpayer-funded Public Defender's Office and work their way through the federal court system. It is indeed ironic that the next time Keith LaMar arrives at Lucasville, the same facility in which he committed several murders, it will be for his own execution. Justice cannot come too soon for convicted murderer Keith LaMar.

Aerial photograph of SOCF as it appeared on April 11, 1993. K-corridor is on the right, and L-corridor with its eight cellblocks is on the left. The L-corridor gymnasium is at the extreme left of the picture.

Close-up aerial photograph of L-corridor. The large eight cellblocks are well identified, and the gymnasium is located at the bottom of the picture. A large amount of debris is located at the corner of a cellblock and the main L-corridor.

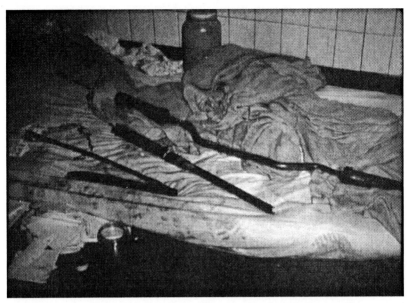

A small sample of the large amount of weapons found during the post-riot investigation. Note the 45-pound universal weight bar that was utilized to break through the concrete block walls of the safe havens to take several officers hostage.

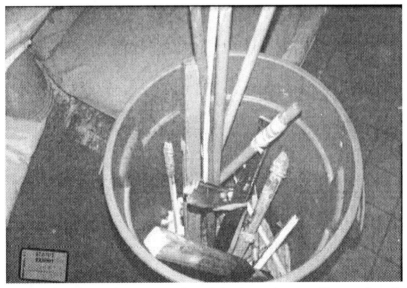

Dozens of additional weapons found by investigators. Broom handles, metal bed frames, and pieces of wood were used for beatings, tortures, and murders.

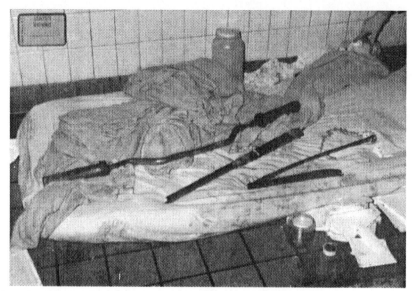

Another view of weapons and the 45-pound solid-steel universal weight bars. These weight bars broke through the concrete safe haven walls with several blows.

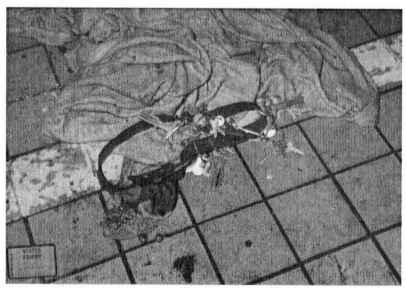

Keys taken from correction officers during the initial takeover. Note the large 5-inch Folger-Adams keys used to access the eight large cellblocks in L-corridor.

Blood-stained aluminum baseball bats used in the assault of other inmates and correction officers. The baseball bats were obtained from the recreation area in the L-corridor gymnasium.

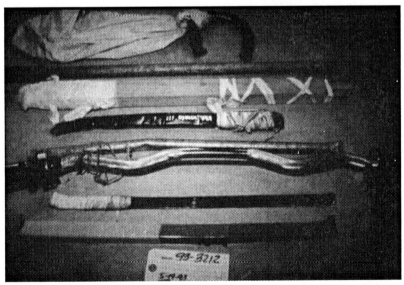

Another sample of the large amount of weapons obtained during the investigation phase following the riot. Numerous weapons were tagged by investigators as evidence that was later used in numerous trials.

A picture representative of the damage and destruction of one of the dayrooms in L-corridor.

Damage that was representative of one of the L-corridor cellblocks. In the center of the picture are the two console panels that controlled the cell and shower doors.

A view from the upper cellblock range of the massive damage caused by rioting inmates.

Another view of the extensive damage and sheer destruction of one of the L-corridor cellblocks.

View from the upper range of an L-corridor cellblock. The two control panels are on the right just inside the cellblock door. The upper barred area is one of the cells where hostages were initially housed during the early hours of the riot.

One of the many booby-traps designed by rioting inmates to be used against troops if an assault would occur. This is a steel locker box filled with concrete pieces to be dropped on anyone entering the cellblock.

One of the steel doors to the officer safe wells. The window was smashed out, and the officers inside were sprayed with a fire extinguisher while the inmates pounded through the concrete block wall on the right to pull the officers out of the stairwell.

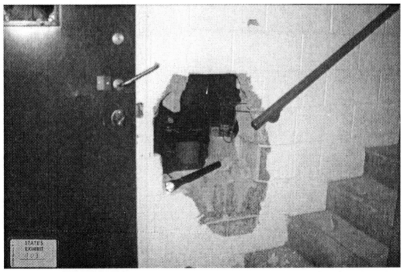

Another view of the above safe well. Notice the total lack of reinforcement in the concrete block wall. Other than the window being broken out, no damage was done to the door. There was no need.

A sample of the Muslim gang graffiti that was painted on the walls of the cellblock that was controlled by the Muslims during the 11 days of the riot.

Aryan Brotherhood gang graffiti.

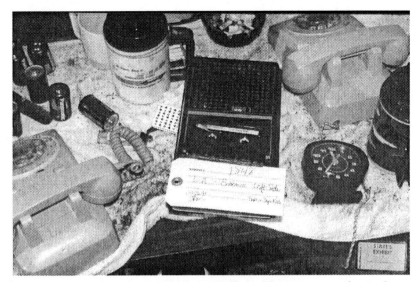

The inmate negotiation area in Unit 3 offices. The tape recorder is the one used by the inmates to record the negotiations and to make audiotapes of the hostages to be sent to officials.

Destruction to one of the cellblocks. Notice the sheets hanging from the railings. These were placed by the inmates under the ventilation ducts to catch any gas canisters that were lobed into the cellblocks by troops assaulting the institution.

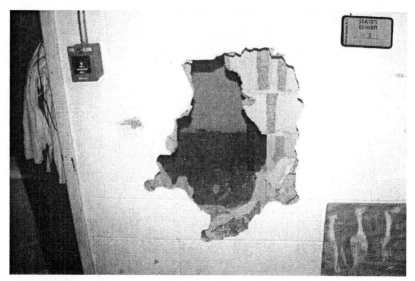

A view inside one of the safe wells designed for officer safety. One concrete block thick with no steel reinforcement. The concrete was no match for the steel 45-pound universal weight bars.

One of the two "death chambers" used by rioting inmates to murder other inmates. It was one of the lower shower cells in the cellblocks. It was in a cell such as this that Larry Dotson was first placed.

Another view of the wall inside one of the death chambers. Notice the large amount of blood splattered on the tile wall. Inmate David Sommers was murdered in this cell.

One of the many pieces of bed linen that were used by rioting inmates to make signs that hung out of cellblock windows to communicate with the media and the public.

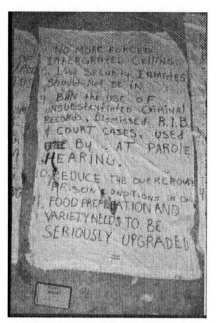

Another sign that contains several of the initial inmate demands that were given on the first night of the riot. This sheet contains demands 7-11.

One of many signs hung from cellblock windows. This sign contains the demands 15-17.

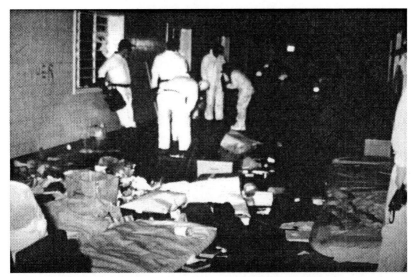

Ohio State Highway Patrol investigators going through the L-corridor, the largest crime scene in Ohio's history.

Rioting inmates sit in the gymnasium after being processed following their televised surrender by DRC and Ohio State Highway Patrol investigators before being sent to various other Ohio prisons.

SOCF officials and staff welcome staff hostages as they are being brought to the institution's infirmary following their release.

Officer Jeff Ratcliff (left) being assisted by Officer Brian Cox to the infirmary following his release after 11 days as a hostage.

Ohio Highway Patrol Colonel Thomas Rice (left), SOCF Warden Arthur
Tate (center), and Deputy Warden David See (right) discuss the situation
during the course of the riot.

The incident command center at SOCF during the riot. Several Ohio
Highway Patrol officials discuss various aspects of the riot with DRC
Southern Regional Administrator Eric Dahlberg.

One of the numerous Tactical Assault Teams from DRC and the Ohio Highway Patrol who were on standby in case an assault was mounted to re-take the prison during the riot.

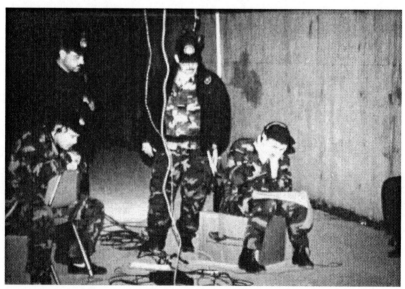

One of the many teams located in the security tunnels under L-corridor listening to rioting inmate conversations. All of these were tape recorded and proved very valuable in the subsequent prosecutions that followed the riot.

Chapter 5: Reality

Outside L-Corridor

On April 12, day two, Officers Nagel and Schroeder were released from the Southern Ohio Medical Center in Portsmouth. Attempts by the DRC to obtain a condition report from Grant Medical Center on Officer John Kemper were unsuccessful because the hospital would not release any information.

Plans were made to clear the K-side gymnasium into the recreation yard. The yard would then be cleared and the inmates would be strip-searched and locked down in K-corridor. A team comprised of Ohio Highway Patrol and SOCF staff would be utilized—the same teams that removed the bodies from the recreation yard hours earlier.

Rioting inmates at 2:10 a.m. demanded a media interview or a "dead CO will be thrown out onto the yard." The telephones being used for negotiations no longer worked, and an alternative telephone system was set up. The processing of the non-rioting inmates was continuing without incident. Warden Tate placed a call to Director Wilkinson and informed him that there had been no contact with the inmate negotiators for over forty-five minutes and that 178 inmates had been strip-searched and secured and another 125 were still not secure.

DRC Public Information Officer (PIO) Sharron Kornegay worked on a media lottery. Reporter Michael Sangiacomo from the Cleveland *Plain Dealer* would talk to the inmates on the telephone, and Channel 4 WCMH-TV from Columbus would film the interview.

Recreation Yard Secured

By 3:00 a.m., all inmates were removed from the recreation yard and locked in K-corridor's eight cellblocks. A total of 303 inmates were now secure. The DRC conducted a media conference at the Valley High School directly across from the SOCF. OSP Post 40 in Jackson, Ohio, had two dispatchers on duty but was being deluged with media inquiries from all over the United States. Inmate negotiators stated that in exchange for a media interview they would release one hostage, but due to the conflicting nature of the inmate negotiations amongst themselves regarding the release of a hostage, Warden Tate agreed to permit a media interview with inmates in exchange for talking with CO Larry Dotson. Up to that point, SOCF officials knew that Larry was missing but had not confirmed his hostage status. This would allow them to do so.

Mr. Whittenberg of the American Red Cross contacted the SOCF Command Center to verify that Officer Bobby Vallandingham was a hostage so that notification could be made to his son who was in the United States Navy in California. At about 7:00 a.m., the inmates demanded a live news broadcast and informed DRC negotiators that "bombs were now attached to COs."

Dotson Family Notified

Following a conversation between Larry and Jack Bendolph, an SOCF unit manager who was negotiating on behalf of the administration at that time, the Dotson family was notified that Larry's location and safety had been confirmed. Emma Dotson spoke directly with Warden Tate and questioned how sure they were that they had indeed spoken with Larry. Warden Tate smiled and explained that they had asked a series of questions that only Larry would know the correct answers to and that they were confident that they had indeed spoken with him and that he was safe. Now DRC and SOCF officials had spoken with and confirmed the identity and safety of all of the staff hostages.

Renewed Demands for Media Interview

The inmates began demanding to speak to reporter Tim Waller from WBNS-TV Channel 10 in Columbus, whom they had seen on TV offering to negotiate on behalf of the inmates. As a result, the warden ordered the electricity cut off to L-corridor at 8:00 a.m. DRC negotiators were having a difficult time negotiating because there were so many different inmate negotiators; therefore, the DRC advised the inmates to select a lead negotiator, while the Ohio Association of Criminal Defense Lawyers notified the DRC that it was available to assist with negotiations. The offer was declined.

FBI Assistance Requested

Warden Tate telephoned Paul Mallet, an FBI technician, for assistance with possible listening technology. Tate, a former FBI agent, was able to draw upon his FBI contact network for assistance. The FBI sent Ed Poore and Mark Hopper to evaluate technology needs, and Mike Hellard and John Linn of the Ashland Federal Prison in Ashland, Kentucky, were sent to the SOCF at noon. Later in the afternoon, inmates in L-corridor hung two sheets out their windows stating, "We want to talk to the FBI now."

A process was established for gathering intelligence by audio from the maintenance tunnels under each of the cellblocks by 8:00 p.m. DRC officials were also successful in placing ladders up into the cellblock walls and were able to hear well within cellblocks and dayrooms. Twenty-four-hour audio listening teams were established, and they recorded constantly until the resolution of the riot.

By 11:00 p.m., the inmates were requesting medications for Officers Buffington and Dotson in exchange for an interview with the news media. The DRC denied the request, to which the inmate negotiator replied, "It doesn't matter; we're doing life anyway."

Weapons Reinforcement

Late that evening, William O. Kempton, training supervisor at the Corrections Training Academy (CTA) just south of Columbus, serving as the duty officer of CTA, received a telephone call requesting that he bring a load of shotguns to SOCF. Kempton lived in Marion, Ohio, approximately ninety minutes from CTA. He telephoned M.T. Schwartz, the other training supervisor at CTA, who lived an hour closer to CTA, and enlisted her assistance. By the time he arrived at CTA, the requested shotguns and ammunition had already been signed out of the CTA armory and securely loaded into a CTA van for transport to SOCF.

Both Kempton and Schwartz delivered the weapons, arriving very late. After turning over the weapons to SOCF security forces, both CTA supervisors were "drafted" for additional duties and were quickly brought up to speed on the situation as it was known at that time and provided with a quick tour. They were then assigned to the incident command post serving as backup members of the Hostage Negotiation Team listening to both inmate and staff negotiators.

Because of his extensive military background and decades of DRC experience, Kempton was briefed on the three tactical plans that had been drafted. The three tactical assault plans were:

1. Blowing a hole in the ceiling of a cellblock and dropping in, making a dynamic entry;
2. Blowing a hole in the floor of a cellblock and coming up through the floor, making a dynamic entry; and
3. Entering through the rear of opposing cellblocks, one from the north and one from the south, making a dynamic entry.

Kempton weighed in on the tactical plans, informing commanders that without a visual confirmation on the location of the hostages, along with no verifiable intelligence on what was occurring inside L-corridor, each of these plans was a "prescription for disaster." None of these tactical assault plans were utilized. After several days' assignment in the command post, Kempton was relieved and returned to his duties at CTA.

Inside L-Corridor

Day two for Larry Dotson and his fellow hostages, started like no other day they had ever faced. Severely beaten, cold, hungry, tired, scared, and confused ... an emotional roller coaster, but there was little time for such thoughts. Blindfolded and still dazed from the beating he had endured during the initial takeover, Dotson remembered being in somewhat of an open area—not in a cell, but what he believed was a unit office. He was lying on a couple of mattresses with a lot of activity and chaos going on around him. No activity was directed toward him, but there was a lot of activity, yelling, screaming, banging, and mass chaos. The riot leaders had assigned several "wrecking crews" with the responsibility of totally destroying each of the eight cellblocks, which would render them inoperable and beyond repair following the riot.

It was difficult to sleep under such circumstances, but he knew he had to sleep to keep both his mental and physical strength as sharp as possible. Sleep provided a relief, although brief, from the pain—both physical and emotional. He was also uncertain when he would have to act to protect himself. He had to remain sharp.

He was able to sleep from about 12:00 a.m. until what he believed was about 5:00 a.m. Several inmates entered his cell, his security zone. They came in and removed the binding from his feet and took him to what later proved to be the inmate negotiation area, which was located in the L-3 and L-4 unit offices. He was given no directions but was given a telephone. On the other end of the line was Jack Bendolph. To ensure that it was indeed Larry Dotson on the telephone, Bendolph asked a series of questions to which only Larry would know the answers. Thirteen years later, he still remembers. The questions were:

(1) Does your house have a basement?
(2) Do you drive a red car?
(3) What is your wife's maiden name?
(4) What is your clock number?

After answering the questions to Bendolph's satisfaction, Larry was asked how he was doing and if he had had any contact with the other staff hostages. Unfortunately, he had not. After about a minute or a minute and a half, the telephone was jerked away from him.

Hostage Reunion

Blindfolded, Dotson heard familiar voices—it was then he realized that fellow officers and hostages Bobby Vallandingham and Kenny Daniels were in the same room. One of the inmates asked Vallandingham if he wanted a cigarette. He accepted. Officers Dotson and Daniels were each offered a cigarette as well, which both declined. Officer Dotson requested water but was denied. At that time, the three officers were permitted to converse for several minutes.

Officer Daniels complained of severe wrist pain but didn't have much else to say. Officer Vallandingham complained of severe right shoulder and rib pain ... he wasn't sure, but he thought that he had had his ribs wrapped and complained of a great deal of pain. They talked about their families and their wives primarily. Officer Vallandingham stated that he was not sure if they were going to get out of there. Larry was concerned by his tone of voice.

I tried to reassure both Bobby and Kenny that we just had to be strong, and why I took this role I don't know, but at that point, I just thought that we could all use a little positive reinforcement.

He attributed his attitude to his military background. Dotson had served twenty years as a military policeman and as part of the United States Air Force Hostage Negotiation Team.

He completed four weeks of training at Quantico, Virginia. Twenty years later, his intense training would help save his life and the lives of his fellow hostages. Larry states:

The situation we were in was just like the textbook training. I went through the initial stages of denial, "This can't be happening to me"; however, reality quickly set in that we were indeed hostages and severely injured. That moved me to the next step of trying to keep a positive outlook and give the situation an opportunity to work itself out. I just decided that I wanted to be part of the solution and not a part of the problem. The problem already had many participants; I needed to be part of the solution.

He told them that he was very confident that the department would do whatever it needed to do to resolve the crisis in a positive manner and to get everyone out alive. There was some negativity voiced, but not much else was said. The three hostages focused mainly on their families. They were hoping that their families were coping with this nightmare ordeal in a positive manner and not worrying too much about them.

We knew that they would be worried, but we were hoping that they were dealing with it as best they could, but all three of us kept our families first and foremost.

They heard inmates saying that they were bent on destroying the prison and could certainly hear the destruction: pounding and banging. It was an endless barrage of noise and destruction, an onslaught of mayhem. The wrecking crews were active.

The most significant thing about talking to Bob and Kenny was that Bobby said to me, "If you get out of here and I don't, please talk to Peg and tell her that I love her." As I look back on that, I don't think that he was giving up, but I just think that he wanted to be assured that someone else could give her the message that he was thinking of her constantly if he couldn't.

Larry replied affirmatively and said:

"Please do the same for Kenny and I." After that, the inmates shut us up and wouldn't let us talk. We remained there together, and we tried to talk, but it was hard. However, they still gave Bob a cigarette each time they had one. When they would smoke, he would smoke.

They remained together for about thirty or forty minutes after that. Although all the voices were quite distinct, Larry was unable to accurately identify any one inmate in particular at that time.

When they were separated again, he was taken back to a similar area but didn't think it was the same because there were two inmates there, and they told him who they were.

They assured me that they were there to make sure that nothing happened to me. The two inmates were Mike Bishop and Freddie Frakes. I had seen those two guys around the institution, so I knew who they were. I never had any problem out of them. As far as inmates go, they were pretty decent. Both had strong Aryan Brotherhood affiliations. When I first had gotten to Lucasville in February of 1991, it was a total culture shock. I had worked for three years at Ross Correctional Institution, but the security level was completely different. At

Ross, the inmates had freedom of movement. When I got to Lucasville, Warden Tate had just clamped down on security and really started to restrict inmate movement. When Bishop was in K-block and I was working there, I remember that he always got newspapers, about three or four a week, and I would ask him what was going on and he would tell me. Bishop never disrespected me, but Freddie Frakes was a different story. He was always in and out of trouble. Freddie would tell everyone that he was "fried"; he had used so many drugs on the outside that he was just burned out. He was a follower; he was just looking for someone that would take him by the hand and tell him what to do next. For the next two days, whenever they would eat, I would eat; whenever they drank coffee, I would drink coffee.

However, Larry was constantly reminded that as long as things remained calm they would protect him, but if the department mounted an assault on the prison, "we will kill you." He had no doubt that if an assault came, they would kill him. Most of the time was spent sitting, waiting, and thinking. He spent quite a bit of his time thinking about his family. A man really gets a chance to do some real soul-searching in times of extreme crisis—time to determine what is really important, time to determine real priorities, and time to reflect.

I am a devoted Christian. I spent a lot of time praying. Praying for me, praying for my family, and believe it or not, I was even praying for the inmates, and for a peaceful ending to this situation. However, my strongest prayer was for my family. I was praying that regardless of what happened that they would be able to deal with the situation whether I got out of there or not. The answer was revealed to me in a very personal, very private way later, but I knew that they would be all right.

After that assurance, it just became a matter of a waiting game. His injuries were becoming more tolerable, his mind was becoming more focused, and he was becoming more aware of his surroundings and what was going on around him. He didn't lose focus of where he was located. He was in the L-3 administrative area. He could picture it in his mind's eye. Knowing his location was critical in case he had to act quickly.

> *The noise and activity level was elevated and seemed to ride a steady tone except when something would occur and the inmates thought that there was going to be an assault. Things went wild. In my mind's eye, as long as the noise level didn't elevate any more than it was I thought that things were calm and that things were going to be smooth for a bit.*

During this same period, there were constant threats from other inmates who would go by his cell and yell in to him. There were several times that the yelling and taunting became so intense that he became very worried. But inmates Bishop and Frakes kept reassuring him that he was going to be fine and that they were there to make sure that nothing happened to him. It wasn't all that reassuring, but it was the best he could get at the time.

He didn't hear any of the inmate leaders discussing demands. He was glad he wasn't privy to those conversations; knowing too much in a situation like that could be very dangerous. He was given snack foods to eat, specifically Little Debbies and two iced raisin cookies. He did not hesitate to eat because he knew he had to keep up his strength—he had to be ready at a moment's notice. When he was given something to eat, he did not hesitate if it was wrapped. He figured that if it was cellophane wrapped, it was safe to eat.

In addition to all of the noise and activity inside L-corridor, he could also hear some of what was going on outside. He could hear the very distinctive sounds of a helicopter overhead. Because of his military training and background, he knew that there was a HU1E flying overhead.

> *I knew it was a HU1E because it was what I flew in as a door gunner in countless missions in Vietnam. It was making a lot of passes overhead. It may sound funny, but I drew a lot of strength from hearing that helicopter. I knew that as long as I heard that chopper, that in my mind they were still out there and doing whatever they could to get us out of there alive. It became a personal issue with me. I felt as if it was my chopper and that they were looking for me.*

91

In a situation like the one Larry found himself, a person draws strength and support from a variety of unlikely sources. It was also reassuring that God was in control and could use something like a helicopter from a war to provide comfort to one of his children. Larry distinctly remembered that at about 8:00 a.m. the inmates became very upset because the administration had just cut the electricity and the water off, and they were trying to find water resources. The noise and activity level reached a fever pitch. It was a very frightening and uncertain time.

> *Everyone was running around yelling and screaming. Many of the inmates believed that it was the beginning of an assault. The tension was very tense ... so tense you could cut it with a knife. I don't mind telling you I was really scared. As hectic and frantic as the situation became, it was very difficult to anticipate what was going to happen next.*

When the water and electricity were cut off, the inmates looked at that as the department giving up on resolving the riot peacefully. The inmates told the hostages that it was an indicator that the department had also given up on them as well. Larry knew that it was a mind game, but it was clear that the situation had changed dramatically, and not for the better. Comments from the inmates such as, "Your people don't care about you"; "Your people are playing hardball"; and "We can play hardball too" were frequent. Larry believed that if something was going to occur, like a tactical assault to re-take the prison, it was going to occur very soon. He had to be ready. It was going to put his training to the ultimate test. This was it; he could feel it.

The inmates began yelling about the snipers on the roof and in the security towers. They knew that there were high-powered rifles in the towers and that the staff in those towers would not hesitate to use them when given the order. There were increasing numbers of men in black fatigue uniforms that greatly concerned the inmate rioters. They did not know who they were or what their orders were. There were a great number of vehicles of all types that made a tight perimeter around the institution's fence. The inmates were well aware of the buildup of arms and troops but were unsure what to do about it. Larry knew that when people became very frightened, they also became increasingly unpredictable and irrational. That was not good.

Negotiations continued with the inmate leaders and Jack Bendolph. The negotiations soon stalled as it became quite clear that the inmates did not like or trust Bendolph. Inmate negotiators soon demanded that Bendolph no longer continue negotiating and refused to negotiate with him. Dotson was very surprised at the vocal hatred of Bendolph. He knew that this was another ominous sign.

As the minutes and hours passed, tension inside L-corridor tempered somewhat. Larry had no further contact with any of his fellow hostages, but the psychological torture from the inmates dramatically increased. They would frequently come by his cell and say, "Your people aren't negotiating in good faith. They don't care about us, and they sure don't care about you. How does it feel to be locked up? You're nobody now … you never were nobody."

The inmate medic, Mason, who had provided first aid to Larry returned to his cell and redressed his wound above his eyes. Larry was told that his wounds were very serious and needed stitches. Inmate Mason appeared to have a genuine concern for the wounds. Larry's wounds were painted with some type of medication and wrapped. This fully blocked Larry's ability to see.

Up until he redressed my eyes, I could see out of the bottom of my blindfold, but after that, I was completely blind. This made me even more concerned, especially since I really believed that there was going to be an assault. It was going to make defending myself even more difficult.

Larry remembered being asked about any medical conditions he had. Despite taking a low dose of medication for high blood pressure, Larry had been trained in these types of situations to always deny medical conditions as they could be used against him or exploited later. That was all part of his military training, which he remembered with increasing clarity.

The psychological warfare of the inmates toward the hostages continued. Realizing what they were doing made it somewhat easier to take, but it still was mentally exhausting—at a time when he needed to remain fully focused. Larry was never interrogated in the sense of the word *interrogation*. There was no need.

> *The inmates knew more about the institution structure and operation than I did. They had been locked up there for years. They had our policy and procedure manuals, our hostage negotiation manuals, and our disturbance control manuals. They had it all and were reading it to me. They knew if an assault came what to expect and how DRC would do it.*

To the best of his recollection, both sides were trying to get their negotiation strategy set. The inmates really thought there was going to be an assault. They discussed the weapons they had and the type of booby traps they had set up, but nothing specific. This made him even more concerned because the inmate leaders were rounding up the inmates who had military, special forces, and martial arts experience to assist them.

> *Many people think that everyone in prison is illiterate, dumb, or stupid. That is not true. While there are certainly those type of people incarcerated, we have many, many veterans with all types of military experience … special forces, special operations, boxers, wrestlers, marksmen, counter-intelligence personnel. Those types of skills were what our people and we were up against. I had absolutely no doubt whatsoever that they would utilize those skills to their maximum advantage.*

After a while he became numb to the mind games that they were trying to play. He asked no questions of the inmates who were protecting him. Although he believed that Bishop and Frakes would answer any questions he asked, the risks were too great. The less he knew, the better his chances of staying alive. He kept his questions to himself. Except when trying to reassure himself that the two inmates assigned to him were going to protect him from other inmates, there was not a time when he was not afraid. It was crystal clear to him that he was not in control.

Due to the unique type of woven restraint the inmates had applied to his hands, Larry had about a five-inch movement with his hands. As a result of the increased inmate activity and tension, he spent a great deal of time trying to think of ways to defend himself with his limited movement.

> *I knew that I could get the blindfold off real fast, but my mentality was that I was not going to be killed without a fight. I was going to use the skills I had been taught. I was not going to go quietly. Every minute that you are here is precious. I am not an aggressive individual by nature, but I was convinced that I was not going to allow them to do to me what they had planned without as much resistance as I could offer.*

It was late in the evening, he believed. At least that is what the inmates guarding him told him. He had all but made it through his second day in captivity, so he spent time praying to live for day number three.

Chapter 6: Impasse

Outside L-Corridor

Tuesday, April 13, day number three, started out as an impasse from not only the inmates' point of view, but the hostages and the negotiation team as well: "kind of like a couple of boxers in the first few rounds trying to feel each other out." Each side was willing to make concessions to the other side to get what they wanted.

However, outside forces and influences were having a major impact on the Lucasville riot and to a degree continued to dictate the events in which Larry Dotson and his fellow hostages were pawns. The media, in all too many instances, created news when none was forthcoming from officials. There was absolutely no question that these sensationalized claims, assertions, and rumors from unnamed sources compromised efforts to bring the riot to a close.

DRC officers found the body of inmate Dennis Weaver, who was the first black inmate to die in the riot, in a cell in K-block with nine other inmates. All surviving inmates claimed that Weaver had committed suicide. Earlier in the day, a mini-riot broke out in K-corridor, forcing officers to use tear gas to end the disturbance.

SOCF Warden Tate and Director Wilkinson met with hostage families at 11:30 a.m. to update them on the status of the riot.

At 3:15 p.m., DRC officials began moving inmates housed in other areas of the SOCF to other prison facilities. The first bus left with eighty-nine non-rioting inmates.

At 3:30 p.m., the incident command center received a call from hostage Jeff Ratcliff, who was pleading for the restoration of power and water. The call was referred to the Hostage Negotiation Team, which was responsible for all internal riot communication.

As a result of the FBI installation of listening and intelligence-gathering equipment, many forms of intelligence were being obtained from microphones and cameras placed in L-corridor.

Late in the evening, at 10:55 p.m., thirty-six inmates boarded a bus for transfer to Lebanon Correctional Institution, some two hours west of Lucasville.

Inside L-Corridor

On day number three, Dotson recalls:

Really, not a lot got accomplished; the only thing really that sticks in my mind about this day is later the inmate medic came back around and put some salve or something in my head wounds. I remember thinking that this wasn't going to accomplish a whole lot, but I was thinking that it wasn't going to hurt anything either. At that time, I am not having a lot of pain, but I was having a lot of numbness around my eyes, the right side of my face, and my head. I really didn't even remember that until about two or three years ago. I also remember how grateful I was because even though the inmates had the upper hand, it was like someone was trying to ensure that we did get some type of medical treatment and that we were being cared for.

As a former negotiator, Dotson knew that one of the things the negotiators strove for was to try to ensure that the hostages were being properly treated. As far as food was concerned, the inmates had pilfered through all of the locker boxes and cells of the hundreds of inmates who were not participating in the riot, so they had quite a food storage built up. He also remembered having a cup of coffee. Since the power had been cut off, the inmates had built fires to heat food and coffee. Even though the coffee was instant, it still tasted good. It's the simple and little things that one takes for granted that become important in a time of extreme stress.

Although he couldn't see anything, he was able to hear a great deal. He remembered clearly hearing the uneasiness of the inmates and how they were preparing for an assault. He could hear bits and pieces of conversations such as, "We have our demo man setting up booby traps."

The inmates had been methodically searching the unit and inmate files for those with military backgrounds, and the evidence after the riot clearly demonstrated that there were indeed booby traps and incendiary devices set up. So they did have the knowledge and capability to do that.

This would be a day of waiting. The mind games continued unabated. Several times throughout the day, the same voice would come by and state, "Your people don't care about you; they want you to die. They are playing hardball." Larry was finally able to identify this voice; it was that of Leroy Elmore, a Muslim.

Despite his best efforts to the contrary, the mental strain was beginning to have an effect. He certainly knew that his own death was a distinct possibility, but he tried to stay focused and thought of what might happen if they did come in to kill him ... what positions he could take up to protect himself. But when your hands are tied and your feet are bound, there is little you can do.

Sleep was difficult. Despite knowing that they needed to sleep, the mental and physical strain the hostages were under precluded any real meaningful and restful sleep. The noise level throughout the L-corridor was elevated and constant. There was really no "good" time in which to sleep. Larry could hear the telephone ring frequently. Even though he was isolated and on several mattresses in the L-3 inmate negotiation area, he remained curled up in a near fetal position—it was safer.

He was very reluctant to stretch out because of the physical vulnerability to which he would open himself. Inmates Frakes and Bishop were still closely guarding him, although they were now switching off with two other inmates who talked very little. Larry was unable to identify those two captors. He only spoke when spoken to and tried to be the "perfect hostage." He received pillows and blankets from his captors but didn't believe he was the recipient of any special treatment. He believed that all hostages received similar treatment; therefore, he didn't get lulled into a false sense of security by believing that he was receiving any special treatment. He didn't expect any and certainly didn't get it.

Frakes and Bishop took an interest in me. They would frequently ask me how I was doing and asked if I needed anything. They sat me up in a chair several times and even walked me around a little bit. Walking was difficult because I was still quite wobbly when I stood up from my head injuries.

Throughout the day and night, the destruction of the cellblocks by the inmate wrecking crews continued unabated. During that time, the inmates were concentrating on the cellblock consoles that controlled access to the cells and showers. They were destroying and burning the consoles and the wiring. The smell of burning electrical equipment was quite distinct. The attitude of the inmates was best described as cocky. There was the constant yelling of vulgar language directed toward the state and department officials and the frequent assertion that they were going to refuse to negotiate with the state or department and that they were going to take their chances with the FBI, which had arrived to assist with the crisis.

Larry continued to believe that there was going to be an assault, certainly during the first few days—yet another thing for which he had to be mentally and physically ready. How was he to keep all of this mental activity straight in his mind? It was exhausting, but there was no time for such exhaustion.

I knew that we did not have any females working on the L-side ... I really believe that if there were females held hostage that it would have changed the dynamics dramatically. That is just my opinion, of course, but I knew there weren't any females because Nedra Chapman had called off, so they could not misuse or abuse the females. Although, I knew that the same fate could also happen to me and the rest of the male staff. I was particularly concerned about Darrold Clark. He was twenty-two at the time, and even though he was a fairly mature young man, I spent a lot of time praying that he would be able to handle the situation and hold on and ride this thing out.

Testimony later showed that the inmates spent a lot of time mentally torturing Clark by dropping an aluminum baseball bat next to his head and sharpening their shanks so that he could hear them, as well as constantly threatening him with sexual and physical assault.

Even though the water had been shut off for a couple of days, Jason Robb had been an institutional plumber and knew where water accumulated in the pipe chases, so they were able to break through the water pipes and obtain water. "Water with the Aryan Brotherhood was plentiful. I got it anytime I asked for it," Larry adds.

Larry was beginning to get his mental bearings back ...

I knew where I was; the denial stage was now long gone, and I was dealing with reality. I was constantly thinking of my family; I was praying that they could understand what was going on. I knew that they didn't, but I was mentally trying to get the message to them that I was going to be okay, so that was my biggest concern at that time.

For Dotson, day number three ended like it had begun—an impasse. But he remained alive and was really beginning to rely more and more on his past negotiator training. He was fully aware of the Stockholm Syndrome and how under extreme circumstances a hostage could easily fall into a sympathetic mindset.

I appreciated the fact that I was still alive. I appreciated the fact that I was being given food and water, and I appreciated the fact that my injuries were receiving first-aid care.

However, Larry adds:

I did at that time, still do today, and always will blame the inmates solely for the uprising. They are responsible for the physical and mental abuse they inflicted upon the hostages and their families. They are solely responsible for the physical damage done to SOCF. They are solely responsible for the physical and mental injuries done to the SOCF and departmental staff, and solely responsible for the death and destruction they caused.

Chapter 7: Movement

Outside L-Corridor

Outside events complicated the entire hostage crisis, and April 14, day four, was no exception. Intelligence information gathered began to document a marked change in the inmates' attitudes toward the hostages. There was increased talk about killing the hostages. Colonel Thomas Rice was the incident commander in the early morning hours. Colonel Rice sensed such a marked change that Warden Tate and DRC's Eric Dahlberg were summoned to the prison and briefed on the "Slammer Plan."

The Slammer Plan

The Slammer Plan was believed to be the tactical plan developed early in the riot by command officials. This plan was to utilize bulldozers and other heavy equipment to create a hole in the corner of the gymnasium, thereby facilitating a dynamic entry into L-corridor. This was the fourth tactical plan developed.

DRC officials authorized the mobilization of several pieces of heavy earth-moving equipment. That rattled the inmates considerably. The DRC claimed that the inmates were tunneling in an apparent escape attempt and that the earth-moving equipment was brought in to check for tunnels and a small hole was knocked in the southwest corner of the gymnasium. Later this same equipment would secure three holes: two in the southwest walls of the gymnasium and one on the north side. Despite attempts to verify tunneling activity, none was found.

The word among the numerous tactical teams present was that they would be on the move soon. Tactical team commanders were briefed that incident commanders expected the following causalities:

- Hostages: 100%
- Tactical Team Members: 40-50%
- Inmates: 70%

These statistics were staggering even to seasoned tactical commanders. William Kempton's initial concerns were confirmed. Commanders briefed their team members.

Loss of OSP Helicopter

An OSP helicopter with pilot Ed Clevinger and DRC's Joe McNeil was sent up to assess the situation. Within minutes after take-off, the chopper crashed. All passengers received only minor injuries but were transported to Scioto Memorial Medical Center. The incident was reported to the Federal Aviation Administration (FAA) as required by law. Investigators were scheduled to arrive at approximately 0900.

Out of Control

While on assignment, Correction Reception Center Officer Troy Howard, assigned to K-corridor, punched an inmate while working in the K-corridor in an alleged unprovoked attack. Officer Howard was placed on indefinite administrative leave and removed from the institution. The nerves of all DRC staff were on the very edge.

Activating the Ohio National Guard

In direct response to DRC's request, Ohio Governor George V. Voinovich ordered the activation of numerous Ohio National Guard (ONG) troops. ONG units activated were:

- 16th Engineer Brigade, Columbus
- 135th Military Police, Brook Park
- 838th Military Police, Youngstown
- 385th Medical Company, Tiffin
- 684th Medical Company, Westerville
- 251st Combat Communications Group, Springfield
- 134th Engineers Group, Hamilton

- 216th Engineering Battalion, Portsmouth (Company A, Chillicothe; Company B, Manchester/Ironton; Company C, Felicity; Company D, Columbus)
- 372nd Engineers Battalion, Company A, Dayton

As if the DRC and command officials did not have enough to maintain their attention, rifle fire was heard about a half-mile northwest of the SOCF. Two units from the Scioto County Sheriff's Department reported that it was a single shooter taking shooting practice in a field away from the institution. To further complicate the crisis situation, State Representative Rhine McLin from Dayton called and expressed her opinion that calling out the national guard was an overreaction.

Hostage Threatened

At 9:00 a.m., inmates hung a bed sheet out of one of the L-corridor windows stating that a hostage would be killed if their demands were not met. At 10:45 a.m., DRC spokeswoman Tessa Unwin was facing an increasingly hostile media. They questioned her about the demands on the bed sheet. Unwin responded, "They've been threatening something like this from the beginning. It's part of the language of negotiation." She also characterized inmate demands as "self-serving and petty."

Negotiations deteriorated rapidly after those comments. Inmate negotiators began yelling at DCR negotiators over the telephone, and tensions rose significantly. Unwin left Lucasville for her Columbus home soon after the news conference, emotionally distraught.

At 11:00 a.m., with negotiations stalled, Dave Michaels from the Dayton Police Department was brought in to head DRC negotiations. Immediately, a food drop to feed 458 people was offered to rioting inmates as a good-faith effort. In the meantime, inmates were continuing to be moved out of the SOCF to other DRC institutions.

At 3:45 p.m., General Hughes from the ONG joined incident commanders in the command center, and final preparations were made for the negotiated food drop. Included with the food was medication for the staff hostages, one of them Larry Dotson.

Six hundred seven ONG were on site at their staging area at the Scioto County Fairgrounds. The Beightler Armory Emergency

Operations Center in Columbus was re-activated because of the involvement of the ONG, and the no-fly zone around the SOCF had been increased to three miles around and 3,000 feet above the prison area.

Progress

The hostage standoff would enter yet another day, although progress had been made on at least two fronts. The first being negotiations; a professional hostage negotiator was now the lead negotiator and had made a good-faith overture toward the inmates with the food drop. On the tactical front, three access points had now been secured should a tactical assault be necessary.

Lansome Newsome, deputy commissioner of operations from the Georgia Department of Corrections, arrived at the request of DRC Director Wilkinson. Newsome had over thirty years' experience in post-crisis troubleshooting and was recommended to DRC officials by the National Institute of Corrections (NIC) in Washington, D.C. Newsome's job during the riot was to assist prison managers in managing the non-rioting part of the prison.

Inside L-Corridor

Day four began a little differently; Larry sensed it. He was moved from the Aryan Brotherhood and the Unit 3 office area to a cell controlled by the Black Gangster Disciples. But, because of their lack of numbers and organization, the hostages were left unguarded and in open cells. As a result, Larry was taken by the Muslims into the L-4 cellblock.

Larry knew of the Muslims' hatred for whites and especially white correctional staff. This greatly increased his fear. He knew that even though the entire situation was extremely volatile and dangerous, he believed that he was safer with the Aryan Brotherhood than with the Muslims. This was not good, not good at all. A very bad situation had gotten much worse.

It certainly appeared that both sides of this hostage crisis now knew where the other stood and what each other's positions were going to be—what they were and weren't going to be able to get from the other.

The inmates told Larry about the crash of an OSP helicopter:

*They were laughing and quite pleased by that. In fact, I
didn't even know that there was a Bell Ranger helicopter up
because they are quite different from the HU1E. The Bell Ranger
is extremely quiet, unlike the HU1E. I could tell the second that
the aircraft commander turned the rotors on the HU1E. It had
a special whine to it. I flew 327 missions in a HU1E. The Bell
Ranger is a very effective observation helicopter, and I am sure
that that is what they were trying to do.*

That morning, inmates hung bed sheets with messages for the
public, the media, and officials to see, warning that a correction
officer would die if authorities ignored their demands. The reporters
were demanding information, and the DRC, by design, was offering
very little information. Unwin responded to the increasingly hostile
media. The inmates had recorded Unwin's comments and began
using the tape to whip other inmate rioters' emotions into a frenzy.
The inmates viewed the department as apathetic.

Later, inmate negotiator George Skatzes yelled into the telephone
to DRC negotiators, "You people think that we're playing games! That
lady from the Department of Corrections stated right on the radio
today, she might as well come right out and said she knows ... it's a
game more or less ... Whatever happens, it's on you people."

Dotson heard the dramatic increase in verbalized tensions within
L-corridor. Shouts of "They don't think we're serious" and "We are
going to have to give them one before they will take us seriously"
were now frequent. The inmates' attitudes had changed dramatically.
They verbalized even more intent to destroy L-corridor and threats
against Larry personally. He was unaware of what had precipitated
the escalation in tension—but again, he knew it wasn't good.

At the request of DRC officials, Governor Voinovich called up
the national guard at noon. There was a report that inmates were
tunneling under the prison in an escape attempt, and for that reason,
equipment was moved into place. That was the official reason given
by the DRC. The inmates were not fooled—the heightened activity
increased the talk and fear of an impending assault.

The inmates clearly saw the mobilization of the guard. They were
taking up perimeter locations with their vehicles and were moving

in heavy equipment. This elicited an immediate response from the inmates. With that, the threats of death were renewed.

Larry was fully aware that both sides were still "feeling each other out."

I knew that the longer things continued, the better chance we had of getting out alive and relatively unharmed, but this was a scenario that no one could train for. Most circumstances are for a couple of hostage takers and a relatively small crime scene. This was hundreds of hostage takers and the largest crime scene in Ohio history. This was rapidly becoming a double-edged sword for both sides.

Many things were going through Larry's mind. With the national guard on the scene, the dynamics changed considerably. Larry had been through negotiator's training, and he knew a little about tactics, but very little. Yes, a lot of things were going through his mind, and none of them were good. He spent a considerable amount of time trying to think of how an assault would occur … how much time he would have before the inmates' strike to kill him … how much time he would have to get his blindfold off … how he would defend himself … how many attackers there would be.

I knew that the inmates were concerned about an assault because an inmate came into my cell at this point. I knew that because things got very quiet. I knew he was there for one reason. He tried to get me to lie down. I didn't say anything, but I did not comply. I just sat there. That was the only recourse I had. I positioned my hands close to my blindfold, because I knew that I would have a second or two before the inmate struck, and hopefully I could get the blindfold off. He didn't say anything other than trying to order me to lie down. He stayed for about an hour until the perceived threat of the assault was lessened.

When an inmate came down the range and told the inmate in Larry's cell, "Come on, man; ain't nothing happening," the inmate left. Larry felt a great sense of relief and again thanked God for bringing him through another life-threatening situation. Nothing can describe the emotional stress incurred when you have been physically beaten, received minimal medical care, been physically restrained and blindfolded, and are in a very confined space with someone who has orders to kill you when given the order.

Later in the day, he thought things were improving because the inmates had told him that the DRC had provided them with food and medication for several of the hostages, including Dotson. He received his medication, Metoprolol 20 mg, for his blood pressure and recalls:

> When they sent in the food, I thought that things were going better. I was not lulled into a false sense of hope, but I thought that DRC's delivering of food was a positive occurrence. As a result of that food drop, I received a very cold drink of Kool-Aid, a piece of fruit, and a bologna and cheese sandwich. I drank the Kool-Aid and ate the fruit but did not eat the bologna and cheese. I love bologna and cheese but just couldn't eat it even though I was very hungry.

Day number four for Larry Dotson and his fellow hostages came and went with no resolution in sight. However, he was still alive—that was all that mattered. He knew that the longer the ordeal went on, the better his chances of survival. He thanked his Lord and Savior for another day in the hands of his enemies. He was unaware of the events of the day outside of his "world." His world at that time consisted of a prison cell with outside "guards" who had orders to kill him at a moment's notice.

Death Council

During the day, there was a meeting of the inmate riot leaders, including Lavelle, Robb, and Sanders. The group discussed killing a correction officer and, without dissent, decided to do it. After the meeting, Lavelle told Sanders that he did not think that killing an officer would accomplish anything. Sanders agreed that they should hold off on killing an officer that day. Later in the day, the news media quoted a DRC employee's statement suggesting that the inmates were bluffing.

Another leadership meeting was held that was attended by Sanders, Robb, Skatzes, Snodgrass, and Lavelle. At this meeting, all agreed to issue an ultimatum and, if authorities failed to comply, to kill one of the officer hostages. It was agreed that a person from each of the three inmate gangs would participate in the murder, and Sanders pledged that his security officers would select a Muslim inmate to participate.

At about 10:00 p.m., inmate Miles Hogan overheard Aryan leader George Skatzes and Muslim Stanley Cummings tell riot leader Sanders "about somebody that was supposed to kill a correctional officer and had backed out of it." Sanders replied that he was "sick of the [expletive] saying they was going to do something and then backing out of it at the last minute." Cummings assured Sanders that he "would make sure this got done," and Sanders replied, "Well, somebody'd better do it."

Chapter 8: Death of a Hostage

Outside L-Corridor

Thursday, April 15, 1993, marked day five of the riot. DRC officials, while methodically trying to resolve the hostage crisis through negotiations, held a meeting at 6:00 a.m. with the Ohio State Highway Patrol and the Ohio National Guard to further develop the tactical assault plan.

The 10:30 a.m. inmate deadline for DRC staff to leave the SOCF tunnels or a hostage would be murdered had come and gone without consequence. At 11:05 a.m., 380 Ohio National Guard troops were interspersed with Ohio State Highway Patrol troops on the outer perimeter security. DRC personnel located in the maintenance tunnels under L-corridor were, through their listening devices, able to hear James Were and others in a riot leaders meeting where Were was reported to have stated that he wasn't afraid to die and that he would kill another hostage if necessary.

At 11:10 a.m., four inmates in a mock funeral procession with a mattress carried out a body wrapped in plastic and a sheet and laid it on the recreation yard.

At 12:10 p.m., SOCF SRT troops recovered the body of forty-year-old Correction Officer Robert "Bobby" Vallandingham. The inmates had now crossed the line; they had murdered a staff member. Officer Vallandingham's body was taken to the SOCF infirmary.

Vallandingham Family Notification

Robert Vallandingham's wife, Peggy, and their son, Robert, Jr., had left Valley High School earlier that morning to return to their home to shower and retrieve needed personal items. DRC officials came to the school and took Vallandingham's parents, Homer and Wanda, into another room and informed them of their son's death.

Emma Dotson relates:

> *When they came in, we thought that they were here to tell us that another hostage had been released. There was a rumor that DRC officials were anticipating another hostage release. Then we all heard this agonizing scream. We all looked at each other because we knew something terrible had just happened. Terror struck each of us in that room.*

Vallandingham's wife, not at the school when DRC officials arrived, learned of her husband's death over the radio while returning to the school. When she arrived, she was emotionally distraught and demanded to know why she had to learn of her husband's murder over the radio.

Inmate Disturbance at TCI

Just when things seemingly could not get any worse, the SOCF Command Center was notified by Teletype that the 225 inmates transferred from the SOCF to Trumbull Correctional Institution had created a major disturbance at 12:15 p.m. The order to lock down all the DRC prison facilities by 4:30 p.m. was dispatched. This was an extremely difficult time for all of the department's prisons.

Anthony Brigano, Ohio's senior warden, was serving at the Warren Correctional Institution. He had numerous staff assigned to the SOCF. Brigano stated:

> *This was the most difficult time during the riot. I had staff at SOCF; one correctional officer had been killed. This was a terrible and tense time, but I had an excellent staff. We were getting limited direction from Central Office because they were directing most all of their resources to SOCF. As warden, I listened to my staff. They told me when to lock down and when*

*to ease inmate restrictions. My staff got us through those tense
times, and I am sure that is true for all of our institutions.*

Vallandingham Announcement

At 2:30 p.m., it was announced that Officer Robert Vallandingham
had been murdered within the last two hours. Institutions throughout
the state went to lockdown status. Colonel Thomas Rice called out
his 6:00 p.m. shift three hours early. Tensions rose considerably.
Negotiations continued, although the complexity and sense of
urgency on both sides had clearly escalated.

Media Broadcast Negotiated

Negotiators on both sides were brokering a deal to release a
hostage in exchange for a live radio broadcast on Portsmouth radio
station WPAY-FM. Prison officials contacted station manager Frank
Lewis, and he readily agreed.

If DRC officials had any luck, it was bad luck, because there was
a tornado watch until 11:00 p.m. for western Ohio, and DRC troops
had to quell a small minor disturbance in L-corridor with a single
canister of tear gas.

Hostage Release #1

Despite constantly changing logistics and inmate demands, at
7:44 p.m., hostage Darrold Clark, wrapped in a brown blanket, was
escorted by inmate negotiator George Skatzes to the negotiation table
in the center of the recreation yard. After being seated at the table and
before a "live" international audience, George Skatzes began:

> *All right, this is inmate negotiator George. I'm out here
> at the negotiating table, my brothers. If you can hear me
> on that radio, please holler at me. [Sound of yelling in the
> background.] Okay, I'm out here. I know there's a lot riding
> on my shoulders right now. I'm gonna do the best job I can.
> Everything's kinda tense. Everybody's a little nervous, but before
> I come out here, everybody in the world had something they
> wanted to say. I can't possibly remember everything. Okay. All
> right, here we go. I can't possibly remember all of the demands,
> but I'll touch on some and what I feel's the most important.*

But first off, I'd like, I'd like everybody to understand that to the best of my knowledge, tomorrow morning at 8:00 a.m., I believe, we are going to have live coverage of this on Channel 10 news. To the best of my knowledge, one more hostage is to be released in the same process we have just went through. That is upon negotiation approval here. You still hear me up there, brothers?

Okay. From the offset of this, we have tried desperately, desperately, desperately to get in contact with the news media. We have beat our brains out. We have been stopped by this administration. They think that they can confine this incident within the walls of this prison like none, like no other part of the world can hear this. They think that they can hide everything like they've been doin' down here for years and years. This is not the case. We are oppressed people; we have come together as one. We are brothers. We are very oppressed, and we are very sick of it. We're not going to take it anymore. We are a unit here; they try to make this a racial issue. It is not a racial issue. Black and white alike have joined hands in SOCF and have become one strong unit.

We have endured pure hell in there that they have put us through. We are still standing strong, and we will remain strong until we either negotiate this to our likings, or they will kill us. We are prepared to die. If need to be. And we hope it doesn't come to that. We hope that there is no more violence; we hope there are no more unnecessary murders. We as a convict body send our condolences to Bobby's family. I can't pronounce his last name so I'll have to use his first. But that is something that had to happen. A lot of us didn't want it, but that ... I'm sorry. That's all I can say now. First off here, we want to continue to have news media coverage. We want to work and negotiate. We want all of our moves babysitted by you people out there on the other side of this fence—people other than people attached to this administration or sympathizers of this administration.

We preferably would like to have an FBI negotiator. We want to get away from this administration. They are oppressing us, and they act like this is a joke. I have worked very closely with the hostages. We are in agreement. They have seen right beside me, eye to eye, firsthand, as to how this administration has acted like this is a joke; it is not a joke. Lives are involved here. Now, there are people, we are releasing one Darrell Ray Clark, Jr. here. I guarantee you folks, he is not gonna be coerced, pressured, or otherwise when he goes on the other side of this fence, and he is gonna tell you what it's like in here.

He's going to tell you. I guarantee you he has seen it side by side beside myself, Jeff Ratcliff, and a few others, as to how this administration has acted and act like this isn't nothing. This is something.

List of demands. Excuse me if I seem to rattle on; I've got so much on my mind, and I can't possibly keep it in order. There's a lot of pressure, you know?

One thing that we want to get rid of in this oppressed condition is our father oppressor, King Arthur Tate. He has got to go. Talk to me! It's nepotism. I hear a lot of complaints about that in the inmate population. They have got to stop that. What's the sense of dealing with one person when one person over here cracks your head and they turn around and look over here and their uncle cracks your head too? What's the difference? They all see eye to eye. We're not gonna take no more oppression.

There's another thing that I personally have in my heart. It's about this TB thing in here. Now, they give us those tests, and there's some rumor maybe, I don't know, but there's something like 33 percent of the people in this inmate population, not talkin' about the guards, that have tested positive, but approximately 33 percent of the inmate populations, if that's true, that tested positive. Am I still on the radio up there, brothers?

Okay, I'm very limited in time. I'm sorry. I'm in the, the, uh, list of demands and all, like, that is by no means short. I could rattle on forever. Uh, I do have one more thing. A man asked me to do him a personal favor. He asked me to bring a note out here to his people. I wasn't permitted to bring a note; that's fine. I will say Jeff Ratcliff sent his love to his mamma and his papa and his people, and he said that he is in there hanging in there strong. He was with Darrold Ray Clark all the time; he's doin' good, and I hope that we will have him out of here soon, too.

And, Jeff, if you can hear me, Darrold Ray said he loves you, brother. I don't know, like I say, there's so much runnin' through my head, and I know there's a lot of pressure on me out here. I'm a strong individual. I can hand [sic] it. Handle it. I know perhaps I haven't pleased everybody because I haven't touched on everything. I've tried, like, again I say, I'm limited on time.

There's a lot running through my head. But one thing I would like to say, in the past in my time here at SOCF, I have said that there are a lot of passive mother [expletive] in this population. Because of everything they seem to be so passive about takin'. I'm man enough to stand up and say I'm wrong. These people here, these my fellow convict brothers, have done nothin' at this time, and you are standing strong and a lot of you feel, like me, that you are ready to die, and I'll tell you what, brothers, every damn one of you, I'm proud of you and I take my hat off to you. And there is one more thing that I would like to say to you people out there on the other side of this fence that can hear me. Please try to help us get some type of electricity and water in here. Cuz we are not gonna bow down; we are not gonna give up; we are going to remain no matter what they put on us. If we die, we die. But we would like to have some light in there, and some water. If we're still alive, I hope that we can continue to negotiate, and I hope that this is not a trick. I hope we have the live TV coverage in the morning.

The live broadcast ended at 8:15 p.m., and George Skatzes re-entered L-corridor.

Officer Clark was initially provided first aid in the SOCF infirmary and transported to the Southern Ohio Medical Center via ambulance for treatment. At 8:29 p.m., the Corrections Command Center, located at 1050 Freeway Drive North in Columbus, Ohio, received a telephone bomb scare, and the command center was relocated to the Youth Land Building. A satellite uplink between the SOCF and the Beightler Armory was operational and secured through encryption.

Inside L-Corridor

The dynamics inside L-corridor had changed dramatically after what had become known as the "Unwin statement" made the day before. Things had gone from bad to worse. Larry believed that the chances for a peaceful resolution of his ordeal were dwindling rapidly. Sleep for Dotson was becoming more elusive. Physically, he was gaining strength, and he had prepared himself both physically and spiritually for what he believed would be the ultimate resolution of this crisis. He was ready.

I am proud to say that, even at this point. That to me is still a very comforting thought. The peace and serenity of that time was very comforting. The prayer that I had been praying that my family would understand was answered in a very meaningful way, so I was ready for whatever may befall me. I am actually as calm at that stage than at any time in my life.

Larry remained with the Muslims. He was treated differently from a racial perspective. The Muslims with whom Larry found himself had a vocal and violent hatred of white people. At this time, he was in L-6 cell 61. He knew exactly where he was because it was at the very top of the range; the first cell on the range was a shower cell and the first living cell was cell 61. The inmates were using the shower cell as a bathroom. He became aware that he was not the only hostage being held in L-6 because he heard them bring Officer Richard Buffington down for a bathroom break. Larry knew it was Buffington because he recognized his voice. This was reassuring. He was not alone.

I would then ask frequently about Buff because I knew that he was an insulin-dependent diabetic and needed his insulin and proper diet, and I also knew that he wasn't getting either of those. I was very concerned about Buff, but the inmates just kept saying, "Don't worry about him, man; just worry about yourself."

Dotson could hear parts of conversations occurring in the console area, which was about thirty-five to forty feet from Dotson's cell. He heard no specific plans but frequently heard the comment, "Man, we are ready for them when they come; we got somethin' for them." Larry knew what those comments meant, and he knew that not only was his life in grave danger if an assault came, but many other DRC lives were also at extreme risk.

The food rations became a whole different issue when he was moved to the Muslims. Before, he ate what the Aryan Brotherhood ate; now his diet became peanut butter and tuna. Water was strictly rationed. Before, he could get water for the asking. The Muslims limited his water to three to four ounces twice per day, which meant that eating tuna and peanut butter was nearly impossible. With his water ration so limited, Larry chose not to eat.

Time passed agonizingly slowly. Overwhelming physical and mental exhaustion now clouded his mental clarity. This increased his frustration, because he knew he had to remain mentally alert, but his physical reserves were being rapidly depleted. He also knew that if his reserves were becoming depleted, those of his fellow hostages were also being depleted. He renewed his prayers for physical and mental strength and clarity.

While he was acutely aware of his own treatment at the hands of the inmates, Larry had no way of knowing that two of his fellow hostages held captive by the Aryan Brotherhood were being treated in a completely different way. Hostage Officers Ratcliff and Clark were sharing a cell and holding regular prayer sessions with Aryan leaders Skatzes and Snodgrass. They were being permitted to shower and bathe and talked on behalf of the inmates to DRC negotiators on numerous occasions as documented by the HNT tape transcripts. In fact, each of the four was recorded as referring to each other by their first names.

Death Council Reconvenes

At approximately 9:30 a.m., another leadership meeting was held. Muslim inmate James "Namir" Were loudly proclaimed that he would "take care of it." Sanders urged Were to calm down. It was decided that one hostage would be killed. Sanders then instructed Were to "take care of business" if Sanders did not get back to Were in half an hour.

Little is known about how the hostage victim was selected, but what is clear is that at about 10:00 a.m., James Were, Alvin Jones, and

Darnell Alexander took Officer Vallandingham from his holding cell that he was sharing with Officer Anthony Demons and took him to the lower shower cell and proceeded to murder him by strangulation.

Despite being outnumbered three to one, Officer Vallandingham did not go quietly or easily. According to the coroner's report, Officer Vallandingham fought for his life for approximately ten minutes before succumbing. Later that morning, when questioned by other inmates why Officer Vallandingham had been killed, Sanders replied, "It was one or many."

As the body of Officer Vallandingham was being placed on the recreation yard by Muslim inmates, Aryan leaders Skatzes and Snodgrass were sitting with Officers Ratcliff and Clark listening to radio news coverage of the crisis.

As a result of Vallandingham's murder, the Aryan leaders now believed that the DRC officials would mount a tactical assault and that during the assault the Muslims would use the opportunity to commit racially motivated murder. Thinking that that would occur, the Aryans believed that it would be "every man for himself" and knew that providing protection to Officers Ratcliff and Clark would be impossible. As a result, Officer Ratcliff was provided a shank by George Skatzes to protect both him and Clark. It was kept under the lower bunk mattress for easy access if needed.

Alone in the Dark

Larry Dotson was totally unaware of the day's happenings. He states:

> *I heard a bunch of yelling in the evening like some sort of cheer, but I didn't know what was happening or anything like that. I had no idea what was going on, but if the inmates were cheering, I figured that it couldn't be good for our side; I knew that.*

While the day's events were far from uneventful, Larry Dotson was unaware of the death of his fellow officer and the release of Officer Darrold Clark. Tension remained high, and Larry remained on his own high mental alert. Another day of captivity was ahead.

Chapter 9:
Beaten and Betrayed

Outside L-Corridor

On April 16, 1993, day six, action continued unabated. At 12:07 a.m., a tornado touched down in the city of Zanesville, not far from the SOCF. Additional tornados were reported in Blue Ridge in Salem Township and in Bernice in Washington Township—areas surrounding the SOCF.

In the early morning hours, the Ohio National Guard took up positions on the institution's perimeter, which was completed at 4:00 a.m. A briefing at 6:00 a.m. was held for the Ohio State Highway Patrol and the Ohio National Guard. In the Ohio Penal Industries shop area of the SOCF, 180 OSP and 200 ONG troops conducted a "training exercise." Troops were being deployed into strategic positions.

Position Compromised

At 11:36 a.m., as troops were being deployed on the rooftop of SOCF, the Channel 4 news helicopter piloted by Rob Case violated Federal Aviation Administration (FAA) flight restrictions and flew over the institution at a low altitude and broadcasted the troop movements and location over the television. The inmates now knew the location of the tactical forces. The inmates were in possession of a battery-operated television that was delivered with the initial food drop by DRC. As a result of his irresponsible actions, Case was arrested and later fined.

Hostage Release #2

Negotiators were able to broker a deal for a "live" television broadcast in exchange for the release of one hostage, which was James Anthony "Tony" Demons. Already seated at the negotiation table was DRC negotiator Dirk Price and OSP Sgt. Howard Hudson. Demons and Stanley Cummings walked out to the media table. Both men were dressed in Muslim garb. In Tower 6, sniper John Wood kept Stanley Cummings sighted in his rifle scope. To prevent any further hostages from being taken, DRC and OSP officials had a prearranged signal to indicate trouble. Sgt. Hudson would be wearing a white baseball cap. If Sgt. Hudson took his hat off, it indicated trouble. Since it was a windy day, Sgt. Hudson pulled his hat down tightly to prevent it from being blown off his head accidentally. The broadcast began at 1:37 p.m. Cummings began:

> *I greet you with the greeting of As Salam-Alaikum [peace to you], which is the universal greetings of Muslims. My name is Abdul Samad Mulin. I represent the Islamic community. We have been oppressed here at SOCF and threatened by Warden Arthur Tate with abusive force to take tuberculosis testing by injection, which is forbidden by the Sharia [Islamic law] ruler, which governs Muslims ...*

After Cummings completed his statement, Correction Officer Demons, in a determined and angry voice, stated:

> *My name is officer CO Demons. My Muslim name ... means the chosen strong one. I would like to say some things. First of all, the Muslims did not kill those seven [sic] hostages. The institution wants the media to make people believe that the hostages were killed by the Muslim brothers. That is not true. Those boys were killed because they were snitches. That's what it boils down to. The Muslims did not touch them. The Muslims have kept every officer in there alive. I feel the institution has done everybody just wrong by keeping everybody in there so long. Now I knew Vallandingham. He was a friend of mine.*

The only reason that man is dead is 'cause he stayed in there so long, 'cause they went to cut off water and turn off electricity, which had me scared for my life in there. So I adjusted to the nation of Islam. I am going to tell you that now I'm proud of that. I fear no man, nothing. The only thing I fear is Allah himself. I'm telling you all that.

Upon Demons' release, OSP negotiator Sgt. Howard Hudson escorted Officer Demons. As they walked, Hudson attempted to place a uniform jacket over Demons' shoulders. Demons defiantly shrugged off the jacket. Sgt. Hudson was able to catch the jacket before it hit the ground. Thousands of Demons' fellow correction officers around the world saw the same open defiance and betrayal. The betrayal would not be forgotten.

After being taken immediately to the SOCF infirmary, Demons was then transported by ambulance to the Southern Ohio Medical Center at 2:26 p.m. Inmate negotiator "George" (Skatzes) called the HNT at 2:25 p.m. and stated that he would call again at 3:00 p.m. "with a way to end this."

At 3:10 p.m., inmate negotiator "George" gave three general surrender demands:

(1) TV coverage of surrender process,
(2) Safety of inmates assured, and
(3) An HOC committee to investigate conditions at SOCF.

Surrender Preparations

By 4:00 p.m., 557 inmates had been transferred from the SOCF with a DRC goal of 655. At 5:00 p.m., the inmates notified negotiators of their nineteen demands, and the DRC agreed. At 6:36 p.m., preparations were rapidly made to initiate the surrender process. Media equipment was put into place on the recreation yard and was ready at 6:45 p.m. The DRC public information officer (PIO) contacted Chaplain Wali Muhammad from CCI and asked him to come to the SOCF at 7:04 p.m. At 7:12 p.m., Chaplain Warren Lewis and Rev. Johnson from the A&E Church in Portsmouth were also brought into the command center to oversee the surrender process.

123

By 7:15 p.m., a briefing agreement had been reached on all inmate demands. Preparation of the signing table was made. The inmates were to exit the building by twos, and the building would be searched for booby traps. However, because of inmate security concerns due to darkness, the surrender would be delayed until 8:00 a.m. the following morning.

The inmates did agree to verify that the hostages were alive and safe by use of an audiotape. The surrender process was put on hold. The local Super America and the Subway shop in Lucasville informed the command center that they were getting calls from Cleveland stating that blacks from Cleveland were en route to destroy the town of Lucasville.

Director's Conference Call

Director Wilkinson held a teleconference at 10:12 p.m. with the DRC's twenty-four wardens and other key staff to discuss the hostage situation and the impact of the Rodney King verdict on the prisons. The riot would enter another day. The DRC couldn't seem to get a break.

Inside L-Corridor

Day six brought a whole new set of challenges for Larry Dotson—both mentally and physically. Larry says:

> *I began thinking a lot about my father ... just things people begin to think about when they think that the end may be near. This was just part of the mental evolutionary process and maturity for myself as an individual. I was also thinking a lot about my mother, because in November of 1992, she had had open-heart surgery, and I remember going and spending several days with her when she was in the hospital, and I can remember how weak and fragile she would still be at this stage six months later. I was wondering how she was coping—how she was handling all of this. We had a family pact that we did not keep anything from each other. I knew, I believed that my family would still be operating under that pact, so I knew that she would know that I was in harm's way at that point.*

Early in the morning, at approximately 7:00 a.m., just after the Muslims had finished their morning chants, Larry heard two distinct voices right outside his cell door. He recognized these two voices but couldn't think of the names of the two owners of these voices. Larry continued to listen with increased interest. It was a conversation between two individuals discussing the creation of the Muslim faith, the Koran, Elijah Mohammad, Allah, and some serious conversion issues. One voice was saying to the other, "This is what you have to do once you accept the faith. This is what we expect out of you," and "You will be the voice when you get out to let the people know what is going on in here." After listening to this conversation, it suddenly dawned on him whom one of the voices belonged to—fellow hostage Correction Officer James Anthony "Tony" Demons.

The other voice belonged to inmate Muslim leader Stanley Cummings, who was schooling Demons on how he would have to carry himself: "Be proud and show that Islam is an honorable faith. You will be our spokesperson on the outside." Dotson was livid. He was absolutely beside himself. He couldn't believe that he and the rest of the hostages, as well as all the DRC staff, were being betrayed in that manner.

"Is That You, Demons?"

The more he listened, the more livid he became. He knew that Tony Demons was one of the biggest inmate advocates among the staff and had a track record of taking the side of the inmates against the staff, but this…. As he listened, and without thinking, and out of sheer anger and frustration, Dotson yelled out, "Is that you, Demons?" As soon as he asked the question, he knew he had made a mistake.

You could have heard a pin drop. I mean, it got real quiet. Almost immediately after I said that, I remember saying to myself, "Larry, you have really done it now." Just after thinking that, I knew that there was going to be severe repercussions. Immediately, the cell door opened and two people came in and grabbed me by the arms and forcibly slapped me repeatedly, which re-opened my head wounds. They forcibly pulled me off the bed and dragged me out of the cell and then dragged me completely around the upper range. I was being dragged so

*hard and so fast that I could not get my feet underneath me. I
was thrown down in cell 37 and told, "Sit your fat [expletive]
down and shut the [expletive] up."*

Larry realized that he had made a serious mistake. He had spent
nearly five full days following his training to the letter and being
the "perfect hostage," and now one verbalized statement made in
sheer anger and frustration caused any goodwill he had garnered to
have been erased. Larry was very disappointed that he had allowed
his emotions to get the best of him. Even though the Muslims had
dragged him to another cell, slapped him around, and left, he fully
expected them to return and kill him. It was just a matter of time,
he thought.

As he sat in that cell expecting to be killed, one of the inmates
told him that one of his fellow hostages was "next door." Actually, it
was two cells down, and that cell held Larry's friend and fellow officer
Richard Buffington. There was an inmate Muslim leader housed in
between them named Darnell Alexander, who was one of Sanders'
lieutenants and went by the Muslim name of "Mohammad."

Dotson found this interesting because Darnell Alexander was the
last inmate he had talked to before the riot began. Dotson relates:

*Alexander was housed in L-3 cell 72, and he knew that
this was going to go down because he came out of his cell fully
dressed and his boots on. Normally he wore a T-shirt, flip-flop
shoes, and boxer shorts. He asked to be let out of his cell to
empty his trash. Conrad let him out, and he was down range
talking to me, telling me how he was getting his act together
and that he was short to the parole board. Looking back, I
know that he knew that the riot was going to begin when it did
because he was a major Muslim player in the institution and
he came out fully dressed. He hardly ever came out on Sunday
evenings—not even to evening chow. There is no doubt in my
mind that he knew what was going to happen. But things have
a way of working out because he was the first inmate convicted
in the post-riot trials, and he got some major time tacked on
his already-heavy sentence.*

Larry came to realize that there were two inmate "guards" outside his cell, then there was Alexander's cell, and two inmate "guards" on the cell that held Officer Buffington. The voices of the inmates were very familiar, but he could not put names to the voices. The inmate "guards" passed messages between Dotson and his friend, but they were never permitted to speak directly to each other until the night they were released.

Dotson had a severely upset stomach that would not subside. The inmates assigned to him asked him what his trouble was, and Larry explained his stomachache. He wasn't sure if the stomachache was from tension, stress, his diet, lack of water, or a combination of all of them. Unknown to Larry, Officer Buffington had already been treated for the same illness earlier and had several antacid tablets left over. Officer Buffington had his remaining antacids delivered to his friend. Larry was greatly relieved and received much comfort from knowing that his friend and fellow Christian was close at hand. Again, the Lord had provided—this time through a fellow believer.

Although he did not know it at that time, Officer Michael Hensley was also being held nearby, in cell 21, but the inmates did not tell Dotson about Hensley. At least three of the hostages were now under the direct control of Carlos Sanders and his Muslims. Also unknown to Larry Dotson was the fact that following the release of Darrold Clark the previous evening, hostage Kenny Daniels was moved into the cell with Jeff Ratcliff. Many of the special privileges that Ratcliff had enjoyed up to that point were somewhat curtailed when Daniels moved in because the Aryans did not know or trust him.

Death Notice

Late in the afternoon, inmate Leroy Elmore came to Larry's cell and sarcastically told him that one of the staff hostages had died.

> *Elmore would come by a couple times a day to play his usual daily mind games with me, and he sounded like he had started to walk away then he stopped and said, "Oh yeah, one of the hostages died. I just thought I'd let you know that."*

Larry inquired as to the identity of the hostage and was informed that it was his friend Bobby Vallandingham. Dotson also inquired as to how Vallandingham had died. Elmore stated, "Well, you know, he was injured pretty bad during the takeover, and his injuries finally got him."

Larry believed Elmore because Bobby had said that he was severely injured. Elmore continued, "Man, we were hopin' to get your people to cooperate a little bit so we could release all you guys before something happens to another one." Larry took this last comment by Elmore as a threat and also assumed that Vallandingham had died earlier that same day. Several minutes later, he heard Elmore tell his friend Richard Buffington the same story about Vallandingham. Larry recalls:

> *I was dealing with the news I had just heard. I could accept it because of how badly I knew Bobby had been injured. I said a prayer for my friend Bobby, and then my thoughts turned to the promise I had made to him to deliver his message to his wife, Peggy, and to his son. I was not looking forward to that, but it was something I had promised to do, and now I had even a stronger resolve to see this thing through and make good on my promise.*

That was an extremely difficult day for Larry Dotson. His fellow officer and hostage Tony Demons had betrayed him; he had received a severe beating from Muslim inmates; and he had learned of the death of his friend and fellow officer and hostage "Bobby" Vallandingham. He knew that with the death of a hostage, things would escalate and begin to move rapidly. All bets were off now. The inmates had crossed the line, and he was unsure how both the inmates and the DRC would react to Vallandingham's death.

Very late in the evening, inmate George Skatzes "made his rounds" and was told of Larry's upset stomach, and he offered him some medication he had in his possession. Larry recalls:

> *Of course, I didn't accept it. No telling what it was. At this point though, any doubts I had about Skatzes' position or authority in this riot were dashed. There was now no doubt in my mind whatsoever that George Skatzes was one of the leaders. Even though the Aryan Brotherhood was no longer holding me, Skatzes would make his rounds to check on all the*

hostages. At least I assumed he checked on all of us. He checked on Buff and I every day.

He also recalled hearing vague comments among the inmates late in the evening: "We're going for it" and "eleven days." He wasn't sure what it all meant, but if the inmates were happy about something, it couldn't be good for him or his fellow hostages. He was right.

Chapter 10: Mental Survival

Outside L-Corridor

On April 17, the hostage crisis entered its seventh day. Intelligence teams maintained their constant listening and recording of all sounds and conversations that were coming from inside L-corridor. In many cases, they were fully aware that the inmates knew that they were being "bugged," and many times, comments and conversations were spoken louder, seemingly for their benefit.

Tensions were expected to increase as the Rodney King verdict was scheduled to be made public at 10:00 a.m. No one was sure how an event happening over 2,000 miles away in California would impact the delicate negotiation process in southern Ohio.

Preparations continued unabated toward a peaceful surrender process. At 7:55 a.m., thirty MPs and thirty Highway Patrol troopers were being readied as the escort force, as the inmates would be surrendering in manageable groups of twenty. The surrender process would have the inmates process through four outdoor tables for fingerprinting and handcuffing. Each of the inmates would be arrested and charged immediately with aggravated rioting before being escorted to K-block holding cells.

Repeated attempts to contact the inmate negotiators by telephone were unsuccessful until 8:19 a.m. The inmates believed that they were in the better bargaining position at that time, for several reasons: they were in a multiple hostage, multiple hostage-taker situation; they held five hostages; the crisis had already entered its seventh day; they had murdered a hostage without consequence; they had received food and water on two separate occasions; they were in possession of the institution's *Disturbance Control Manual* and the *Hostage Negotiation Manual*; and they had aired their grievances to the world via the media.

Based on those beliefs, the inmate negotiators informed, "We will not be rushed into this. We have all of the cards and are playing hardball. We want food and water now." Negotiations appeared to have taken a turn for the worse. Inmate negotiator George Skatzes stated that "things are not going well in here" and that there were "too many people talking and to try to get a hold of." He wanted a peaceful end, but he would get back to the HNT as soon as possible. Less than one hour later, George Skatzes resumed conversation with negotiators. Demands had now changed. Inmates now were demanding food and water. When questioned about the holdup of the resolution, Skatzes replied that he was "not at liberty to say. Things are not well in here."

In an attempt to get stalled negotiations back on a productive track, a face-to-face meeting on the recreation yard was proposed. Ron Milton of WLWT-TV Channel 5 in Cincinnati agreed to air the inmate surrender process live and uninterrupted as a condition of surrender, and preparations were being made for another food and water delivery to the inmates.

To prove that all of the hostages were alive and well, at 2:00 p.m., the hostages were permitted to make an audiotape answering in their own voices a series of questions submitted by negotiators. Finally at 4:17, all five hostages were verified and the truck was moved around the gymnasium for the food and water delivery. Colonel Rice and Warden Tate met with the hostages' families to inform them of the tape and the most recent developments.

Meanwhile, in response to Scioto County Coroner Thomas Morris's request, the Ohio Funeral Directors Association activated its Disaster Response Team and had approximately twelve funeral directors assembled at a staging area near the prison. Rumors perpetuated by the media claimed that dozens of dead bodies were located in the gymnasium. Tensions had decreased but remained on a roller coaster path.

Inside L-Corridor

Larry Dotson got very little sleep during the night. Between having been betrayed by Tony Demons, physically beaten, learning of his friend Bobby Vallandingham's death, as well as suffering an upset stomach, he was very restless and slept very little.

Vallandingham Was Murdered

Early in the morning, after the Muslim chants, Leroy Elmore came back around to Larry's cell and said, "Mr. D., I can't do you that way, man; you know that officer that died—he was murdered. You don't need to know how it happened; all you need to know is that he was murdered. Your people were not taking us seriously, and we had to make a stand. He was murdered."

That was devastating for Larry. It was one thing to be told that one of your friends had died and to come to grips with the emotional and physical loss, but now he'd been told that his friend had not just died, but was murdered. That was a whole new shock phase for him. Larry states:

> *I was just trying to comprehend what I had just been told. I had met Wanda and Homer, Bobby's parents. I knew Peggy and their young son in the navy. I now realized that I was going to have to deliver that message—something I never thought I would have to do. As I sat there, I began to get increasingly angry and disgusted. I'm thinking out loud, "Lord, how much more are we going to have to endure?" As soon as I said that, the answer came to me, and it brought that inner peace back.*

Larry was thinking of the effect Bobby's death was going to have on the hostage families, the negotiations, and the local community. Larry relates:

> *I knew that this was going to create such a firestorm of resentment that the people were going to demand that something be done because of Bob's local standing. He was a local boy and a high-school sports hero and was very well liked and respected in the local community. Something was going to have to happen. That was another crisis point. I geared up to make the last stand. I just knew that it was crunch time. I*

have had a long time to reflect on this specific period, and I was running the gamut here of "do I do something stupid here" or "do I back off and let this thing play out." The inner peace came back. I think that that speaks volumes about me as a person and the God I serve. I was also thinking that I was still alive and breathing; Bobby can't do that. My priority became to get out of there and deliver the message that I had promised to do.

Larry never dreamed that he would have to deliver that message. Even after Elmore had told him that Bobby had died, and as tragic as that was, he could deal with having to deliver the message because he knew how badly Bobby was injured, given the nature of the situation. However, when he found out that his friend had been murdered, that completely changed everything. He knew he had to deliver the message, but he just didn't know how he was going to do it.

Larry remembers how sad that day was for him. The physical and now extremely volatile emotional roller coaster of the past seven days was really beginning to take a toll. He began to feel the life, both physical and emotional, drain from him. Up to that point, his faith and training had carried him, but his training was never meant to handle that type of situation because it had never been faced before. There was no training for that type of situation, for that length of time.

I remembered becoming increasingly angry with the Muslims. Every morning I could hear them down there chanting and praying to Allah. I was thinking, "How can these people be so stupid?" Allah is not even a living icon. I was thinking how grateful I was that I have a living God that I could call upon and listen to. The more they chanted, the more I prayed. I fought them like that. Almost like a "my God is better than your god" type of mentality. I know that sounds kind of silly, but that was where I was at that time. At that time, I was grasping at any straw I could get, because that is what I needed at that point. My mind was starting to go. I will be honest with you; the mind was starting to go at that stage. I was also consciously aware that my mind was starting to go. I was tired from the lack of proper rest, the emotional strain, I could feel it ... my senses were not as keen, I could no longer smell. I was thinking that I want my family to be proud of me. I knew they would be regardless, but I wanted to be as emotionally stable as I could.

He now had to concentrate and verbalize his thoughts of what he had to do ... it had come to that. Mental verbalization was no longer working. He had to physically talk to himself to maintain his sanity and thought processes. He had lost a friend to murder. He had a family to get back to and a message to deliver. At that point, it became all about him.

Did I know any elaborate survival skills? No. Did I know any elaborate mind survival techniques? No. I was having to deal with me as a person, and I was going to do what I had to do to contend with the surrounding circumstances. I knew that I was okay, but I was just unsure just how much more I was going to have to endure.

Larry was grateful to have had the four weeks of training as a hostage negotiator to draw upon. He credits his training for his being able to so effectively fight off the mind games the inmates were playing. As a result of his training, he knew that his coworkers cared what happened to him; he knew that there were many people trying to effect his release; he knew that the negotiation phones were being manned at all times and that there were people calling in the command center and that his fellow staff were willing, able, and ready to "come in at the drop of a hat" to effect his rescue when the time was right. He knew that they were still trying.

Another source of strength was that he could still hear the HU1E helicopter going up frequently, reminding him that they were not forgotten. The training was extremely critical at this point. It was day number seven, and he was still alive. He remembered that the longer a crisis goes on, the stronger the chances of hostages being released alive.

He also knew something that the Muslims did not know. He knew the strength of his God. His thoughts turned to his fellow hostages, and he began thinking about their faith.

I knew that Buff was strong. I knew that Kenny had a strong walk. Most of the others were fairly young, and I didn't know about them. I was saddened by the fact that I did not know about Bobby. I was praying that he had had the opportunity to make peace and accept Christ as his personal savior before his death. I was praying for his soul. My faith is very important to me. I know that He is why I am here today, and I will never deny His loving touch on my life. My faith had gotten me to that point; my concern was if my faith was strong enough to see this thing through to its conclusion. I was praying for a resolution to the whole thing. I prayed for each of my fellow hostages, although my prayers were different for them. The believers, I was praying for Him to deepen their faith and trust; for the others, it was intercessory prayer.

Chapter 11:
Hurry Up and Wait

Outside L-Corridor

On Sunday, April 18, DRC surveillance equipment indicated that there were no more dead inside. Activity outside L-corridor was hectic but somewhat organized. Activity was at times driven by the extreme highs and lows of the highly emotional negotiation process. As per one of the inmate's initial demands, DRC officials were attempting to contact John Rion, a Dayton area attorney and past president of the Ohio Association of Criminal Defense Lawyers. He was in Florida after his initial offers of assistance were rebuffed on the 12th.

Inmate Legal Assistance

Meanwhile in Cleveland, Nikki Schwartz received a telephone call from DRC Chief Legal Counsel Greg Trout asking him to enter the negotiation process. Schwartz was a prominent member of the Ohio Association of Criminal Defense Attorneys who had a long history in dealing with the DRC in numerous lengthy inmates' rights cases in the 1960s. Schwartz was then an attorney appointed by U.S. District Judge Don Young to represent the inmates of the Marion Correctional Institution.

In the mid-'70s, Schwartz was hired as counsel to the Counsel for Human Dignity, which brought a federal suit against the State of Ohio because of conditions at the old Ohio Reformatory in Mansfield.

The counsel was a coalition of groups that included the American Civil Liberties Union (ACLU), the National Association for the Advancement of Colored People (NAACP), and the Roman Catholic Church.

Schwartz agreed to enter the negotiations and was picked up at the Burke Lakefront Airport by an Ohio State Highway Patrol plane at 11:30 a.m. and flown to the Greater Portsmouth Regional Airport, where he was met by Trout and DRC attorney Austin Stout and then driven the eleven miles to SOCF. Upon arriving at the SOCF negotiation room, negotiator Dirk Price picked up the speakerphone and dialed the extension to put him in contact with the inmate negotiators.

After establishing contact at 1:40 p.m., Schwartz immediately warned the inmates that the conversation was being monitored by the others in the room with him. Those in the room included Warden Arthur Tate, Jr.; Allen K. Tolen, special agent of the FBI; Thomas W. Rice, superintendent of the State Highway Patrol; and Eric Dahlberg, southern regional administrator of the DRC.

With Schwartz's arrival, the DRC anticipated a quick and peaceful end to the siege. Officials requested WLWT-TV Channel 5 to ready their satellite truck to move inside the SOCF compound to broadcast the surrender process.

Robb's Ultimatum

DRC negotiators attempted to secure the release of two hostages with the arrival of Schwartz, but the inmates, believing that they now had the upper hand, refused. In fact, a conversation with inmate negotiator Jason Robb was quite abrupt. He simply said that the inmates refused to release any hostages until after their meeting with Schwartz, claiming that they "may not even like him," and further demanded that "if we don't do it our way, then we'll stay until the end of the month or you can come in after us. Meet it or beat it ... that's how it is." Robb abruptly hung up, and there was no further contact between the sides for the remainder of the day.

Meanwhile, the DRC moved ahead with its surrender preparations despite the lull in actual negotiations. A makeshift public address system was constructed to inform the inmates throughout the prison of the inmate demands the DRC had agreed to. A tape informing the inmates of the DRC's acceptance of each demand was broadcast continuously throughout the evening and the overnight hours.

Inmate Tunneling

On the 19th, surveillance reported scraping and banging sounds coming from various locations beneath L-corridor and other locations outside of L-corridor. The DRC believed that rioting inmates were attempting to tunnel out. An SOCF maintenance worker provided DRC officials with a map of area pipes. It was noted that fire hydrant lines ran in the area near where the sounds were being heard. The sounds were initially reported at 4:16 a.m. by an SRT from the Marion Correctional Institution that consisted of Roger Knaul, Larry Yoder, Jeff Bisel, and Rudy Mason, among others. Could the inmates be trying to escape, or were they trying to obtain water? No one was sure, but the answer had to be determined. A plan would be drafted to obtain the answer.

At 7:00 a.m., OSP Sgt. Fisher stated that the *Cleveland Post* had just notified them that four busloads of inmates' families were leaving Cleveland en route to Lucasville.

Autopsy Report

At around 8:30 a.m., the preliminary autopsy report of Officer Vallandingham was released by Scioto County Coroner Tom Morris. The cause of death was strangulation with no other signs of torture or injuries. That dispelled the widespread sensational and "yellow" journalistic media reports of Vallandingham's mutilation.

At the same time, DRC officials contacted Nikki Schwartz at the Comfort Inn in Chillicothe and requested that he report immediately to the SOCF. Warden Tate conducted a briefing with all pertinent agencies. All were informed of the status of the institutional operations, intelligence being received, morale, buses of inmates' families, Vallandingham's autopsy report, the need to restrict access to the command center, and the memorial service scheduled later that evening for Officer Vallandingham at the SOCF.

Caravan from Cleveland

Upon hearing of the buses of inmates' families being set to leave Cleveland, Governor George Voinovich telephoned Cleveland NAACP President George Forbes and asked that the buses be cancelled and said that he would send Director Wilkinson to Cleveland to meet with the inmates' families. Governor Voinovich had a personal friendship with Forbes, as Forbes was the president of Cleveland City Council when Voinovich was mayor. Forbes agreed. Director Wilkinson met with the families and explained to them what was happening and assured them that he was committed to ending the siege peacefully but reserved the right to use force should the need arise.

After the meeting, Wilkinson flew to the SOCF. At 3:10 p.m., a briefing was held to implement "Operation Mole," which was designed to determine if the inmates were attempting to tunnel their way out of L-corridor and the SOCF.

The inmates hung a bed sheet message out of an L-5 cellblock window that stated, "State is lying to public want to end this ordeal meet face to face with attorney, EME."

Operation Mole

Operation Mole was initiated at 5:00 p.m. and involved the use of a backhoe and ten OSHP troopers. The area between the two perimeter fences would be dug up in the vicinity of Tower 7.

Warden Art Tate telephoned Officer Darrold Clark and had a cordial conversation. Tate made numerous attempts to contact Demons to no avail. Consequently, Warden Tate was unable to talk with Demons. A memorial service for Officer Vallandingham was conducted at 6:30 p.m., and the hostages' families were given a tour of the SOCF and updated on the negotiation and operational progress. Operation Mole concluded at about 8:00 p.m. with nothing being found. The DRC had the answer: Inmates were not tunneling their way out.

Late evening, at about 11:00 p.m., OSHP Colonel Rice was informed of surveillance reports from L-4 and L-2 that reported inmate conversations about "killing Officer Ratliff in two days or possibly by 4:30 p.m. tomorrow." Colonel Rice immediately relayed the latest information to DRC officials.

Operation School House

In the pre-dawn hours of April 20th, OSHP Captain Welch conducted "Operation School House," which was the not-so-subtle operational name given to the security of Valley High School directly across from the SOCF where the hostages' families were being housed. Upon his inspection, all was quiet. At about 8:00 a.m., negotiations resumed with the HNT talking with inmate Jason Robb.

Face-to-Face Negotiations

Inmates, buoyed by the arrival of Nikki Schwartz, stated that no hostages would be released until all of the demands had been met and that the inmate negotiator wanted a direct face-to-face meeting with Nikki Schwartz. At 9:25 a.m., hurried preparations were made for a face-to-face meeting along the inner perimeter fence.

After all plans for the meeting had been agreed to, negotiators for the DRC (Dirk Price, Sgt. Howard Hudson, and Colonel Tom Rice), Allen Tolin of the FBI, and Nikki Schwartz began their slow and deliberate trip to the negotiation table, arriving at 10:45 a.m. After several minutes of waiting, DRC officials and the FBI agent left the negotiation table, leaving only Nikki Schwartz at the table. The HNT established telephone contact with inmate Robb, who stated that they would be out in seven minutes. Finally, after nearly an hour of tense waiting, at 11:53 a.m., three inmate negotiators began walking out of the gymnasium toward the negotiation table.

The DRC had snipers in all of the SOCF towers, including Tower 6, which was again manned by members of the Warren Correctional Institution SRT, including Lt. Troy Lynch and Officers Keith Lawson and John Wood. Tower 6 had an unobstructed 300-yard line of sight of the negotiation table and the recreation yard. Officer Wood sighted in the approaching inmates with his scope-equipped .308 sniper rifle mounted on a tripod. Tower 6 radioed physical descriptions of the inmate negotiators: inmate Robb, wearing a black sweatshirt and pants, blue bandanna on his head, and a gold watch on his left wrist; inmate Carlos Sanders, with a blue knee-length robe, blue bandanna, blue prayer cap, and dark sweatpants; and inmate Anthony Lavelle, wearing a black full-length robe, black pants, blue bandanna, and a gold watch on his left wrist.

Tower 6 kept the command center fully informed of all activity at the negotiation table. Negotiations between the inmate negotiators and Schwartz continued until 1:30 p.m., when three members of the HNT and Colonel Rice joined them at the table. Then at 1:58 p.m., the HNT and Colonel Rice departed to the base of Tower 6 and waited on Nikki Schwartz. At 2:20, again, the HNT and Colonel Rice re-joined the negotiations.

At 2:50 p.m., the negotiations concluded and all parties left the negotiation table. DRC officials retreated to the command center, and the inmates re-entered the L-corridor gymnasium with all of the details of the surrender hammered out and agreed to by all parties. At about 3:00 p.m., the HNT made contact with inmate Robb in reference to the laundry bags and tape to be delivered to the previously used food drop areas by the SRT, and these items were subsequently picked up by the inmates.

Later in the early evening, the command center received word of a protest march being organized by Janet Spears in Lucasville. OSHP Captain Marshall stated that it would be a peaceful march in support of SOCF staff. It was scheduled to last thirty minutes in Lucasville, not near SR 728 or the institution.

The inmates re-established telephone negotiations with Nikki Schwartz at 5:30 p.m. to finalize the surrender process details and supplies. All parties came to the agreement that a food, water, and supply drop would be made to the inmates in exchange for a newly made audiotape of all hostages. Warden Tate notified the hostages' families of the tape and the status of the negotiation process. The news media was briefed by command center staff at 8:00 p.m. A late-night meeting between inmate negotiators and Schwartz was rescheduled for the next morning at 9:00 a.m. No further contact occurred, and all remained quiet for the remainder of the night.

Inside L-Corridor

April 18 through 20 marked days eight through ten for Larry Dotson and his four fellow hostages. The hours seemed to drag on. The unrelenting banging, yelling, and screaming of the wrecking crews continued almost around the clock as the inmates continued to destroy everything they possibly could. The smell of human waste and smoke permeated the stale air.

Blindfolded, restrained, weak, tired, confused, scared, thirsty, and hungry, Larry lay on his bunk in a defensive fetal position. His senses became dull to the noise, the smell, and being blindfolded. Dates and times were becoming increasingly difficult to keep straight and had taken on a more cognitive role. Thought processes required much concentration. He thought to himself, *How much longer can this go on?*

In a "Routine"

As perverted as it sounds, Larry was into a routine, both mentally and physically. He had survived a full week of being held hostage and had gotten a "feel" for his surroundings, his inmate "guards," and the different noise levels inside the besieged L-corridor.

He could tell by the comments and activities of the inmates that they were becoming increasingly restless and were feeling almost the same way as he was: tired, hungry, thirsty, and scared as well. He also was well aware that when physical and mental demands increased, people became increasingly unpredictable. He was powerless to control anything that was happening around him. He had an increasingly difficult time controlling what was happening inside of him, but he was keenly aware that if he lost control mentally, it was all over. Mental control, that was the only thing he had left that he had full control of; he couldn't lose that.

Those three days were pretty "routine." Larry remembers:

> *The inmates, while tired and hungry, were feeling pretty cocky. You could tell it in their comments and the attitudes in their voices. They had held out this long and were proud of it. They were demanding to talk to an attorney, and there was comments being made back and forth about who it should be and what they wanted. One thing was always clearly evident, and that was that the inmates did not trust one another. The distrust between the whites and the blacks was first and foremost. They trusted each other much less than they trusted the state and the department. If I remember correctly, it was on day nine that I kept hearing the name of attorney Nikki Schwartz. I had never heard of him, but the inmates kept talking about him like he could get all of them out of this thing*

unscathed. I seriously doubted that, but anything or anyone who could help bring this nightmare to a peaceful conclusion was more than welcomed by me.

Larry continues:

I was still able to pass an occasional message to my friend Buff, and the inmate "guards" did provide us with some very limited information, but information was hard to obtain because I really don't think anyone really knew what was going to happen next. When the inmates told me that they didn't know something, I really believed that was true. Things just seemed to happen from one minute to the next, and there was certainly no real plan. The inmates were constantly thinking that there was going to be an assault by outside forces; that was the only thing that they were fairly sure of. I knew that negotiations were continuing because I occasionally would hear a telephone ring and yelling. I know that when I say that I had gotten into a routine that that sounds incredible, but that's the best way I can describe it. We are all creatures of habit, and regardless of where we find ourselves, we try to adapt to some type of order or routine in our circumstances and our environment. I was desperately trying to do the same thing under the most intense and trying of circumstances. Plus, I had the ultimate ace in the hole; I had my very own personal savior who promised to never leave me or forsake me—and he didn't.

Larry's world had taken on a new reality. His world consisted of a nine-by-twelve-foot cell, being constantly watched, and being given very limited food and water. He knew that the siege could not go on much longer, but he was unsure of two things: how and when it was going to end. Things remained "routine" with inmate Elmore making his daily "mind-game" rounds and George Skatzes his evening rounds—until April 20. Larry recalls:

On the twentieth, I knew things were going to come to an end, one way or another. I had a good feeling when the inmates began to take an increased interest in our physical condition. They came in and walked us several times a day and tried to clean up as best they could our wounds, but with the limited supplies it was pretty much a waste of time. The inmates who walked me around slipped a couple of hard oatmeal cookies into my shirt pocket. My training told me that things were beginning to move. I remember the inmates making reference to their attorney, and I believed that the negotiation process had finally become productive. I was now just praying that neither side did anything stupid that would upset the delicate balance that I felt had been achieved.

Larry recalls that when he was instructed to come out of his cell for walks,

I really didn't want to do it because I had grown to have a sense of security in my cell. I was still weak from all that I had been through, and we really hadn't done any activity for over a week except lay down, so any upright activity was a real challenge.

Resolution Talk

Throughout the evening on the 20th, Larry heard numerous vague references to a "resolution" the following day. The inmates never referred to a surrender process but always a "resolution." Even though the rumors were flying about an end to the siege the next day, it did not deter the wrecking crews from going about their never-ending task of destroying as much of L-corridor and its eight cellblocks as possible.

Larry's thought process after several hours of hearing the rumors was "Right, wrong, or indifferent, tomorrow something's got to happen." That wasn't so much anticipation as it was reality.

I somewhat anticipated a peaceful resolution the following day, but I just knew that it could not continue much longer. The inmates knew that and so did we. One way or another, there was going to be an end to the siege—peaceful or otherwise.

Eleven days seemed like an eternity, and the tension level was already at maximum. As for Larry, he knew that the time for action, one way or another, was rapidly approaching.

Taped Message to Family

However, Larry's emotions were buoyed by the fact that at about 8:00 p.m. each of the hostages was permitted to audiotape a message to their respective families. Larry recorded the following message:

> *Honey, how are you? I miss you like crazy. You hang in there. The Lord is essential to me, and He is with me. I am willing to accept whatever may come of this. I love you and the kids with all my heart. Hopefully soon we'll be together. I love you.*

Larry believed that the making of that tape could be viewed two ways. One was that it was verification to both the negotiators and the families that each of the hostages was alive and well; or two, that it was going to be the last time anyone heard from the hostages. Larry chose to concentrate his thoughts and energies on the first.

Chapter 12: The Resolution

Inside L-Corridor

There was very little sleep to be had late evening on the 20th and throughout the night going into the 21st. The early morning hours were filled with Carlos Sanders and his Muslims conducting their morning ritual of chants and prayers, which was not unusual. However, this morning was different. Up until then, Larry had never heard anyone make any attempts to disrupt the Muslims. He heard someone yelling and chiding the Muslims. The voice was very loud, so Larry thought that it was coming from a cell very close to his on the upper range.

It turned out to be inmate Bruce Harris. He was actually on the lower range in cell 14. Harris was a black inmate and had become uncontrollably violent and verbally abusive following a beating at the hands of the Aryan Brotherhood, with the permission of the Muslims, for the rape of a white inmate during the initial hours of the riot.

On orders of Carlos Sanders, the Muslims made several visits to Harris's cell and told him to stop making noise and interrupting the Muslim prayer activity. Harris responded with vocal racial slurs and increased yelling, screaming, and destruction of cell fixtures. Larry remembered that the Muslims made two trips to Harris's cell in the late afternoon and early evening. The third time they entered the cell, they tried to physically persuade Harris to comply. He refused to do so and continued his activity. On orders of Sanders, Muslims Stacy Gordon, Reginald Williams, and others proceeded to kill Harris.

However, Larry was not overly concerned with Harris. Positive activity was occurring that could lead to his freedom. He was concentrating on that goal. Larry knew that there was some type of surrender process going on because he was hearing constant yelling and bargaining going on in the cellblock and the corridor. "Hey, man, you got to get me out of here"; "I got something for you if you let me go next"; and "I got all my stuff packed; I'm good to go" were frequently heard. Larry was unsure of who was in charge of how the inmates were being released and in what order. In his mind, this was a very positive sign. If there was indeed going to be a peaceful resolution to the eleven-day-old siege, this was the best opportunity. Larry sat in his cell and was told nothing about what was occurring until Muslim Elmore came around to make his rounds. When Larry questioned Elmore, he responded, "Man, we don't know what's going on ourselves; things could turn any time. Just keep your [expletive] mouth shut." Larry sat alone in his cell throughout the day, as he had now for the ten previous days. Waiting. Wondering. Praying.

Outside L-Corridor

Throughout the night there were no negotiations. But at 9:20 a.m., contact was made with inmate negotiator Jason Robb, who demanded a meeting between the inmate negotiators, Attorney Nikki Schwartz, OSP Colonel Rice, and FBI negotiator Allen Tolin. A meeting table and arrangements were quickly put into place, and all parties met at 10:05 a.m. Negotiations continued until 12:50 p.m. At approximately 1:00 p.m., Warden Tate, Colonel Rice, and Nikki Schwartz announced to the media that a settlement had been reached and the resolution process would begin with the injured inmates being removed first, beginning at about 4:00 p.m. The entire surrender process would be carried live and uninterrupted on television via WLWT-TV Channel 5 in Cincinnati. The afternoon was busy with the logistics of obtaining the materials and devising a procedure to ensure the peaceful resolution.

At about 3:30 p.m., DRC SRT delivered portable lighting, flashlights, and stretchers to the recreation yard outside the L-side gymnasium for the removal of the injured inmates. Inmates retrieved the materials at 3:37 p.m. with the surrender process scheduled to begin within minutes.

The "Resolution" Commences

As scheduled, at 3:56 p.m., the injured inmates began evacuating the L-side gymnasium: some limped, some utilized crutches and walkers, and several were carried on stretchers. Negotiators had agreed that inmates would place all weapons in one of two large plastic trash cans on each side of the gymnasium exit doors, then exit the gymnasium in groups of twenty, carrying their personal belongings in the provided laundry bags, walk slowly to the designated OPI box truck, place their materials inside, immediately place their hands on top of their heads, and walk slowly to awaiting authorities who would handcuff and escort them to the K-side gymnasium for processing.

Processing would consist of the inmates being strip-searched, fingerprinted, given a cursory physical examination by medical staff, placed in white jumpsuits at four separate tables (A, B, C, and D), and held in the gymnasium to await transfer to another prison via large DRC buses. The first inmate processed was John Fields, #246-513, at 4:06 p.m. As the surrender process continued, Nikki Schwartz met with the inmate leaders.

At 4:17 p.m., the first major problem erupted. The OSP and Ohio National Guard were placing troops in strategic locations to monitor the surrender process. As the troops entered the recreation yard, the inmates went "crazy," again thinking that they were being assaulted. Mass chaos erupted in L-corridor. Larry remembers:

> All of a sudden, there was mass chaos, and an inmate began running on all four ranges yelling, "Calm down; they aren't going to do anything stupid now. We've already got some of our people outside."

Finally, after both sides calmed down and cooler heads prevailed, the troops were relocated and the surrender process resumed. It ran smoothly but agonizingly slowly. At 4:30 p.m., Warden Tate telephoned Scioto County Prosecutor Lynn Grimshaw and advised him to ready his prosecution team, and Scioto County Sheriff Sutterfield was also notified of the tentative surrender.

149

Another Media-Created Crisis

The process was continued methodically until 4:50 p.m., when a member of the media announced that four of the hostages had been brought out on stretchers. That was blatantly untrue; however, it created a media frenzy that caused a great amount of tension and distress among the inmate negotiators, as well as the DRC and the hostages' families. Immediate steps were made to issue a retraction, and DRC spokesperson Tessa Unwin, who had returned to Lucasville from Columbus, immediately briefed the hostages' families that the injured on stretchers were inmates and not hostages.

The Surrender Continues

The tired and riot-worn inmates continued to surrender in groups of twenty throughout the late afternoon and evening. However, again media reports threatened to compromise the surrender process and the lives of the five hostages. Inmate negotiators contacted the HNT complaining about the live news coverage being provided. The media was speculating on the number of inmates to face criminal charges and the possible laws that had been broken by the rioting inmates during the course of the eleven-day siege, including the murder of Officer Vallandingham.

Inmates were also balking because the Muslims were worried that the DRC wouldn't take all assigned inmates on a bus together to Mansfield as agreed in the negotiations earlier in the day. Attorney Nikki Schwartz persuaded the Muslims that the DRC would honor its commitment regarding transfers, and DRC officials were able to persuade media personnel to stop speculating regarding legal matters. The surrender and processing of inmates resumed. The fifth group of twenty inmates exited L-side at 8:10 p.m.

The Beginning of the End

With about a quarter of the inmates processed, finally at about 8:30 p.m., following the Muslim evening prayer service, Leroy Elmore came back to Larry's cell and said, "Okay, man, come with me; it's time to go. I've gotta put you in a spot where I can keep an eye on you." Larry, usually reluctant to leave the security of his cell, was much less reluctant this time. Larry remembers:

Too many positive things were happening, in my mind. I could tell that a lot of inmates had been released because the noise level kept dropping throughout the day and evening. I figured that was a good sign. I was near certain that I was getting out of there.

Elated, relieved, but cautious and afraid, Larry shuffled out of his cell, still blindfolded, hands and feet bound, and led by his captor to the other side of the range. Elmore said, "Okay, we've gotta stop here and pick up Hensley." Both hostages were then taken to another cell. He was now unsure of what was going on. He had a fleeting moment of fear and hesitation. However, those emotions evaporated almost instantly.

Hostage Reunion

Larry had been unaware of Hensley's location prior to their reunion. Elmore told both hostages, "Both of you sit down and keep your [expletive] mouths shut." Hensley immediately asked, "Where's Buffington?" Elmore replied, "I've got to go get him." Elmore left and came back a couple of minutes later with Officer Richard Buffington. All three hostages were placed in the same cell, each given a blanket, and Officer Hensley was given a couple of cigarettes. Hensley asked Elmore, "What's up? What are you going to do with us now?" Elmore responded angrily, "Man, all of you have been nothing but a pain in the [expletive] for the last eleven days. Just sit there and keep your [expletive] mouths shut." Hensley, a feisty and defiant individual, responded, "Well, [expletive] you too!" Larry was unsure of what the response of Elmore would be to that comment. While Larry shared Hensley's attitude, he had already taken a severe beating for making comments. He was in no hurry to take another beating, especially this close to what he believed was his release. Larry's attitude could best be described as guarded optimism.

Elmore did not respond but slammed the cell closed and locked the door. Elated, the hostages talked among themselves in low voices, asking each other the typical questions about their respective injuries and their families, and about their anticipated release. Larry recalls:

After the typical questions, we all agreed that we believed that we were going to be released. We all agreed that both they and the inmates knew that this siege could not continue much longer and that this was their best chance of being released alive. We were together for about an hour or an hour and a half. We talked about Bobby, because we all knew that he had been murdered, and how each of us was dealing with that fact. We also expressed our relief that Darrold had been released early and hoped that he was doing well both physically and emotionally.

Taking Care of Business

During a meeting in L-2 between gang leaders Robb, Lavelle, and Sanders, it was decided that inmate David Sommers, who controlled the telephones and ran the inmates' tape recorders throughout the negotiations, "had to die because he knew too much." Sommers had a reputation as a snitch before the riot. Aryan Robert Brookover also had a reputation as a snitch, but he was given an all-too-familiar choice: kill or be killed. Brookover asked Skatzes if he was going to be killed. Skatzes replied, "Just take care of business; be cool."

The surrender was held up for a period of time because Skatzes, Robb, Sanders, and Cummings told Lavelle that they had some things they had to take care of. Brookover was given a white kitchen uniform, a shank, and an extension cord. Skatzes, Snodgrass, and Bocook also changed into different clothing. Upon Robb's arrival, the inmates went to L-7, across the corridor from L-2. When they arrived in L-7, no one was there. Bocook screamed, "Where's that [expletive] Sommers at?" Robb immediately left to get Sommers from L-2, and a few minutes later, Sommers was seen following Robb into L-7. Brookover tackled Sommers and stabbed him. Skatzes ran up and kicked Sommers in the head. Brookover then followed orders to choke Sommers with the extension cord, and then Skatzes struck Sommers in the head with a baseball bat at least three times. Brookover and the others beat and stabbed Sommers until he was dead. Following Sommers' murder, the killers cleaned themselves, burned their clothes, and surrendered to authorities.

The Gauntlet

After about ninety minutes, Elmore returned to the hostages. As he unlocked and opened the cell door, he said, "Come on; it's time to go." Each of the three hostages was directed out of the cell, still blindfolded, feet and hands bound. They were instructed, "Don't move too quick and keep your mouths shut." They walked single file with their hands on the shoulders of the person in front of them. Hensley first, then Buffington, followed by Dotson. They were led down range, down a short flight of steps, out of the cellblock, and into the L-corridor. As they entered the hall, Larry could hear the continuing racial arguments being made among the inmate groups.

Aryan Lt. Roger Snodgrass, who had been dispatched by Aryan leaders to murder Muslim Emmanuel "Buddy" Newell, was screaming and threatening Newell, who had been handcuffed and left locked in an empty cellblock by Carlos Sanders. Sanders had earlier agreed to Aryan demands for the murder of Newell. Despite repeated attempts, Snodgrass was unable to open the cellblock door. With all of the yelling and screaming, Larry was unsure if he and his fellow hostages would make it down the corridor alive. Dotson remembered the corridor being like a gauntlet. Racial tensions were extremely high and an all-out racial war could have erupted at any time, with each racial group barely tolerating the other. Time seemed to move slowly, as did his progress down the long corridor.

Once they entered the hallway, fellow hostages Kenny Daniels and Jeff Ratcliff and their Aryan captors joined Mike Hensley, Richard Buffington, and Larry Dotson. All five hostages shuffled down the long L-corridor and down the short ramp to the gymnasium. They could feel the cold breeze coming through the hallway. Larry recalls:

I was concentrating on walking and not falling. I kept my prayer chain going. When I felt the cold breeze when we entered the gymnasium, I really started to cry. I was concentrating on Emma at this point. I was focused on her. I was praying that she would soon have the closure that she had been waiting for the past eleven days. She is so critical to my existence. My kids were very important to me, but at that point, it was all about Emma and what she has had to endure as my wife. I was praying for the Lord to give her peace to deal with this. With all of the racial tension going on around me, I tried to remain focused and kept moving.

Larry recalled having his worst case of nervous tension at that point, more so than at any time during the past eleven days. Being so close but yet so far from freedom created an extreme amount of nervous tension.

Free at Last

Muslim Leroy Elmore released hostages Mike Hensley, Richard Buffington, and Larry Dotson at 10:25 p.m. As they exited the gymnasium, Larry felt the mist of a light rain and the cool breeze of the spring night. He then heard his pastor, Charles Bryant, from the Southshore Church of God say, "There's Brother Larry." He immediately responded, "Thank God, Pastor Bryant." Pastor Bryant was one of five members of area clergy selected to observe the complete surrender process. This was one of the surrender demands and points of agreement.

Larry knew that he was again a free man. He praised God. Within seconds, an OSHP trooper came up to Larry and pulled him off to the side and said, "Okay, big boy, you're free. Don't look up; I'm going to take these blindfolds off of you." All three officers and their OSP trooper escorts walked over to the K-side gymnasium, where each was placed on a hospital stretcher and sent on his way to the SOCF infirmary.

Fourteen minutes later, Aryan leader Roger Snodgrass escorted hostages Kenny Daniels and Jeff Ratcliff over to the waiting Ohio Highway Patrol troopers. As Snodgrass removed the blindfold of Jeff Ratcliff, he proclaimed, "In the name of the Aryan Brotherhood, I return your officers safe and unharmed," and immediately surrendered to authorities. Daniels and Ratcliff joined the other former hostages in the infirmary hallway on separate hospital stretchers.

A Hero's Welcome

Once in the hallway leading to the infirmary, as Larry recalls:

The institution had lined the halls with hundreds of staff members. They were cheering and clapping. It was incredible.

I think that they needed to see us as much as we needed to see them at that point. I remember near the end of the line just before entering the infirmary, Art Tate was standing there with big tears in his eyes and said, "It's really good to see you, Larry." He shook my hand and patted me on the shoulder. It was clear to me that Art couldn't talk at that point. People see Art Tate as a big, tough ex-FBI agent. He is, but he is a very caring individual. It was clear that he was overcome with emotion. He personally checked in on all of us a couple of times when we were in the infirmary. They just don't come any finer than Art Tate.

Hundreds of SOCF and other DRC personnel lined the hallway, many reaching out, patting the hostages on the shoulders, yelling and cheering. It was clear that the staff who had worked around the clock for eleven days needed to see the hostages as much as the hostages needed to see those who had worked tirelessly for their release. It was a moment Larry Dotson would never forget.

As he was wheeled into the infirmary treatment room, the first person he saw was Nurse Patsy Taylor, Lt. Wayne Taylor's wife. Larry immediately asked, "How's Wayne?" Patsy just looked at him and her eyes filled with tears, and she turned and walked away. Larry did not know what had happened to Lt. Taylor, but he knew that he was on duty and would have been in the thick of the fighting.

Another nurse immediately came over and quickly began cutting the inmate clothing off of Larry and gave him a very quick physical exam and cleaned up some of his wounds. After a couple of minutes, Patsy Taylor came back over to Larry and said, "Wayne is doing okay. He has a lot of cuts and bruises and a broken arm, but I just can't believe you. You go through all of that hell in there … you look like death warmed over, and here you are, and your first question you ask is about my husband."

Larry responded that he was concerned about Wayne and knew that Wayne would have been directly involved in the riot response. SOCF staff then brought in new uniforms, and all of the hostages changed and readied for transport to the Scioto County Medical Center via ambulance. Five wheelchairs were lined up to take the hostages to the awaiting ambulances at the front entrance.

However, none of the hostages were in any mood to be wheeled out of their institution. All demanded to walk, and walk out they did. Larry walked out with his shift captain, Randy Holcumb, and Lt. Jim Swan, who were both elated to see their fellow staff members alive and well, considering their ordeal.

Each of the five awaiting ambulances was staffed with a nurse, paramedics, an HNT member, and a psychologist. As they exited the infirmary hallway, again the entire route to the front entrance building was lined with cheering staff. After entering the awaiting ambulances, they slowly exited the SOCF grounds and turned left onto SR 728. Larry remembers:

> *The entire route to the hospital was lined with cheering people, hundreds of them. It was a sight that I'll never forget. We had a police escort to the hospital. When we arrived, there was another big cheering crowd in the parking lot. I didn't know there were that many people in the area. It was incredible. Seeing the response was really heartwarming for me personally, and I'm sure for the other guys as well. I have no words to describe the emotional high that I was on at that time, and I couldn't wait to see my family.*

Once he arrived at the hospital, Larry was demanding to see his family. However, hospital personnel responded, "They're here and waiting on you, but we have to get you checked out and cleaned up first." A team of nurses and Dr. Charles Wheeler looked him over and tended to his wounds and ordered a series of tests. After that, Dr. Wheeler said, "Well, I think this young man needs to see his family."

Part 3:
Post-Riot

Chapter 13:
Hospitalization and Debriefing

A Short Family Reunion

A few minutes later, at just about midnight, the door opened and in came Emma, Joe, and Kimberly with her husband. Larry just looked at them for what seemed like an eternity. Larry remembers:

> Other than the decision to give my life to Christ and my kids being born, seeing my family was probably the most important moment in my life. You could tell just by looking at them that they had been through the wringer. I just felt so bad for them, because I felt like it was all my fault for causing all of this for them. That is a moment that is vividly captured in my memory.

The family all joined hands for a moment of prayerful thanksgiving and praise. After that, the tears started flowing. Larry's sister, brother, nieces, and nephews entered the room. One of those family members was his brother-in-law, who said to him, "You'll never know how much these people care for you. I have been with them now for the past eleven days. Your family is so devoted to you ... I just wanted you to know and really appreciate that."

Larry was thankful that once his family was notified that he was a possible hostage victim, his sister and brother-in-law left their jobs in Kentucky and notified their respective supervisors that they would return when there was a resolution. They remained with his wife, Emma, throughout the eleven-day siege.

> *I really appreciated their standing by Emma like they did, because if I had been in Bobby Vallandingham's position, Emma would have really needed their help and strong support. The fact that they cared enough to leave their jobs and family in Kentucky to stay with Emma is something I will never forget. How do you thank people for such unselfish behavior? I don't know, but it is important that I let them know that I will never forget that.*

The joyous family reunion was heartfelt and sincere but all too brief.

First Debriefing

After what seemed like a very short period of time, Highway Patrol Trooper and Investigator Mark Roegles entered the room and requested a meeting with Larry to conduct a debriefing and an interview. Roegles, permanently assigned to the Circleville Post, was still dressed in his black duty fatigues. He sincerely apologized but stressed that the investigation must begin. Larry was somewhat agitated by the interruption of his family time. Understanding why the interruption was necessary did not make it any easier.

SOCF, being a state owned and operated penal facility, fell under the jurisdiction of the Ohio State Highway Patrol, specifically the Investigative Services Unit. Sgt. Howard Hudson was the officer in charge. Emma stayed with Larry during the debriefing while other family members were taken to a nearby waiting room.

Investigators were very interested in what Larry had seen and heard, and inquired if he could put names and faces together. Larry assured them that he knew plenty. During that first one-hour interview, doctors and nurses continually entered and left the room. Larry's heart rate was somewhat erratic and caused great concern. Roegles was attempting to verify previously obtained information implicating Jason Robb, Carlos Sanders, George Skatzes, and Keith LaMar. Investigators were trying to pinpoint who was involved in the very early part of the riot. This was just the first of many interviews and depositions yet to come. Following his joyous family reunion and answering the initial questions of investigators, Larry spent his first of seven nights in the hospital. Attributed to the tension and stress of his hostage ordeal, Larry's blood pressure and heart rhythm were irregular. Intravenous medications were required to correct what eleven days of brutal captivity had caused.

Physical Healing

His head injuries were healing well, but he was plagued with frequent and severe headaches. While at the Southern Ohio Medical Center (SOMC), he met daily with Psychologist Tom Haskell to deal with his posttraumatic stress disorder (PTSD). Six months prior to April 11, Larry's mother underwent open-heart surgery. As a result of the stress of her son's captivity, she was re-admitted to SOMC. Larry and his mother visited frequently while both were patients.

While hospitalized, Warden Art Tate and many SOCF staff visited him. No one from the DRC Central Office visited, although he did receive telephone calls from DRC Director Reginald Wilkinson and Lt. Governor Mike DeWine. Larry did not accept their calls. Several high-ranking members of the labor union to which Larry belonged were frequent visitors.

Going Home

Larry was the last of the hostages to leave the hospital after the riot, and the media was "camped out" at the SOMC front entrance. On the day of his discharge, April 28, 1993, Larry was taken out the back service entrance/exit to avoid the media. He arrived at a home filled with flowers, cards, family, friends, neighbors, and many members of his church family for a welcome home dinner.

On the morning of April 11, 1993, Larry left home for his shift at the SOCF. Before his return, he would be beaten, held hostage, lose a friend to murder, betrayed by a fellow officer, be released after eleven days, spend seven days in the hospital, and undergo psychological counseling. Larry now had come full circle. Due to the medication he was prescribed for his frequent and severe headaches, Larry was restricted from driving for ten days.

Chapter 14: A New Normal

Psychological and Spiritual Healing

The following day, Sunday, Larry and his family drove to the Southshore Church of God for morning services. As his wife, Emma, pulled into the church parking lot, he noticed the large message of "Welcome Home, Brother Larry" on the large marquee. He smiled to himself. After entering the building, he was enthusiastically met by Pastor Charles Bryant, who respectfully asked Larry to speak to the unusually large congregation. Larry readily agreed. Pastor Bryant escorted Larry and his family to the only empty pew in the building, in the front row, clearly marked with a large yellow ribbon. After seating his family, Larry followed Pastor Bryant to the dais and was seated. After a traditional and reverent opening, Larry was introduced.

The packed house erupted into a prolonged and sustained standing ovation. There was not a dry eye in the building. Overwhelmed, Larry just stood and looked out over his church family—over two hundred of them. After several minutes, the ovation faded and the congregation seated themselves, and a deafening silence permeated the crowd. The same congregation had a well-organized, twenty-four-hour-a-day prayer chain maintained throughout the siege. The same congregation had provided numerous meals to his family over the previous three weeks, and the same congregation had sent dozens of cards, letters, and flowers to him and his family since his release.

Larry made his way to the podium and just stood and looked out over the sea of tearful faces. After what seemed like an hour, he tried to speak, but there was only more silence. With tears flowing, the crowd again erupted into another sustained standing ovation. This provided Larry with the precious time to compose himself. With both legs pressed up against the back of the podium and both hands firmly gripped on the podium's sides, he began:

> *I thank Jesus Christ, the Son of our Living God, for the opportunity to be with you today. It is clear to me that after those horrifying eleven days that you and I had a mutual need to be together today. I am here as a result of your hours of intercessory prayer and the grace of a Loving God ...*

That service began the mental healing process. Physically, his wounds were healing with little visible scarring. To deal with the mental scarring, he continued to see Dr. Haskell every week. At the same time, he was receiving frequent calls and visits from both the DRC and OSP investigators and SOCF personnel staff to complete the enormous volumes of paperwork. The SOCF had assigned one member of the personnel staff to each of the former hostages.

A Setback

Larry was only home from SOMC for two days when he was notified that his friend and fellow officer John Kemper, beaten and left for dead during the initial takeover, had suffered a major stroke and was critically ill. Larry took this news very hard. Psychologically, he was now caught in a downward spiral of what has been described as survivor's guilt syndrome.

Return to L-Corridor

Fifteen days after his hospital discharge, to assist investigators and in what he thought would be an aid to his own emotional health, Larry toured the riot-torn prison with OSP Investigator Mark Roegles and Sgt. Howard Hudson. He recalls:

> *Up until I took that tour and saw the near total destruction and devastation for myself, I really had no idea how bad the riot really was. I know that sounds odd since I was in the middle of*

it, but I really had no comprehension. We were beaten, dazed, blindfolded, bound, and moved around for eleven days. Our senses at times were not all that sharp. When I think back on what I saw on that tour—it's really frightening.

During the sixty-minute tour, investigators and Larry retraced his steps during the riot as best he could remember. While psychologically troubling, the most difficult was physically. The overwhelming stench inside L-corridor was nearly incapacitating. Many of the investigators wore biohazard body suits and respirator masks.

At the end of this emotionally exhausting tour, Larry was informed that investigators had found many of the personal belongings of the former hostages, including him. Although he was not interested in retrieving any of his personal items, he did go through the box and took what belonged to him, including his car and house keys.

Offers of Assistance

Cards, letters, flowers, and gifts continued to arrive at the Dotson home for nearly a month. He was grateful for all well wishes and offers of assistance. Far and away, the greatest sustained assistance came from the labor union of which Larry was a member. That union was the Ohio Civil Service Employees Association (OCSEA), Local 11 of the American Federation of State, County, and Municipal Employees (AFSCME). OCSEA provided him and all of the hostages with counselors, financial assistance, legal services, experts on worker's compensation and insurance law, and tax assistance. Individuals who went far and above the call of duty were Del Evans, Paul Goldberg, Don Sergeant, Nate Miller, Dave Justice, Mike Hill, and Charlie Williamson. Larry fondly recalls:

I can never thank them enough for all of the help and assistance that they gave to the families during the siege and the unbelievable amount of assistance and support that continued until we were all back on our feet again.

Unlike a few DRC officials and politicians who attempted to capitalize on the former hostages for personal or political gain, the support he and his family received from his union was sustained, substantial, and sincere. His union clearly demonstrated solidarity.

165

For their selfless giving of support and assistance, Larry will always remain grateful to his OCSEA/AFSCME brothers and sisters.

Other assistance came from the California Corrections Association, which sent $2,500 in two checks to each former hostage. The Correction and Peace Officers' Foundation held a formal dinner in honor of the former hostages in Portsmouth. As they were formally introduced, they were each presented with a check for $2,000.

By this time, Larry's headaches had become less frequent and less severe. He was getting out more and had become more and more restless. He needed to return to work and a sense of normalcy, but he wasn't at all looking forward to returning to L-corridor and the SOCF.

On May 14, 1993, Larry received a letter on behalf of Governor Voinovich, Lt. Governor Mike DeWine, and signed by Director Wilkinson. The letter wished him a speedy recovery from his injuries, thanked him for his service to the DRC and the people of Ohio, and promised "to take care of you." Subsequent conversations between Director Wilkinson, Assistant Director Thomas Stickrath, and Larry resulted in Larry being promised a position at the CTA as long as he wanted.

Transfer to CTA

One of Larry's friends at the SOCF was Jim Hineman, who served as the administrative assistant to Warden Arthur Tate. Larry and Jim had both graduated from the United States Air Force Security Police Academy in San Antonio, Texas. Larry served as a law enforcement trainer. Both Hineman and Warden Tate telephoned CTA Superintendent Janis Lane and arranged a visit for Larry and his wife. They spent two days touring the campus in Orient, Ohio, talking with the other training officers and reviewing the curriculum. After extended talks with Superintendent Lane, arrangements were made for Larry to transfer to the CTA as a training officer. On the advice of his psychologist to make a gradual transition, he and his family moved to the small town of Ashville about twenty miles south of Orient in September 1993. After a few weeks of adjustment, on October 17, 1993, he began his duties as a training officer at the CTA. Larry believed that he could continue his healing process while at the CTA.

On his second day at the CTA, he was asked to accompany Superintendent Janis Lane to the American Correctional Association ceremony at the Hocking Correctional Facility. While there, Director Wilkinson introduced him to the large crowd. No one had informed Larry of his expected role at the ceremony, and he was taken aback. Larry believed that he was being used for propaganda purposes, but there was little he could do at that moment.

He continued to be the "poster child" of the DRC and CTA. He spoke several times a week to both pre-service and in-service classes at the CTA and attended events at the Warren Correctional Institution, Lebanon Correctional Institution, Hocking Correctional Facility, and Lima Correctional Institution. He made two hostage training videos for Paul Farmer and *LockUp USA*, spoke at hostage events in Minneapolis, Minnesota; St. Cloud, Minnesota; Sumpter, South Carolina; Chester, Pennsylvania; and Philadelphia, Pennsylvania. In addition, Larry frequently testified for the DRC at numerous depositions and inmate trials that ultimately resulted in five riot leaders being sentenced to death for their roles.

Seeking Restitution

In early 1995, Larry and the other hostages were referred to the union-recommended law firm of Carr and Sherman, who initiated litigation against the DRC and the State of Ohio for numerous torts before and during the siege. After nearly two years of litigation, the State of Ohio settled with the former hostages and the family of murdered hostage Robert Vallandingham. Larry remembers:

It was a very tense time. The department's attitude toward each of us changed dramatically. It's almost like they were only being kind to us so that we wouldn't sue them. When we did, it was like the gloves came off. They settled with us, but it was nothing in comparison with what we went through.

To the best of Larry's recollection, Robert Vallandingham's widow received $850,000; his son, Robert Jr., received $150,000; John Kemper $300,000; Mike Hensley $300,000; and Jeff Ratcliff $300,000. He remains unsure of the amounts of Darrold Clark and Richard Buffington. Larry received $120,000 despite being the second most seriously injured former hostage. However, the attorneys' share of each award was one-third, which slashed the amount to each victim. Based on the above amounts, the attorneys took over $673,000! The amount was insignificant to Larry; he was glad to have that trauma behind him and to continue the mental and emotional healing process.

World Turned Upside Down

Life was good for the next six years. He continued his assignments at the CTA, served on the Memorial Park Committee, rewrote the department's hostage lesson plans, trained the department's hostage negotiation teams, served on numerous committees, and testified at over seventeen riot-related trials and sentencing hearings.

Then came November 9, 2001. A meeting was called for all CTA staff in the large Parkview classroom. Approximately one hundred people crowded into the room and heard Eric Dahlberg, who was then the deputy director of Human Resources. Dahlberg announced "very deep and painful" layoffs of Central Office staff, including CTA. He gave absolutely no specifics and was vague and evasive in response to any and all questions. When a few of his comments were challenged, he became verbally aggressive and belittling. The questions he did answer resulted in a lot of talk but nothing said. He did announce that the specifics and details would not be available until January 6, 2002, and assured the CTA staff that they would *not* bear the brunt of the layoffs. For the remainder of the year, tensions were high and an air of uncertainty swept throughout the department. The union met several times to inform the staff of their "bumping" rights under the collective bargaining agreement. Rumors of the actual numbers of staff to be laid off circulated and changed by the minute.

As devastating as was this news, Larry really did not believe that any layoff would apply to him—relying on the promises made to him by Director Wilkinson and Lt. Governor Michael DeWine. He would soon learn a bitter lesson in political expediency.

"A Tremendous Success Story"

The following day, November 10, 2001, Thomas Stickrath came to the CTA and met with Larry and CTA Superintendent Tracy Reveal in her office. He told Larry, "You have been a tremendous success story, and we will find a position for you." After that meeting, with a renewed sense of optimism that the department would make good on its promise, Larry believed that he would be permitted to continue his career at CTA. Larry and Stickrath e-mailed each other frequently over the next forty-five days.

Right after the first of January 2002, Larry received a telephone call from Stickrath at his home in Ashville. Stickrath offered Larry a newly created position with the Adult Parole Authority in a pay range lower than his current position. When Larry did the calculations, he realized that he was going to lose $357 per month plus travel expenses.

Two days later, Larry telephoned Director Wilkinson. Larry explained his situation, and Director Wilkinson stated matter-of-factly, "Well, there's nothing else I can do." Larry stated that as the department's director, he could do more should he so choose. Director Wilkinson then asked, "Is there anything else?" Larry said there was not, and Director Wilkinson hung up. Larry would have no further contact with either Director Wilkinson or Assistant Director Stickrath. Larry learned another bitter lesson.

Expendable

On January 6, 2002, another ominous meeting was held in the same Parkview classroom. Eric Dahlberg announced that his office had identified over 1,600 eligible employees for the Early Retirement Incentive (ERI), but not enough had opted to take it, and therefore, "deep and painful" reductions were being made. He did not mention that he was one of the eligible senior employees who opted not to take the ERI.

He announced the layoffs in a trite and matter-of-fact manner. Eleven of the nineteen CTA training officers, or 58 percent, would receive layoff notices, and numerous other staff were also scheduled for elimination. He announced that the Central Office, which included the CTA, was eliminating forty positions, and twenty-five of them were occurring at the CTA. So much for the CTA not bearing the brunt of the layoffs. However, in addition to the layoff, which was being predominately borne by union employees, the CTA was creating four new management positions. There would now be more supervisors at the CTA than there were people to supervise. Larry was one of those whose seniority marked him for layoff.

Despite numerous attempts to have the DRC officials make good on their written promise to him, Larry learned another hard lesson in political reality. The DRC had no further need for Larry. He had testified at over seventeen trials, assisted in getting five death sentences, appeared with Director Wilkinson to enhance the director's political and media agenda, trained dozens of new DRC hostage negotiators, and trained thousands of new correctional officers. The DRC had taken all it needed from Larry and now reneged on its written promise to him.

Going Back Inside

Betrayed by those who promised to "take care of" him, Larry reported to the Warren Correctional Institution (WCI) on February 17, 2002, as one of their two training officers. Initially to report on February 2, 2002, Larry took two weeks off to evaluate his options. During the time off, he consulted with his faithful wife, Emma, and prayed frequently, seeking guidance. Larry received the answer to his prayer when he was told in a very special way to report to WCI and "be strong."

As difficult as it was for Larry to walk back into a prison, especially a prison that housed the very inmates who were convicted of beating him, Larry overcame his initial fear and apprehension.

On his very first day, Warden Brigano arranged for Larry to be met in the front entry building and escorted to his office on the second floor of the institution's administration building. As Larry reached the top of the stairs, he was met with the warm and comforting smile of Warden Brigano. Brigano had both arms extended and welcomed Larry with a vigorous handshake and warm and genuine hug. He took Larry into his office, where they talked for over an hour. He assured Larry that he would not have to walk the facility unescorted until he felt comfortable. After the meeting, Warden Brigano escorted Larry to the Training Office located at the rear of the building's first floor. Waiting for him was his partner and friend from CTA, Gary Williams.

After approximately three weeks, Larry felt fairly comfortable in his new environment. Warden Anthony Brigano, Administrative

Assistant Richard Jesko, and Training Officers Gary Williams and Van Hewitt were critical in Larry's successful adjustment back inside of a prison. Larry knew that if he needed to finish his career at the WCI, he could do it, both physically and emotionally.

Testament to Faithfulness

Fortune and blessing again smiled on Larry Dotson. On April 5, 2002, he was offered a training officer position with the Ohio Department of Job and Family Services in Columbus, where he intends to finish his career. As of this writing, he works alongside his friend and fellow training officer, Stan Sikorski, who also previously worked for the DRC. Larry's adjustment to a new state agency and work environment was hastened by his new supervisor, Adrain McConnell. Since his arrival, Larry and Adrain have become very good friends, and Larry will be forever grateful for Adrain's kindness, support, and understanding.

Chapter 15:
Post-Riot Investigative Reports

The post-riot investigations began even before the riot ended. In addition to the obvious massive criminal investigation spearheaded by the Ohio State Highway Patrol, nearly a dozen committees and task forces were established to evaluate the SOCF disturbance and to make recommendations.

The following are executive summaries and/or recommendations from three of these committees. The findings and recommendations of the Lucasville Media Task Force are detailed in the following chapter.

Disturbance Cause Committee

Overview

This committee was appointed by Director Wilkinson to identify facts that caused, contributed to, or triggered the April 11 disturbance. Their report examined the environment of this institution and the systems that were in place to manage Ohio's maximum-security institution. This executive summary was designed to identify the weightiest of those findings as they applied to the disturbance. The committee consisted of Gary C. Mohr, chairman; Morris Bayes; Dr. Maureen Black; Jeff Carson; Gerald Clay; Steven Dix; Susan Dunn; Carole Shiplevy; and Don Teter. The committee issued its report on June 10, 1993.

Leadership

During the six weeks this committee deliberated, leadership became a factor in the management of Ohio's maximum-security prison, which required attention in their report. In fact, it is interesting to note the observation of Lanson Newsone, National Institute of Corrections' consultant during the disturbance, while he commended Warden Tate for his leadership. He stated, "It was evident that problems existed with executive staff and supervisory ... The staff needed many questions answered during the crisis as did the inmate population. Supervisory staff failed to fill the void."

The committee specifically found the following points regarding leadership at SOCF:

- Warden Tate, since his appointment as warden at SOCF, has provided energetic leadership through implementation of Operation Shakedown and regular tours through the institution, and during staff interviews, it was conveyed by an overwhelming majority of staff that Warden Tate provided excellent leadership.
- Warden Tate does not possess confidence in key administrative staff and middle managers (captains and unit managers), and as a result, a team concept does not exist among institution management staff. A disruptive tension exists between custody and unit management staff. In fact, because of a lack of confidence and unproductive performance on the part of key administrative staff, Warden Tate was in a position to deal directly with Muslim inmate leaders regarding TB testing, an event found to have triggered the disturbance.
- The State of Ohio employee classification system compensates deputy wardens at SOCF (Programs Deputy Warden at SOCF administratively directs 500 employees) at the same pay rate as much smaller, less complex institutions. This system proves to be an obstacle in the department's goal of placing its

most experienced and competent people in the most challenging positions.

In pondering the cause of the April 11, 1993, disturbance, several critical elements that are more fully discussed in the body of this report surfaced as being influential to this event. The below stated citings are viewed by this committee, in addition to the leadership issues mentioned above, to have set a stage for this event to occur.

- **Operation Shakedown.** In November 1990, the Department of Rehabilitation and Correction (DRC), under the direction of Warden Tate, implemented a comprehensive plan following recommendations of the House Select Committee and DRC administrative observations to bring increased security and control to the institution. This plan significantly reduced freedom of movement and increased the custody of inmates after a period of much less control. Implementation of this plan proved effective in reducing inmate deaths and increasing a sense of safety and security for both staff and inmates cited in the 1991 American Correctional Audit (ACA). The plan proved effective when fully implemented; however, when one of the fundamental components of the plan, single-celling, was abandoned because of the growing prison population, tension within the institution regarding double-celling and interracial celling negatively impacted institution operation. Groups of inmates being supervised during movement, at recreation, and in the cellblocks grew.

- **Cell Assignments.** Double-celling of the inmate population was voiced by a vast majority of both staff and inmates as a cause of the disturbance. There are specific factors associated with double-celling that required further explanations. First, at the time of the disturbance, the highest security group of inmates assigned to the general population, Maximum Security Level 4, were the most frequently doubled-celled. Secondly, interracial celling increased beginning in 1991 as ordered under *White v. Morris* and as routinely followed throughout the state. A formal and informal process existed at SOCF to provide an avenue for known racists and gang members to be assigned to a same-race double cell or single cell. Double-celling was further aggravated by one of the general population cellblocks being closed down on a rotating basis for maintenance upgrades. It also needs to be noted that both the National Institute of Corrections' security/custody recommendations and DRC classification policy call for single-celling maximum-security inmates. On April 11, 1993, 804 inmates were double-celled at SOCF.

- **Institution Transfers.** Beginning significantly in June 1992, SOCF transferred out a predominately stable group of 424 inmates in exchange for a higher security, younger group of inmates from the Mansfield Correctional Institution (MANCI), following the MANCI disturbance and murder of a correction officer. From June 1992 to April 9, 1993, 96 percent of the inmates received at SOCF from MANCI were maximum-security, compared to 86 percent of those inmates leaving SOCF having a lesser security classification of close or medium security.

- **Staff/Inmate Relations.** Serious problems exist regarding interpersonal communication between staff and inmates at this facility. This disruptive relationship is both racial and cultural in its origin. A review of the use-of-force incidents at SOCF from January 1992 to the time of the disturbance not only reflects a very high rate but also indicates a disparity in use of force against black inmates. Specifically, 74 percent of all reported use-of-force cases involved black inmates compared to their percentage of the SOCF population being 57 percent. During committee interviews, two SOCF employees were physically observed to have lightning bolt tattoos, a sign associated with the Aryan Brotherhood.

- **Security.** DRC implemented a comprehensive management system, unit management, to break these large inmate populations into smaller, more manageable groups with security and unit management staff working together. The relationship between security staff and unit management personnel at SOCF is dysfunctional, which creates an environment where inmates take advantage of poor communication and turf battles. Correction officers are unclear on whether to take direction from unit management staff or exclusively from security shift supervisors. Two correction officers are assigned to each general population cellblock, with the exception of the one "merit" cellblock. While this assignment pattern seems adequate for maximum-security cellblocks, one of the officers per block is regularly pulled for escort duties and supervision in recreation, leaving officers routinely working alone in the cellblocks. The security in the institution is further diminished by inmate clerks performing sensitive responsibilities despite previous security audit citings and direction by Warden Tate. In fact, despite a tightening down on inmate clerk jobs during the past two and a half years, including taking keys away from inmates, duties involving taking sensitive photographs after hours, typing disciplinary reports of other inmates, and having access to employee training and personal information currently exist at SOCF. During the investigation, the influence of inmate clerks assigned to the captain's office was observed as a search was conducted in the captain's office, where large quantities of food taken out of secured areas of the kitchen were found.

- **Classification.** The inmate reclassification process that determines their appropriate security level (e.g.,

Maximum Security Level 4, Maximum Security Level 3, Close Level 3, Medium Security Level 3, etc.) is a source of tension for both inmates and staff. Serious inconsistency exists between the philosophy of SOCF and Central Office. The committee discovered that since January 1992, 75 percent of inmates recommended for medium security by SOCF staff have been rejected by Central Office with no reasons provided for the rejection. Inmates are unable to transfer to another facility until their security classification is reduced to an appropriate level.

- **Institution Intelligence.** As reported, 13.7 percent of the entire inmate population can be identified as members of an inmate gang. There is no centralized system for conducting investigations, authorizing investigations to be conducted, or for the communicating of the findings of investigations to key decision makers. As a result of the absence of a centralized intelligence system, gang information is frequently not available when important decisions like assigning inmates to cellblocks are made. The staff person assigned as the institution investigator is not functioning as part of the administrative staff and is not coordinating all investigations.

While the above elements were instrumental in creating a setting where a major institutional disturbance could take place, the determination to lock the institution down to force the 159 inmates who initially refused to take the TB skin test, and for that determination to be known by the inmates before it was to occur, was the triggering mechanism. Points worth noting about this process include:

- TB testing was a department-wide initiative performed at the initiation of the Department of Rehabilitation and Correction's Central Office.
- SOCF tested the entire population of over 1,800 inmates with the exception of the 159 who refused to

take the "stick test." Of that total, twenty-nine cited religious reasons.

- Warden Tate directly communicated with inmate Sanders, recognized inmate Muslim leader, both in a response to a "kite," written communication from Sanders, and in a meeting during the week of April 5. Both communications clearly informed the inmates that the remaining 159 would be tested through the method "stick test" previously utilized. It is important to note that SOCF and Central Office did discuss alternative methods of testing (x-ray and sputum methods), however, determined that the only way to measure exposure is through the "stick test."
- On Friday, April 9, Warden Tate called a meeting of executive staff, unit managers, and the medical and food service administrators to discuss a plan designed to lock the institution down on April 12 to complete the remaining tests. Despite this meeting being classified as confidential, word widely spread throughout the institution beginning on Friday. Inmate clerks were assigned to areas where the lockdown was being discussed.
- It is important to note that inmate Sanders, the recognized Muslim leader, and four other Muslim inmates refused to leave the chapel on Saturday, April 10, resulting in the chaplain having to push Sanders out of the way in order to gain access to the hallway. This incident went unreported until April 29. The committee also discovered a constitution for the Muslim inmates citing the use of inmate imams, which is contrary to DRC policy.

The planned lockdown of the institution provided a forum for the Muslim inmates to forge a relationship of cooperation with the Aryan Brotherhood just prior to the breakout of violence on April 11. Information in the form of evidence does not exist to support long-term planning of this event by a cross section of the inmate population. The body of the report and relevant documentation will more fully and comprehensively describe SOCF and causal factors associated with the disturbance.

OCSEA, AFSCME Local 11

The Ohio Civil Service Employees Association represents the largest number of Ohio state public employees including over 8,000 correction officers. The union's review and recommendations were drafted with the sole purpose of enhancing the safety and security of Ohio's 15,000 correctional employees. The executive summary of the union's report released on August 25, 1993, was both hard hitting and contained numerous recommendations. The executive summary and recommendations follow.

Understaffing, overcrowding, insufficient training, and inadequate prison management techniques and policies underlie a crisis in Ohio prisons—brought into sharp focus by the riot and eleven-day siege at the Southern Ohio Correctional Facility.

Few problems in Ohio have received the study and attention devoted to the crisis in our prisons over the past decade, yet three prison employees have lost their lives at the hands of inmates in just four years. Further study is not sufficient. Trading lives for money, by continued failure to adequately fund the results of "tough on crime" political rhetoric, is unacceptable.

Based upon research compiled by the union and interviews with scores of staff members and other prison systems across the country over the last four months, OCSEA developed thirty-two sets of specific recommendations for addressing the Ohio prison crisis. Key among them are:

- Increased staff of Ohio prisons.
- Upgraded pre- and in-service training for staff, leading to peace officer certification of correctional officers.
- Comprehensive management policies in the areas of prison gangs, crisis response planning, unit management practices, staff communications, and cultural diversity training strategies.
- Management of prison overcrowding by:

1. Construction of a maximum-security prison in northeastern Ohio;
2. Emergency legislation requiring non-violent inmates with less than ninety days left to serve at the time of sentencing be kept in county jails or released on intensive probation, rather than being sent to the state prison system;
3. Review of early release authority granted to the director, Correctional Institutions Inspection Committee, and governor under existing emergency overcrowding legislation;
4. Expanded community corrections for non-violent offenders; and
5. Required fiscal impact statements for all legislation proposing mandatory, determinate, or longer sentences for crimes.

The SOCF riot is a symptom of what is wrong in the Ohio prison system, not an isolated event. A variety of factors provided inmates with a clear advantage in the SOCF uprising:

- Understaffing
- Mass inmate movement
- Inadequate training and command structures
- Inmate access to sensitive information
- Judgment calls on the part of the administration
- Prison design and construction
- Policies and practices not consistent with the nature of SOCF inmates

Other factors in the riot included:
- The nature of SOCF inmates and a history of loose prison administration
- The warden's response to objections to TB testing by 159 of the 1,822 inmates at SOCF
- Overcrowding
- Racial and cultural tensions among inmates and between inmates and staff
- Inadequacy of mental health programs for inmates

Most of these conditions and problems exist throughout the Ohio prison system. Funded substantially below that of other states, Ohio has the worst-staffed and most-overcrowded prison system in the nation.

Political slogans and empty rhetoric will not resolve the crisis in Ohio prisons. The situation cries out for vision and determination. The union is willing to work shoulder to shoulder with the administration in developing comprehensive solutions to a very complex problem.

Summary of Recommendations
(1) Factor: Worst-staffed Prison System in the Nation
Recommendations: (1) Ohio must make a serious effort to improve the staffing patterns in its prisons, through either a significant reduction in inmates or a significant increase in staff; (2) the state should commit to achieve the national inmate-to-CO ratio by the year 2000; and (3) a joint DRC/OCSEA committee should be established to review staffing patterns and needs and recommend allocation of the new staff positions among the prison.

(2) Factor: Mass Inmate Movement Creates Security Risks
Recommendations: (1) Movement of maximum- and close-security inmates should be sharply curtailed and restricted to reasonable numbers; (2) adequate security staff should be available to supervise all movement; (3) inmates in one housing unit should not be permitted to mix or have direct contact with inmates in another unit, even units in the same block or complex; and (4) the recreation field at SOCF, consisting of three ball diamonds, a football area, and general recreation areas, should be divided with security fencing to preclude inmates from different housing units mixing or having direct contact while on the yard.

(3) Factor: Unit Management Practices Undermine Staff and Threaten Security
Recommendations: (1) Joint teams of line security staff and DRC officials should visit other state and federal prisons to evaluate their unit management practices, benchmarking the best practices for application in Ohio; (2) the current unit management system should be substantially revised to conform with true unit management principles and to give security and safety factors higher priority; (3) the chief of prison security (major) should report directly to the

warden and share equal rank with other deputies; (4) unit managers should be trained to emphasize the primacy of security procedures in all unit operations and policies; (5) the security of unit staff, including clerical support staff working inside the prison, must be considered in planning the physical layout of unit/housing areas and in the security staffing patterns for the area; (6) unit managers who object to inmate tickets or believe that any penalties should be modified should be required to submit a written statement to the RIB considering the matter, with a copy to the officer issuing the ticket, but should have no authority to cancel the ticket; (7) inmate records should be maintained in the Prison Records Office, not in the unit offices; (8) inmate clerks should not have access to telephones, computers, or records in unit management offices and should have no role in the processing of cell assignments or inmate tickets; and (9) line security staff should be included as participants in the unit management summit meeting Director Wilkinson recently announced.

(4) Factor: Prison Command Structure and Training Diminish Security

Recommendations: (1) In the event of a disturbance, the top security officer at the institution should report to the Command Center and establish overall tactical command rather than personally respond to the scene; and (2) the duty officer at a maximum-security prison should have substantial security experience, be well-versed in disturbance response tactics and be required to remain at the institution at all times.

(5) Factor: Staff Training Not Sufficient

Recommendations: (1) A joint union-management committee should review pre-service and in-service training programs in benchmarked prison systems, with the objective of adopting the best aspects of other programs into a major revision of Ohio efforts; (2) a correctional peace officer training program and certification process, similar to that used for other Ohio peace officers, should be established; (3) DRC should allocate training funds to provide the following in-service training to all DRC employees through a jointly administered training project during the current biennium:

- Gang identification and management training
- Stress management in a correctional setting

- Tactical and hostage security procedures
- Communicable diseases in corrections;

(4) DCT and TRT teams should receive full support and training from the department, including issuance of standard uniforms and equipment for all team members; (5) tower officers should receive clear tactical training and orders concerning control of inmates in the yard under riot conditions; (6) DCT and TRT team members should be selected from among the most qualified volunteers by a joint committee at each prison; and (7) DCT and TRT team members should receive a wage premium whenever the teams are activated or engaged in training.

(6) Factor: Inmates Have Weapons

Recommendations: (1) To reduce injuries to both inmates and staff arising from outbursts of violence in the prisons, a joint committee should be established to review and recommend advanced devices for the control of violent persons, such as pepper gel and stun guns or shields; (2) only the warden should be informed of a shakedown to be conducted under Operation Clear Out—and wardens should keep such knowledge confidential until the team has arrived at the prison; and (3) a strong effort should be made to increase uniformity in the designation of contraband items.

(7) Factor: "Safety Zones" Not Secure

Recommendations: (1) A true security envelope for staff should be constructed at each end of the blocks in maximum-security prisons; (2) each security envelope should be on a television monitor with a roof or tunnel security egress wherever possible; (3) all walls, floors, and ceilings in a maximum-security prison should be built as true security barriers; and (4) a joint committee should be established at each Ohio prison to review escape training plans and procedures to determine if flaws similar to those at SOCF exist.

(8) Factor: Lack of Gang Management Strategy

Recommendations: (1) All employees should receive at least six hours of gang training on an annual basis; (2) DRC must accelerate development of overall policies and tactics for establishing control of intelligence systems on prison gang behavior; (3) joint management-union gang coordinator teams should be established at each prison, with a statewide network linking them for purposes of developing solid staff training programs and intelligence networks for sharing gang information between prisons; and (4) gang coordinator teams at each prison should participate in other law enforcement gang training programs to ensure that DRC staff remain aware of developments on the streets.

(9) Factor: Sunni Muslims Met Unsupervised

Recommendations: (1) Prison employees should receive in-service training on the fundamental tenets of all non-traditional religious groups within the prison population; (2) no religious groups should be permitted to meet without direct security staff supervision; (3) security tenets must outweigh religious tenets in a prison environment; and (4) DRC should hire qualified Islamic leaders or imams to provide leadership and chaplaincy services for Muslim inmates in the same manner as for Judeo-Christian inmates, and with the same manner and criteria of background checks.

(10) Factor: Inadequate Security Awareness by Chaplain

Recommendation: Security monitors should be installed in the chapel areas to permit constant observation of inmates and to relieve the chaplains of security obligations or instincts which may run contrary to their traditional values and beliefs.

(11) Factor: Inmate Access to Critical/Sensitive Information

Recommendation: DRC should establish a joint committee at each institution to regularly review the number and nature of inmate job assignments, with the objective of eliminating those which allow inmates access to security information or data regarding staff or other inmates; influence over cell assignments or inmate movement; access to Rules Infraction Board charges or results; access to intra- or inter-departmental security communications; or access to computer systems or software.

(12) Factor: Lockdown Delay Allowed Inmates to Prepare

Recommendations: (1) Prison officials must act promptly and directly when confronted with inmate resistance to prison rules or procedures; delays in responding to group threat behavior allow inmates to plan for increased resistance; and (2) prison officials should reevaluate steps in preparing for a lockdown to avoid providing advance notice and information to the inmates.

(13) Factor: Crisis Response Staffing and Training Inadequate

Recommendations: (1) Prisons housing maximum- and close-security inmates should have a full complement DCT team on duty at all times, while all prisons should have trained cell extraction teams on duty at all times; (2) prisons housing maximum- and close-security inmates should have a full complement TRT team on duty throughout first and second shifts; and (3) utilization of a full-time DCT squad as institutional "police" should be examined for all Ohio prisons, using the Minnesota Oak Park Heights prison as a model.

(14) Factor: Poor Communication with Staff

Recommendation: DRC should invest substantial energy and planning in strategies for improving its internal communication effectiveness with staff.

(15) Factor: Dangerous Inmate Recreation Policies

Recommendations: (1) A joint committee should be established to investigate the safety and appropriateness of alternative exercise equipment, such as Nautilus or SolarFlex; (2) in all other prisons, free weight bars should be regarded as dangerous tools or weapons, used only under direct supervision of an officer and safely secured when not in use; (3) muscle-building supplements should be eliminated from commissary sales; and (4) DRC should adopt a weapons-free recreation policy.

(16) Factor: Poor Prison Design

Recommendations: (1) Correctional officers should be included on every prison design review team and utilized throughout construction to help detect and correct the following shortcomings, which are common in Ohio prisons: blind corners, lack of overhead security and protection for staff, inadequate or improperly installed locks, missing inner crash gates to prevent inmates' access to the main entrance, missing bars on prison administrative buildings, and inadequate or missing fencing in prison yards; (2) a joint committee should examine the practices and policies in other states regarding the construction of security gun ports or galleys in maximum-security prisons and the installation of automated gas injection devices; (3) staff safety equipment and devices should be tested on a regular basis and replaced when newer, more comprehensive devices become available, and this should include regular testing of devices such as the rear stairwell telephones; (4) remote radio monitor speakers should be installed in unit offices and other administrative offices within the prison so that non-security prison employees can stay informed regarding man-down alarms and emergency situations.

(17) TB Testing

Recommendations: (1) DRC should continue to screen all inmates for TB, using the most appropriate medical procedures; and (2) DRC should participate in an aggressive educational program to inform inmates and staff of the threat of TB, particularly the new drug-resistant strains, and of the medical necessity for testing programs.

(18) Racial/Cultural Differences

Recommendations: (1) DRC should develop a serious, long-term strategy for dealing with racial and cultural differences between staff and inmates, including a significant training component; (2) because of the shortcomings of prior efforts, effective new training strategies should build the appropriate learning content into the overall curriculum rather than focusing on a presumed need to "fix" staff under labels like "cultural sensitivity training"; (3) the state should construct prisons closer to major urban areas in order to increase effectiveness in recruiting and retraining qualified minority staff; and (4) training on street and prison gangs should be recognized as a factor in assisting staff in dealing with cultural differences between inmates and staff.

(19) Inmate Classification System

Recommendations: (1) A step-down system that allows inmates to earn their way into less restrictive environments must be an integral part of any prison management strategy; it is imperative that such step-down procedures be followed if the system isn't to collapse; (2) Inmate Classification Committees at each institution should include a correctional officer familiar with the inmate being reviewed; and (3) a joint committee should be established to review existing inmate classification standards and procedures and to benchmark such practices in other prison systems.

(20) Inadequate Mental Health Services

Recommendations: (1) The legislature should review mental health needs and practices in the prison system, including an examination of whether prison inmates can be required to take psychotropic drugs that are important to controlling their behavior without hospitalization and court review; (2) adequate mental health facilities should be established in all Ohio prisons to ensure treatment and to allow the prison to deal with the special problems and conflicts that mentally ill inmates present for other inmates and the staff; (3) mental health workers in the Ohio prison system should be trained regarding security procedures and report all inmates who have refused to take their medications or exhibit other unusual behaviors to prison security staff at the end of their shifts; and (4) mental health workers in state prisons should report directly to DRC.

(21) Alcohol and Drug Treatment

Recommendation: Ohio should increase funding of alcohol and drug treatment programs, both in and out of institutional settings, to reduce recidivism.

(22) Lack of Staff Input

Recommendation: DRC should develop a plan for the systematic and sincere inclusion of union leadership in efforts to improve employees and improve security and operations.

(23) Inmate Assaults on Staff

Recommendations: (1) Every assault on a staff member should be reported to the Ohio State Highway Patrol within twenty-four hours of occurrence; (2) the state should aggressively pursue prosecution and reimburse county prosecutors for costs associated with the prosecution of inmates who have assaulted a corrections employee; and (3) a monthly report of assaults and other safety hazards should be prepared by each Ohio correctional facility, using the format developed at SOCF, with a copy forwarded to the statewide and institutional Health and Safety Committees.

(24) Prison Crisis Response Planning and Policies

Recommendations: (1) The crisis response plan for each Ohio prison should be mandatory reading for all staff, and refresher training on the plan should be incorporated into the regular in-service training program; (2) DRC should establish and enforce a policy that prohibits the carrying of a disturbance control manual into the interior of a prison; and (3) a joint committee should conduct a benchmarking review of disturbance control plans and procedures in other prison systems.

(25) Community Corrections

Recommendations: (1) Ohio should continue to expand community corrections programs and operations, but not at the expense of prison safety and staffing; (2) policy-makers must be careful in efforts to distinguish between "violent" and "non-violent" offenders when establishing guidelines for the return or placement of convicted felons in Ohio communities; and (3) DRC should engage in a serious discussion with a broad spectrum of OCSEA leaders to explain departmental plans regarding community corrections and determine joint strategies for promoting them.

(26) Use of County Jails

Recommendation: Legislation to require non-violent inmates with ninety days or less remaining on their sentences at the time they are to be sent to a reception center to serve their remaining sentences in the county detention facility or under intensive probation should be pursued on an emergency basis.

(27) Mandatory/Determinate Sentencing

Recommendation: Prior to final passage in either legislative body, the Legislative Budget Office should be required to attach a ten-year fiscal impact statement to all legislation imposing new, mandatory, or determinate sentences for criminal activity.

(28) Overcrowding Emergency

Recommendation: The director, CIIC, and governor should carefully examine existing statutory authority to reduce prison overcrowding by declaring an overcrowding emergency and reducing the sentences of non-violent offenders by up to ninety days.

(29) New Maximum Security Prison

Recommendation: DRC should build another maximum-security prison in northeastern Ohio.

(30) "Super-Max"

Recommendations: (1) DRC should establish a special committee to determine the percentage of Ohio inmates who should be considered for confinement in a "super-max" environment; and (2) DRC should establish a special committee to evaluate existing and planned prisons for the construction of a stand-alone super-max unit within the prison complex.

(31) False Ceilings
Recommendation: False ceilings should be eliminated in Ohio prisons.

(32) Inmate Transfer Policies
Recommendation: When transferring inmates from one prison to another as a result of a disturbance, a team of correctional officers from the sending institution should brief appropriate security staff at the receiving prison regarding the nature and proclivities of the inmates being transferred.

Correctional Institution Inspection Committee (CIIC)

The CIIC was made up of equal members of the Ohio House of Representatives and the Ohio Senate. House members included Michael Shoemaker, Sam Bateman, Rhine McLin, and William E. Thompson. Senate members were Betty Montgomery, Jeffrey Johnson, Jan Michael Long, and Anthony Sinagra. During the year 1994, the CIIC held six extensive hearings including a public forum in Portsmouth, Ohio, conducted two on-site inspections of SOCF, and conducted inspections at each of DRC's thirty-two prisons. Portions of the CIIC's report follow.

Preliminary Findings of Fact

Trigger Event: Credible evidence and testimony supports a finding that the disturbance was "triggered" by inmates learning of a planned lockdown of the institution, scheduled for Monday, April 12, 1993. The planned lockdown was in response to approximately 159 inmates who had refused to take TB skin tests. Word of this "confidential" plan was widely spread among the inmate population beginning Friday, April 9, 1993.

The committee finds that any number of inmate disgruntlements could have served as the "trigger event" for the riot situation. Many inmate complaints are common, frequent, and have potential for producing major disturbances. Institutional lockdowns are frequently evoked to stabilize an inmate population immediately prior to or immediately after a sensitive situation. Many planned lockdowns in Ohio's prison system have successfully occurred despite advance notice being leaked to inmates.

While the disgruntlement over the TB testing issue may have been a "trigger" incident, it cannot be said to be the cause of the riot. The TB testing issue cannot be directly linked to the brutal murder of Correctional Officer Robert Vallandingham, nor to the murder of nine inmates, nor to the other violent assaults that occurred during the siege. Indeed, it is significant to note that TB testing was not even cited as an issue in the initial list of nineteen demands issued by inmates on the second day of the riot.

Contributory Factors: Several factors adversely influenced the operations and conditions at SOCF, contributing to an environment ripe for a major disturbance. Testimony received from DRC officials was very critical of DRC's own policies and practices, including:

- Dysfunctional unit management;
- Inmate clerks performing sensitive responsibilities;
- Noncompliance with restrictions on inmate movement;
- Improper functioning of inmate informal complaint process;
- Inadequate understanding and enforcement of court-ordered random double-celling;
- Inadequate intelligence system on inmate gang activity;
- Serious inconsistency between the philosophy of DRC Central Office and SOCF staff with regard to inmate classification.

The department acknowledged and accepted significant responsibility for not properly monitoring and correcting many of these long-standing deficiencies in institutional operations and conditions.

Crowding: Double-celling at SOCF was a significant factor contributing to the Easter Sunday riot. Severe crowding produced double-celling throughout Ohio's prison system. Double-celling at SOCF produced a more dangerous atmosphere and environment for those who work there and for those who live there. Double-celling put an added burden and responsibility on a workforce already challenged by inadequate staffing levels and by the disruptive nature of the inmate population. Crowding had an adverse impact on every area of institutional operations and conditions.

Increased violence is linked with increased crowding at maximum- and close-security institutions. Crowding alone reportedly accounts for much of the stress experienced by staff throughout SOCF. There is a certain population (slightly less than design capacity) that existing staff can manage adequately. Beyond that level, negative effects on the staff reportedly begin to be visible in staff attitude, communication, and interaction with inmates and other staff.

The department implemented Operation Shakedown in October 1990 in response to the House Select Committee recommendations for increased security and control of SOCF. A major component of this plan was to single-cell all inmates at SOCF. The opening of the new Mansfield Correctional Institution (MANCI) in October 1990 allowed for the transfer of maximum-security inmates from SOCF. As a result of Operation Shakedown, SOCF's population had been reduced to operational levels of 1,600 to 1,650 during 1991 and 1992. As of the date of the riot, SOCF's population had risen to 1,820, with 804 inmates double-celled. Staff size did not increase.

Change of Security Designation at Mansfield: Until June 1992, the Mansfield Correctional Institution (MANCI) served as the state's alternative maximum-security prison. From its opening in October 1990, MANCI received maximum-security inmates from SOCF, allowing for a gradual reduction in the inmate population at SOCF. Following the fatal assault of a correctional officer at MANCI in June 1992, the department decided to transfer all maximum-security inmates out of MANCI back to SOCF. This was done despite the fact that it was a close-security merit status inmate who had assaulted the officer. The transfer of maximum-security inmates from MANCI was a critical blow to Operation Shakedown, resulting once again in double-celling at SOCF.

Nature of the Inmate Population at SOCF: The particular nature of the SOCF inmate population itself was a contributing factor to the riot. Department officials testified that the re-designation of MANCI as a close-security institution resulted in the transfer of a "predominately stable group of 424" inmates out of SOCF to various institutions in exchange for a "higher security, younger group" of

293 inmates from MANCI. Some inmates are initially classified as maximum-security due to the nature of their criminal convictions—murders, rapists, armed robbers, etc. Some lower security level inmates are re-classified up to maximum-security solely due to their disruptive behavior exhibited at lesser security institutions. Many of the most disruptive and violent prisoners who are now plaguing Ohio's prison system are those younger inmates serving comparatively shorter sentences for drug and theft-related offenses. Many of these same inmates are involved in gang-related activities in the prison.

Until June 1992, both SOCF and MANCI housed maximum- and close-security inmates. The decision to re-designate MANCI as a close-security prison reversed a noteworthy achievement of Operation Shakedown—the ability to effectuate institution separations between general population maximum-security inmates. Many maximum-security inmates require institution separations from each other in order to prevent altercations or to ensure their personal safety. Placement into the Protective Control Unit at the Warren Correctional Institution is not always an approved option for maximum-security inmates. Institution separations are also utilized to frustrate and impede potentially disruptive associations between and among known gang members. The re-designation of MANCI resulted in a significant loss of general population maximum-security beds.

Dysfunctional Unit Management: The improper functioning of unit management at SOCF was a contributing factor to the riot. Testimony from DRC officials characterized unit management as "dysfunctional," suffering from a "lack of communication," "lack of trust," and "lack of shared mission." Other notable deficiencies, as cited in the Disturbance Cause Committee Report, include:

- An inconsistency in the interpretation and enforcement of rules and policies between the units.
- Inconsistent responses to or resolutions of inmate concerns by unit staff and officers resulted in misunderstandings with the inmates.

- In-unit restrictions had an impact on the accessibility and the lines of communication between unit staff and inmates.
- Not all unit management staff had completed DRC-approved training curriculum for unit management.
- Security restrictions and time and space limitations impacted programming in the various units.

SOCF correctional officers have long expressed the following concerns regarding unit management:

- "There is little communication between the unit staff and the block officers. There is poor consistency in how different units operate. Each unit seems to operate under different policies and procedures."
- "Every cellblock is run differently because every unit manager runs his unit differently."
- "Some units are not operated by good teamwork."
- "Unit staff undermine the role and authority of officers in the blocks."
- "Officers must contend with inflamed inmate tensions when unit staff are not available or not responsive."

Testimony further revealed that unit management at SOCF was plagued with "independent, inconsistent functioning of units" and that "a disruptive tension exists between custody and unit management staff." The committee finds that, in some units, there is a schism between unit staff and line officers. In some cases, the result of friction, discord, and confusion tests authority and "pull" with senior administrative staff. Shortage of staff is believed to be one of the reasons why inmates report inadequate access, response, or assistance from staff. It also explains in part why the expected benefit of unit management, reduction in grievances due to the handling of the problem at that unit level, has not been apparent.

The committee is supportive of unit management as a concept. However, serious concerns exist as to whether unit management, as presently structured and understood by SOCF staff, can be successfully implemented. Unit management, properly understood, is one method to accomplish the goal of integrating the equally valuable roles of custody and treatment. Unfortunately, the current concept had been imposed on an understaffed work force entrenched in outdated notions of "custody versus treatment," and without sufficient training, understanding, or acceptance of how unit management can create a more beneficial and safer working environment. Traditional notions of "custody staff" and "treatment staff" must be integrated without sacrifice to real security needs. In this regard, the recent promotion of the former SOCF chief of security (major) to the position of SOCF director of social services is viewed as a noteworthy management decision. Important policies and programs affecting inmate social services are to be administered by a staff person keenly aware of security-related issues.

Inmate Access to Sensitive Information: Advance inmate knowledge of the "confidential" planned lockdown was a contributing factor to the riot. Department officials testified that many inmates at SOCF were performing sensitive responsibilities despite previous security audit citings and direction by Warden Art Tate.

Shortage of staff is believed to be one of the reasons that in some units, inmates are not only allowed to but are expected to take on responsibilities and tasks that they ought not have. A shortage of staff does not explain why many who have been selected for what are regarded as the most powerful, coveted positions are known predators. Use of inmates in duties and decision-making includes but goes far beyond the old habits of using inmates in appropriate record-handling tasks. The level of reliance and dependency of staff on certain inmates is extremely disturbing. While staff have said for many years that the inmates "allow us to control the institution," that statement was especially true in pre-riot SOCF.

Frequent Mass Movement of Inmates: Despite significant curtailment and regimentation of inmate movement initiated by Warden Art Tate during Operation Shakedown, the movement of large numbers of inmates throughout SOCF on a daily basis was a contributing factor to the riot. With only one or two escort officers, hundreds of inmates at one time congregated in the dining room or in corridors or at recreation. Testimony from department officials confirmed that Operation Shakedown established limits on inmate mass movement, such as only one cellblock at a time in the corridor for inmates going to and from recreation or the yard. "However, as had become the practice, inmates were permitted to come into the yard using no particular system to comply with the movement restrictions" (DRC Disturbance Cause Committee Report).

Pervasive Problems: The aforementioned contributory factors of crowding, dysfunctional unit management, inmate access to sensitive information, and frequent mass movement of inmates are also identified as pervasive problems adversely affecting the conditions and operations at many other Ohio prisons. Although not necessarily factors that directly contributed to the riot, the following issues are cited here as additional pervasive problems that need to be addressed not only at SOCF but throughout Ohio's prison system.

Staffing: Testimony from DRC officials revealed that eighty-two out of eighty-six staff reported for second-shift duty at SOCF on the day the riot started. The inmate population at that time was 1,820; total SOCF staff was 673, including 462 uniform (security) staff. Although SOCF was far from being Ohio's most crowded prison, it was unquestionably understaffed. Statements received from correctional officers confirmed that, for the majority of a given shift, one officer had to work a cellblock alone—operating the console that opens and closes the cell doors; letting inmates in and out of their cells, the shower, and the dayroom; conducting the required "range checks" and "cell shakedowns"; "patting-down" every inmate entering the dayroom; and supervising inmates in the dayroom, in the showers, and in other areas of the block. It was not unusual for one officer to be responsible for supervising up to 160 inmates in a cellblock.

Ohio's prisons also suffer from an insufficient number of non-custody staff. Staff positions that are not directly security-oriented may appear as superfluous or less than essential to the perceived basic mission of confinement. However, the functions of non-uniformed staff are also essential to the security of the institution. All prison staff positions have a legitimate and valuable security function. Idleness ranks very high as a factor in disturbances and other breakdowns of security. This applies all the more to crowded institutions. Inmate work assignments, training, education, and recreational activities (properly staffed, directed, and supervised) not only keep inmates busy but direct their attention to positive goals.

Like crowding, inadequate staffing adversely affects every aspect of institutional operations and conditions. Staff shortages (custody and non-custody) in Ohio's prisons are not solely attributable to an insufficient number of Department of Administrative Services (DAS) authorized positions. Large numbers of unfilled vacancies, the customary slowness of the civil-serving hiring process, and the limited capacity at the Corrections Training Academy also contribute to the continuing level of staff shortages.

Historically, staffing patterns at all Ohio prisons have never increased proportionately with the rapid escalation of the prison population. Compared to other state prison systems of comparable size, Ohio's prison staffing had consistently ranked dangerously low. Credible testimony from OCSEA officials, citing comparative ratios of inmates to correctional officers, revealed that "Ohio has been the worst-staffed prison system in the nation for the last two years, and has never been better than third-worst in the last five years."

At the end of fiscal year (FY) 1993, DRC had 5,014 authorized positions for correctional officers, compared to 4,450 actual correctional officers—i.e., 564 officers below the authorized complement. The General Assembly authorized the hiring of an additional 904 correctional officers during the 1994-1995 biennium. Of the 904, a total of 438 officers were allocated to be hired during FY 1994. From July 1, 1993, to April 1, 1994, DRC hired and trained 568 "new" correctional officers: 415 of the 438 allocated positions, and filling 153 "formerly vacant" positions.

DRC officials report that "the Department is authorized by the Department of Administrative Services and the Office of Budget and Management to have a C.O. roster of 5,384." This figure is significantly less than the 5,452 total authorized by the General Assembly for FY 1994 (5,014 authorized at the end of FY 1993 plus 438 allocated for FY 1994). The total legislative authorization for FY 1995 is 5,918 (5,014 authorized at the end of FY 1993 plus 904). In order to satisfy the legislature's total authorization, the FY 1995 allocation must equal 534 (the remaining 466 of the 904 plus an additional sixty-eight).

According to DRC officials, the Corrections Training Academy pre-service classes are "filled to capacity each and every week." Due to limited capacity at the academy, training is limited to approximately fifty persons per month.

Inmate Gang Activity: Credible evidence was gathered for the committee to find that SOCF suffered from an inadequate system of intelligence gathering and monitoring of inmate gang activity. Department officials testified that "as a result of the lack of official investigations initiated and/or completed by the investigator, several other staff were conducting investigations on their own, without authorization from the warden or coordination by the investigators, or any one single person having knowledge of what investigations were being conducted. Each 'investigator' was collecting information that was not often shared with other key staff."

During 1992, the department developed a policy regarding inmate gangs and disruptive inmates. This five-point plan established methods for the identification, stratification, intelligence gathering, monitoring, and management of inmates involved in gang/disruptive group activities. Comprehensive Policy Directives relating to inmate threat groups were subsequently developed. Despite these excellent initiatives by DRC Central Office, SOCF staff did not cooperate in a cohesive, united approach to intelligence gathering and monitoring of inmate gang activity. There is a critical need for all staff at SOCF to work together to address gang issues and problems. SOCF staff could benefit from the gang-related recommendations developed in the aftermath of the death of Correctional Officer Davis at Mansfield in June 1992:

- Establish membership, organization, leadership, and habits of the gangs involved.
- Establish a roster and definitions for gangs, members, and affiliations, since affiliations by non-members can be just as powerful as full-fledged membership.
- Establish a computer database of gang information.
- Continue a more sophisticated education of information source departments—i.e., Mail Office, Identification, etc.— but do not allow gang education to violate intelligence concerns.
- Continue to work progressively toward education and intelligence gathering.

Court-Ordered Random Celling: Contrary to common perception, the federal court in *White v. Morris* did not mandate that inmates be double-celled on a racially integrated basis—i.e., forced integration of double-celled inmates. The consent decree provides for "random assignment of inmates to double cells without regard to race, but provides for exceptions where security is an issue." The court order in *White v. Morris* was "intended to apply the same standard as that set forth by the court in *Stewart v. Rhodes* (1979)." As a result of the *Stewart* case, the department had issued policies and procedures directing that "within an appropriate housing unit, the inmate shall be assigned to the first available (lowest-numbered) cell."

According to Warden Tate and other DRC staff, the problem with racial cell assignments was not so much the court decree as with the manner in which it was interpreted and implemented by prison staff. Many staff wrongly understood the court order and the department's policy to be absolute and inflexible. The SOCF Policy and Procedures on this issue was incorporated by reference into the consent decree and expressly provides that:

"Inmates may be moved within a unit upon the request of the unit manager or his designee. Such request shall be in writing, stating the reasons. If the movement will separate integrated cell mates, or create segregated cell mates, the programs deputy or his designee must determine (a) whether a legitimate penological rationale exists, or (b) the movement creates no significant impact on the overall racial balance within the unit."

Despite the flexibility and security safeguards structured into the consent decree, many unit staff were unduly rigid in their interpretation and enforcement of the random cell assignment policy. Inmates who attempted to relay objections to a particular cell placement were frequently told (regardless of the potential for an altercation with the assigned cellmate), "Too bad; your name was pulled at random for this cell assignment, and that's the way it's going to be." Inmates were being assigned without being afforded meaningful opportunity to express their reasons for objecting to the placement to unit staff, without adequate pre-screening by unit staff of each prisoner, and/or without a careful review by unit staff of the prisoner's master file, upon which to make an informed decision prior to cell placement. In many instances, same-race cell assignments were being made at random without regard to whether an inmate with predatory tendencies was being celled with an inmate who had been victimized or preyed upon in the past.

Moreover, the problem at SOCF on this issue was expressed by Warden Art Tate in a letter to CIIC staff dated December 31, 1991:

> *This issue was specifically addressed by Judge Duncan in 1979 in his Stewart v. Rhodes ruling. The Department is supposed to be utilizing a "random cell" policy with regard to inmate cell assignments. Additionally, when documentation on investigations indicate that a problem would likely exist regarding two interracial cell mates, actions are taken to insure that serious problems are avoided. An example would be celling an Aryan with a Black Muslim.*
>
> *I have repeatedly instructed my staff to closely monitor this entire process to insure that obvious problems are eliminated. My biggest "hurdle" has been the fact that random celling, per-se, had not been practiced here at SOCF prior to my arrival. I am now attempting to implement a policy that has been "on the books" since 1979, but hasn't been practiced. This has created a lot of tension and anxiety among both black and white inmates.*
>
> *In my opinion, most complaints are coming from inmates who object to being told who their cell mate will be. Many inmates have refused to cell with another inmate solely on the basis of race. When this occurs, absent additional documentation, disciplinary actions have been initiated. I have been accused by many inmates of developing a "new policy" for celling simply because existing policies were never implemented. I have also met with some staff resistance to implementation of the random cell policy.*
>
> *The Committee is well aware of the security reasons for not simply allowing inmates to choose their cell mates. However, we are also well aware of the potential danger of forcing certain inmates to cell together. It is understandable why many SOCF staff adhere to the belief that their work environment is made less stressful by allowing most inmates in general population*

to choose their cell mates. Certainly, every cell placement at a maximum-security institution should be carefully considered to avoid any probability of violence. Predatory inmates should not be celled with docile inmates. We recognize that these determinations are often very difficult to make and that they should not be made solely on the basis of race. Appropriate staff at SOCF must closely monitor the entire process to ensure that obvious cell mate problems and conflicts are eliminated.

The key to safe, successful implementation of a policy to prohibit racial segregation in cell assignments is in good communication between the inmate and staff responsible for making or changing cell assignments. If specific problems are brought to the attention of the staff by the inmate, that becomes staff's opportunity and duty to check thoroughly into it, and to make an informed, responsible decision on a case-by-case basis. Leaving cell assignment decision solely up to the inmate's choice is as unwise as any random cell assignment disregarding what the reclass reveals and what the inmate communicates regarding anticipated or present problems. The task of making wise cell assignment decisions is regarded as a difficult one. Staff must make random cell assignments to prohibit racial segregation, yet also make responsible safety and security-based decisions in that regard. Cell assignments ought to take everything into account that is relevant to safety and security of both parties and the institution.

Racial/Cultural Conflicts: Serious problems exist regarding interpersonal communication between staff and inmates. The DRC Disturbance Cause Committee Report revealed that:

This disruptive relationship is both racial and cultural in its origin. Interviews and documents support tension exists at the facility regarding cultural and racial differences between staff and inmates. Three (3) SOCF employees have lightning bolt tattoos, a sign associated with the Aryan Brotherhood. The Correctional Officer interviews revealed that most white Correctional Officers felt that the Aryan Brotherhood was more of a religious group than a gang. Most white Correctional

Officers did not understand that the Muslim group and some considered the Muslims half gang and half religious.

Additional testimony and direct observation by committee members reveal deep-rooted cultural and/or racial intolerance and misunderstandings between significant numbers of SOCF staff and inmates. This issue is viewed as a historical problem deriving from the placement of large numbers of urban black offenders in a rural prison with a scant number of minority employees. Although historical in origin, the committee is deeply concerned that racial and cultural tensions may have been exacerbated by the riot. The need for immediate, ongoing racial and cultural sensitivity training, tolerance, and understanding is evident.

Inmate Classification: Security classification is a process that establishes and adjusts an inmate's security level. It is also directly linked to inmate privileges. Proper, timely, and accurate classifications of inmates are the most important prison management decisions made on a daily basis. The enormous daily challenge for the department's Bureau of Classification is to decide: who should be initially assigned to what particular institution(s); who should be transferred to what particular institution(s); at what security status, for what purpose, and for how long; and which inmates should have institutional separations from each other (for personal safety and/or to prevent potential threat group affiliations). Such decisions are compromised and frustrated by prison crowding, limited transfer options, limited bed space at appropriate institutions, delays in receiving information from sentencing courts, inadequate documentation of critical information by institution staff, and the meager size of bureau staff beleaguered with this responsibility.

Testimony from department officials cited several problems with the inmate classification system as a source of longstanding concern for inmates and staff at SOCF: "The Classification Review Board does not routinely document reasons for rejections of recommendations to reduce an inmate's security status from maximum to close. Inconsistent understanding of classification philosophy between Central Office and SOCF" has long been cited as a concern, as frustration and tension "for unit staff and inmates in that inmates who are decreased to Close security generally do not get transferred out of SOCF to a close security facility."

The department recently announced its determination to single-cell all inmates at SOCF. This is a most laudable goal. However, its attainment is fundamentally conditioned on the strengthening, restructuring, and enhancement of the inmate classification system. Existing resources and staffing at the Bureau of Classification appear to be insufficient to accomplish this task. Existing policies, procedures, and administrative rules pertaining to classification issues may have to be amended. Existing deficiencies, incongruities, and inadequate documentation relating to classification issues must be corrected through proper training and diligent monitoring.

Inmate Frustration with the Inmate Grievance Procedure: Fear of retaliation for using the grievance procedure has been a longstanding concern of inmates. CIIC staff continues to receive correspondence from many inmates who view the procedure as "futile," "ineffective," or "a waste of time." The lack of cooperation on the part of some institutional staff with the inspector of institutional services has also been cited as a longstanding problem with effectively investigating inmate grievances. Clearly, the inspector has the duty to investigate each grievance, and he or she has the authority to take corrective action or to recommend such action to the warden.

A formal written procedure to ensure that inmates are afforded an effective, credible mechanism to provide an outlet for their complaints and dissatisfaction is a fundamental requirement in prisons. The committee is in full agreement with the observations of the National Advisory Commission on Criminal Justice Standards and Goals:

> *A formal procedure to ensure that offenders' grievances are fairly resolved should alleviate much of the existing tension within [the] institution ... Peaceful avenues for redress of grievances are a prerequisite if violent means are to be avoided. Thus, all correctional agencies have not only a responsibility but an institutional interest in maintaining procedures that are, and appear to offenders to be, designed to resolve their complaints fairly.*

The department's inmate grievance procedure is well structured and designed. Questions remain, however, as to its effectiveness. The department continues to face the formidable challenge of establishing credibility to the grievance system. Success in this endeavor is directly related to the department's success in implementing an effective unit management system at every prison. The committee continues to view the inmate grievance procedure as a very important and critical means of addressing many inmate concerns, and it has the *potential* to bring about improvements.

Initial Response to Disturbance: On the basis of credible testimony relating to the chronology of events during the initial five hours of the riot, the CIIC found as follows:

1. The rotary telephone system at SOCF effectively impeded prompt communication of the disturbance to key institutional staff who were not on-site.
2. Within one half-hour of the initial disturbance, the institution's perimeter was secured with the assistance of Scioto County sheriff deputies.
3. Warden Art Tate was at home, available to be reached via telephone. Despite attempts to do so, he was not notified until two hours after the initial disturbance.
4. Tactical command was not effectively established and organized by SOCF staff on-site during the first two hours, thereby forestalling and preempting an early opportunity to rescue five correctional officers and one inmate who had taken refuge in the rear stairwells of L-2, L-4, and L-5. This failure to establish command permitted inmates to erect barricades throughout L-block, move the hostages, and gain needed organization and confidence among their population.
5. Unit Manager Oscar McGraw served as assistant team leader of the SOCF Tactical Response Team. On the day of the riot, Mr. McGraw was also serving his assigned weekend rotation as SOCF duty officer. His dual responsibility of "supervisor" and "implementer" created an unfair conflict of interest. Testimony

revealed that he was not the most senior member of SOCF staff on-site. He arrived at the institution at the same time as one of the deputy wardens. While Unit Manager McGraw performed his tactical responsibility by taking an armed position in Tower 5, the committee remains concerned that no clearly stated policy directive existed to prevent similar "conflicting roles of responsibility" from occurring with other prison staff.

6. The Disturbance Control Team was not assembled until two hours into the siege (5:00 p.m.); the SOCF Tactical Response Team was not assembled until 5:45 p.m.; critical intelligence as to the precise number, identities, and specific location of the hostages was not known; and inmates had erected a barricade at the lower crash gate into L-corridor, thereby negating any real possibility for launching a successful assault on L-block.

Disturbance Control Plan: The SOCF Disturbance Control Plan was not made available or accessible to all correctional officers. All officers had not received adequate training on how to properly respond to a major disturbance or how to effectuate the plan. Credible testimony revealed the inadequacy and ineffectiveness of internal communications and the lack of information-sharing between SOCF administrators and correctional officers regarding critical components of the Disturbance Control Plan.

No comprehensive district-wide plan exists. SOCF officials did have direct involvement with other local responders (police, fire marshal, Highway Patrol, county sheriff) through annual reviews of the Disturbance Control Plan. However, external communications and information-sharing between DRC officials and some local community officials were less than adequate with regard to critical components of the SOCF Disturbance Control Plan and the "chain of command" during the eleven-day siege. Local residents are directly affected by major disturbances at prisons, whether those disturbances are caused by riots or natural disasters. Key local officials and responsible citizens in the affected community need to be involved in the development, review, training, and implementation of Disturbance Control Plans at each prison.

SOCF Leadership Issues: Warden Art Tate should be commended for having made significant improvements to security operations during his tenure at SOCF, beginning with Operation Shakedown. He should also be commended for his effective leadership during the eleven-day siege and for his efforts in securing the safe release of the hostages. Credible testimony and evidence support the committee's finding that many staff believe that Warden Tate provided excellent leadership.

Testimony revealed that Warden Tate did not possess confidence in key administrative staff and middle managers. As a result, a critical teamwork did not exist among institution management staff. In addition to the above referenced problems regarding SOCF unit management staff, the committee is deeply concerned with the following observation of National Institute of Corrections Consultant Lanson Newsome, who was on-site during the siege:

> It was evident that problems existed with executive staff and supervisors from the ranks of captain, lieutenant, and sergeant. The staff needed many questions answered during the crisis, as did the inmate population. Supervisory staff failed to fill the void, which occurred during this process. It was evident that many of the sergeants, lieutenants, and captains did not move throughout their assigned units on a continual basis, assessing the operation and making corrections where necessary. The Consultant observed many of the supervisors sitting in offices or in chairs in the hall when critical decisions needed to be made concerning the operation of their unit. Until proper, competent leadership is established at all levels within the Lucasville facility, problems will continue to be experienced.

Longstanding and wide-ranging problems at SOCF have not been caused by the absence of well-defined written policies and procedures. Nor have all problems been caused by double-celling. Many day-to-day practices of SOCF staff have been at variance with established policies and procedure. Some of those divergent practices are attributable to staff shortages. For example, some post orders for correctional officers assigned to certain cellblocks often required more tasks than could be performed realistically or practicably on a given shift. Other divergent practices, unrelated to staff shortages, are attributable to the staff's misunderstanding and/or unacceptance of Central Office directives on how a maximum-security prison should be run. DRC Central Office administrators should be more vigilant in ensuring that day-to-day practices of SOCF staff are congruent with written policies and procedures. Enhanced training and diligent monitoring are crucial.

Preliminary Recommendations

(1) SOCF should be operated and maintained as a true maximum-security facility. This can and should be accomplished with due regard to well-established constitutional rights of prisoners. Critical measures necessary to operate SOCF as a true maximum-security institution include: single-celling; adequate staffing; enhanced training and monitoring; appropriate restrictions on inmate mass movement; and programs that are commensurate to maximum-security inmates.

Reasonable corrections professionals (as well as informed legislators) differ on what it means to operate SOCF as a "true" maximum-security institution. All parties agree that single-celling and increased staffing are essential components. All agree that daily inmate movement should be more regimented and limited in numbers and frequency than was evident prior to the riot. Serious differences arise, however, on questions such as:

- How much (frequency) inmate movement is appropriate for maximum-security inmates?
- How many officers are needed to safely escort how many inmates at a time?
- To what extent should SOCF house "general population" inmates as well as inmates who are in Administrative Control (disciplinary isolation)?
- How many hours per day should general population maximum-security inmates be locked down?

- To what extent should maximum-security inmates be afforded out-of-cell opportunities to attend educational or vocational programs?
- To what extent should maximum-security inmates be afforded out-of-cell opportunities to work in Ohio Penal Industry Shops?
- To what extent should maximum-security inmates be afforded out-of-cell opportunities to attend treatment programs (substance abuse, sex offender, mental health)?

The most important question is, who should have final decision-making authority to answer the above questions: DRC Central Office? SOCF warden and staff? Correctional employee unions? General Assembly? All parties have a vital role and responsibility in defining how a "true" maximum-security prison should be operated.

(2) Inmates at SOCF should be single-celled. Simply assigning 1,000 of the worst prisoners to SOCF is not a difficult task. However, SOCF does not operate in isolation from the rest of Ohio's prison system, and Ohio has more than 1,600 maximum-security prisoners. Major decisions, such as single-celling at SOCF, adversely affect conditions and operations at Ohio's close-security institutions. Moreover, the department cannot regulate or control its ever-increasing intake of violent offenders.

(3) DRC should aggressively proceed with the hiring, training, and placement of all legislatively authorized correctional officer positions. Department officials should conduct an immediate assessment and evaluation of all practicable means and methods for accelerating the hiring process. The assessment should also include a feasibility study (with appropriate budget estimates) for increasing the number of persons per month who can be trained at the Corrections Training Academy. Full consideration should also be given for possible expansion of the academy's training capabilities.

(4) The mass movement of inmates from cellblocks to other areas of SOCF should be drastically reduced or limited, as compared to the levels of mass movement. DRC should consult with security experts in other states and with line staff at SOCF to determine the appropriate level. More important, DRC should expressly prohibit the actual inmate-to-correction-officer ratio at SOCF from reaching the level it was at for the recreation yard on April 11, 1993.

(5) DRC should consult with national experts and with OCSEA union representatives to review and determine appropriate restrictions and safeguards (as to number and frequency) for mass movement of inmates at SOCF and at close-security institutions. The committee supports the department's gradual easing of the lockdown to allow for "manageable" numbers of general population inmates at SOCF to be escorted to the inmate dining room for all three meals; and to recreation; and for educational, vocational programs; and for OPI shop operations.

(6) DRC should immediately initiate a comprehensive study of the inmate classification system. A critical assessment of existing resources and staffing at the DRC Bureau of Classification is needed to ensure that inmates are timely and accurately assessed and placed at proper institutions. Diligent efforts should be made to address deficiencies, incongruities, inadequate documentation, staff uncertainties, and other lax practices by institution staff relating to classification issues. Enhanced training and monitoring by DRC Central Office staff is warranted. To the extent that the department more effectively structures and utilizes its inmate classification system to ensure that the "right" inmates are appropriately assigned and retained at SOCF, DRC will have addressed a significant problem responsibly.

(7) DRC should ensure true safety zones for employees to seek during disturbances. In addition, the Disturbance Response Plan should provide for the continuous monitoring of and immediate response to safety zones when summoned.

(8) The SOCF Disturbance Control Team should be maintained indefinitely on-site, seven days a week, on first and second shifts. Further, DRC should provide the recruitment of additional team members and support for continuous training and retraining of the Special Response Teams.

(9) SOCF should maintain a Disturbance Response Plan that is clearly defined and accessible to correctional officers. The plan should clearly establish and identify a command structure in the event of a disturbance. Staff should be made aware of, trained, and retrained for the implementation of such a plan. Department officials must develop comprehensive strategies to engender improved communication and understanding between senior level staff and line staff.

(10) No inmate should be used in any position of trust where confidential or sensitive information is accessible. "Confidential" and/or "sensitive" should be clearly defined and should include information that, if known by inmates, could be potentially jeopardous to employees or to inmates.

(11) DRC should develop a communication policy whereby information provided to the media about a prison uprising is carefully evaluated as to its impact and ramifications before release.

(12) SOCF should appoint a community advisory committee (a) to assist in developing a community response plan in the event of a major disturbance and (b) to assist in developing a community relations program.

(13) The department should conduct an exhaustive security audit and study of all recreation equipment, furniture, and other non-stationary implements that are readily accessible to inmates to determine the probable use of such items as assault weapons.

(14) One of the qualifications for the warden position at a state maximum-security prison should be some prior work experience in security operations.

(15) If the governor issues an executive order to respond to a prison disturbance, the clear chain of command should not only be established but also communicated to all levels of government that have heretofore been providing responsive assistance. DRC should make continuous concerted efforts to improve the lines of communication between prison administrators and key officials in the local community.

(16) Consideration should be given to establishing an informal procedure by which the governor, president of the Senate, and speaker of the House would be advised of any proposed federal consent decree (settlement of inmate litigation) at least thirty days prior to acceptance of such a settlement by DRC.

(17) **A select committee should be established to study all relevant issues pertaining to mental health services in prisons, including the current policy of not forcing prisoners to take prescribed psychotropic medications.** At a minimum, membership should be comprised of officials from the departments of Mental Health and Rehabilitation and Correction, legislators from the Senate and House of Representatives, correctional officers, union representatives, and service providers from the private sector mental health community.

(18) **Department officials should consult with appropriate staff of the Ohio Peace Officer Training Council to explore methods and means of enhancing the entry-level and in-service training curriculum for DRC correctional officers.**

(19) **State prison beds should be reserved for violent offenders and those who are repeat offenders.** Additional funding should be made available for less expensive facilities such as boot camp facilities. In this regard, the recommendations of the Criminal Sentencing Commission (S.B. 274) authorizing a "continuum of sanctions" and the expansion of community-based corrections programs should be enacted. Housing non-violent offenders in less expensive settings will provide real potential for meaningful rehabilitation and will make available needed space for longer prison sentences for violent offenders.

(20) **The department should continue its efforts to bring Ohio's prisons into substantial compliance with American Correctional Association (ACA) standards.** The pursuit of ACA accreditation is undoubtedly costly in the short term, especially for the older institutions. However, the comprehensive accreditation process itself greatly serves the department's efforts to develop institutions that are (1) adequately staffed for safe, secure, and efficient operations; (2) adequately programmed for meaningful and effective rehabilitative treatment; (3) adequately supplied and equipped for the delivery of essential services such as food, clothing, and medical care; and (4) sufficiently engaged in preventative maintenance operations to protect and preserve the institution's infrastructures. The reduction in the number of inmate lawsuits and more successful defense of those suits are an additional benefit of accreditation status. Therefore,

in the long term, accreditation status can produce tremendous overall cost savings in the operation and maintenance of a prison.

(21) The department should develop comprehensive strategies for improving racial and cultural tolerances and sensitivities among the inmate population and between inmates and staff. Enhanced training components, structured throughout entry-level and in-service curricula, should be identified and implemented. Inmate grievances alleging "inappropriate supervision" and "harassment" should be vigorously monitored and investigated. Inappropriate behavior with a demonstrable racial animus exhibited by an inmate should trigger swift disciplinary actions and appropriate penalty enhancements.

(22) The department should develop a policy that would ban the public display of racially/ethnic sensitive tattoos or images by staff while on duty at any DRC facility. Such a policy should be developed with due regard to well-established First Amendment freedoms. A narrow range of disciplinary sanctions, including dismissal, should be provided for policy violations.

(23) Immediate and collaborative attention should be given to severe crowding at DRC reception facilities. Prison crowding is exacerbated by the daily delivery of first-time non-violent offenders with ninety days or less remaining on their sentences to DRC Reception Centers. These critical issues should receive prompt attention from the General Assembly, DRC administrators, union representatives, county commissioners, county sheriffs, and local judicial authorities.

(24) DRC should immediately develop a comprehensive strategy and system for identifying and intelligence gathering, monitoring, and management of inmate gang activity at all Ohio prisons. All DRC employees should receive extensive training on all relevant issues related to gang activity.

(25) DRC should make every possible and appropriate effort to increase the level of understanding, acceptance, and cooperation between and among all prison staff with regard to unit management policies and practices. Enhancing the quality of communication, cooperation, and support between unit and custody staff should be viewed by all DRC wardens as a priority consideration. Unit activities and practices should be monitored regularly by DRC Central Office and by senior staff at each prison to ensure consistent application of and proper compliance with established policies and procedures. Increased training on all aspects of communication and cooperation between senior level staff and line staff must be engendered. Line staff should be afforded frequent and meaningful opportunities to participate in unit management operations and decision-making.

(26) **DRC should aggressively strive to enhance the credibility and effectiveness of the inmate grievance procedure at each prison.** Existing administrative rules and policies prohibiting reprisals or retaliation for filing grievances should be vigorously enforced. The inspector of institutional services at each prison should be assured of receiving appropriate cooperation from all staff during his or her investigation of grievances in accordance with applicable administrative rules.

Chapter 16:
Media Feeding Frenzy

There is nothing like a pending disaster to bloody the media waters and trigger a feeding frenzy. This was certainly the case at Lucasville. With a potential disaster not seen since the prison riots at Sante Fe, New Mexico, and Attica, New York, and fresh from the fiery ending to the Branch Davidian Compound in Waco, Texas, the media fought each other for a bigger piece of the Lucasville story. Never in Ohio's history has an event been so massively, relentlessly, and unfortunately, pathetically covered.

Hundreds of news reporters from around the region, nation, and world gathered in the area surrounding the obscure town of Lucasville like vultures, even paying prison neighbors for standing room to get a clear camera shot of the riot-torn prison. In Lucasville, many in the media appeared to subscribe to the belief of not allowing the facts to get in the way of a good story.

Truth Be Damned

Writing for the *Columbia University Journalism Review*, Bruce Porter writes:

> *Glaring mistakes went reported as fact, and were never corrected. Reporters intruded upon the privacy of townspeople, trampling on the grief of families whose relatives had been murdered or held hostage. They vied for atrocity stories. They ran scary tales—totally false, it was later found—that spread*

panic and paranoia throughout the region. And in its general aggressiveness and error, the press ended up greatly hampering the effort to end the disaster peacefully, even in some instances posing a threat to the lives of the hostages.

Television—The Worst Offender

Near the start of the riot, negotiators for DRC were trying to listen to demands that rioting inmates were yelling through a bullhorn, in an attempt to put an end to the riot. However, a television news helicopter flew so close to the prison that the voices of the inmates could not be made out due to the noise.

WCMH out of Columbus went above the prison to televise a live shot of the SWAT unit taking up positions on the cellblock roofs to await further orders. In doing so, it compromised troop positions. In the voiceover for the live shot, the reporter ignorantly stated that viewers should not be concerned because "the inmates are not watching this now because there is no electricity in there." While the electricity had been cut off, officials knew many inmates would be watching on their battery-operated television sets.

In the midst of the riot, the governor's office and DRC Director Wilkinson had to take time away from managing the riot to mediate a battle between two competing television stations over who should be allowed to go in and film the release of hostages and under what conditions. According to Wilkinson, "Managing the media was almost as difficult as it was dealing with some parts of the riot. The stations were fighting over things like the transponder and whose logo was going to be shown. That stuff got in the way of us thinking about how to get this thing over."

Almost all of the media, it seemed, were engaged in atrocity stories, all trying to "out atrocity" the other. Phil Hayes, a television reporter for WCMH, the NBC affiliate in Columbus, reported a total of 172 dead bodies inside the prison. To authenticate his claim, Hayes interviewed a woman who claimed to be a friend of a Lucasville inmate and said that the number 172 came from prison staff. Later it was learned that the number of 172 was not a body count but a head count of the inmates in one of the cellblocks not involved in the riot.

Not surprisingly, neither the television reporter nor anyone with the station ever bothered to advise the public of its gross error.

Second "Honors"—Newspapers

Bruce Porter writes, "In many dramatic cases, when news from official sources dried up, the option the press chose to exercise was to print rumors." According to Bill Sloat, a reporter from the *Cleveland Plain Dealer*, "After a while we'd steeled into this routine siege. Well, there's not much news in a siege, so then the story began to become atrocities. Everybody had to have an atrocity."

It seems that the competition really peaked when it came to seeing who could come up with the most dead bodies. The *Portsmouth Daily Times*, located ten miles south of the prison, ran a story that "rumors of more deaths than officially reported dominated the landscape Tuesday. Callers from inside the prison told *Daily Times* staffers that anywhere from 50 to 150 bodies were in the prison gymnasium."

Not to be outdone by a small local newspaper, on day six of the riot, the *Cleveland Plain Dealer* ran a front-page story quoting anonymous "legislative and law enforcement sources" as saying that "at least 19 more people lie dead inside the Lucasville prison ..." The story also professed to quote one "high-level official" of DRC as saying, "There were some pretty barbarous mutilations of the dead ... and the truth is ... [officials] are deliberately sitting on it to not incite a loud outcry from the public." The newspaper could not have been more wrong, but apparently the truth was not newsworthy enough.

Effect on Staff

In Lucasville, horror stories of high body counts were not only beginning to affect hostage negotiators from the FBI, Ohio Highway Patrol, and DRC, who were negotiating with inmates over the phone; they were also compromising the effort to end the riot peacefully.

David Michael, a Dayton police detective and hostage negotiator, said, "My negotiators were on pins and needles because of the stories. They were scared to death to go home at night because the word had gotten around that so many people had died in there. It got around to the tactical people; it got around to the command people running the situation, who were thinking, 'Are we missing something?' Here these people are fooling around, playing negotiators, when all these people are dead in there. Well, the negotiators got to thinking it might be their fault."

Michael further stated that at one point, a SWAT team became so unnerved over the dead body stories, and by not being allowed to go in and stop the killing, that the prison warden actually had to lock them up inside the prison.

Effect on Rioting Inmates

While the dead body stories were creating a real nightmare for negotiators and staff, the rioting inmates had convinced themselves that these stories were actually being given to the media by prison administrators to lay the political groundwork for an armed assault of the prison. According to Michael, the inmates were greatly upset, for instance, over newspaper stories that said that inmates had "tossed" or "thrown" the murdered body of Officer Vallandingham out of a second-story window, when in fact they had carried it out on a mattress and laid it on the ground—still dead, but, to their way of looking at it, treated with some respect.

According to Cleveland inmate advocate lawyer Niki Schwartz, "The inmates were unhappy that the media was reporting them in a way that made them seem to be monsters. The reports of bodies piled up like cordwood, guards having been mutilated—they felt those things they knew to be false had been planted by the state to make them look bad."

Who's Hurt?

According to Porter, when it came to knocking down the atrocity stories, state officials faced the difficult task of having to prove a negative, of demonstrating convincingly that the bodies didn't exist. In the perverted opinion of some newspaper editors, the burden was not for the press to prove a story was true but for the state to prove it was false. Then managing editor of the *Portsmouth Daily Times* Gary Abernathy said, "The media is going to get out all the information they can get … and if the state doesn't do its job of shooting it down, it's going to keep feeding on itself."

When questioned about his newspaper's reports of high body counts, Abernathy replied, "Although it turned out to be wrong, most in the media felt it was a safe mistake to make, because if you're wrong, who's hurt? The best argument about who's hurt is family members of prisoners who don't know if their family members are alive or dead. You're saying 150 unnamed, faceless inmates are in there dead. No one's going to be able to come back later and say, 'Gee, you were wrong, and we're going to sue you.'"

Compassion and Common Sense Prevails

The *Cincinnati Enquirer*, which threw more than a dozen reporters and editors into the Lucasville riot story, appeared to have covered the riot more conscientiously than any other media outlet. *Enquirer* reporter Ben Kaufman, a reporter who normally covered the federal courts but worked as one of the lead reporters on the riot, stated, "Those of us with any history at the *Enquirer* knew we had blown some major stories in the past. With Lucasville, we wanted to do this story right. Instead of being pushed to get what other people had, we were told what the other papers were running, and it was up to us to verify it or discard it. They said, 'If it's there, get it, but if you believe you don't have it, we don't want you to write it.'"

"Journalistic Integrity"

The news agency that was the most directly involved with the riot was also the one that had the least amount of trouble in cooperating with authorities trying to end the siege in Lucasville. WPAY-FM out of Portsmouth was a very popular radio station with the inmates, which prompted the Ohio State Highway Patrol to request that Frank Lewis, general manager of the station, clear all news stories before airing them, citing erroneous information could compromise the hostage negotiations. Lewis agreed, although it caused him some concern later because he often could not find his police contact to clear stories that had been given to the rest of the media, as well as the fact that as a local media outlet, his station had come up with some good exclusives, which he had to keep confidential.

One such exclusive was that on day five after the murder of Officer Vallandingham had been confirmed and reported, Lewis learned that authorities had received an audiotape confirming that all of the rest of the officers were still alive and well. Lewis, at the request of authorities, held off in reporting this information because the story might in some way compromise the health and safety of the remaining officers. Lewis stated, "We knew the families would have loved to have heard their men were alive. But we were so afraid that if we jumped the gun on it that they would panic inside and maybe take another life."

Lewis was the first broadcaster authorities used in trade of free airtime for the release of a hostage. According to Porter, Lewis signed a waiver while on his way to the prison not to sue should anything happen to him during the broadcast. In fact, he was tear-gassed mildly while passing near a cellblock where state police were discouraging a group of unruly inmates from joining the main riot.

After passing the cellblocks, Lewis was led out to the recreation yard, where the prison staff wove his microphone and cord through the institution's chain-link fence and razor wire to the table in the middle of the recreation yard. From the other side of the fence, Lewis watched as inmate George Skatzes walked across the yard with hostage Darrold Clark and sat down at the table.

Afterwards, Lewis gave his own press conference and appeared on NBC's *Today Show* the following day. Lewis and WPAY reportedly took considerable flak for giving free airtime to rioting convicts. When asked about it, Lewis stated, "What I learned more than anything through all of this is, it's certainly not hard to make a decision on whether you're going to have journalistic integrity or save a life. I'm sure there are some news agencies around the world who would consider that a hard decision. That was not a hard decision on my part."

Lucasville Media Task Force Report

Three weeks after the end of the Lucasville siege, Governor George Voinovich wrote to *Dayton Daily News* Publisher J. Bradford Tillison and asked him to chair a panel on "media lessons learned at Lucasville."

In his letter to Tillison, Governor Voinovich wrote:

> *My goal is to find out how the State of Ohio can do a better job in dealing with the media in future disasters. I would like to come up with a product that can be used by future governors as well as sharing it with my fellow governors ... I believe that the state can and should learn many lessons from Lucasville.*

Your Task Force can provide important information on one of the major areas we need to learn from.

Tillison and the governor agreed that it would not be the purpose of the task force to critique the performance of either the state or the media at Lucasville. Far be it from the media to critique their own actions. Rather, the purpose would be to make constructive recommendations to the state on how it could better handle crisis situations in the future. It was also agreed that the recommendations would be broad enough to apply to a variety of crises in which the state might be involved, not just prison riots.

Choosing the members of the task force was left entirely to Tillison, and over the next two months, ten persons agreed to serve on the task force. Two later had to drop off because of professional or personal conflicts. The final, nine-member task force included five newspaper representatives, a radio representative, a television representative, a wire service photographer, and the director of the E.W. Scripps School of Journalism at Ohio University.

The members of the task force were:

1. J. Bradford Tillison, chair, *Dayton Daily News*
2. Gary Abernathy, managing editor, *Portsmouth Daily Times*
3. Lawrence K. Beaupre, editor and vice president, *Cincinnati Enquirer*
4. Stephen Dean, assignment editor, WCMH-TV (although he covered Lucasville as a reporter for WTVN-AM, Columbus)
5. Gary Gardiner, Ohio photo editor, The Associated Press
6. Frank Hinchey, state editor, *Columbus Dispatch*
7. Ralph Izard, director, E.W. Scripps School of Journalism, Ohio University
8. Jim Otte, Columbus bureau chief, WHIO-TV, Dayton
9. Sandy Theis, president, Ohio Legislative Correspondents Association, Statehouse reporter, *Dayton Daily News*

All members of the task force donated their time and paid their own expenses. All witnesses before the task force appeared at their own expense with the exception of two out-of-state witnesses whose expenses were paid by the *Dayton Daily News*. The governor's press secretary, Mike Dawson, acted as liaison between the task force and state government. The Department of Rehabilitation and Correction provided an employee to keep the minutes of the task force. Witnesses appearing before the task force were:

1. Reginald Wilkinson, director, DRC
2. Sharon Kornegay, public information officer, DRC
3. Colonel Thomas Rice, commandant, Ohio State Highway Patrol
4. Sgt. John Born, public information officer, Ohio State Highway Patrol
5. Major Jim Boling, Ohio National Guard
6. Mike Dawson, press secretary, Governor Voinovich's Office
7. Ann Fisher, Toledo *Blade*
8. Ben Kaufman, *Cincinnati Enquirer*
9. Ron Rollins, *Dayton Daily News*
10. Darrel Rowland, *Columbus Dispatch*
11. Pat Benedict, WCMH-TV, Columbus
12. Stan Sanders, WCMH-TV, Columbus
13. Craig Helfant, WSYX-TV, Columbus
14. Tyn Tolan, WBNS-TV, Columbus
15. Kevin Betts, WCPO-TV, Cincinnati
16. Dave Claborn, WTVN Radio, Columbus
17. Lorna Jordan, WVXU Radio, Cincinnati
18. Mark Nordstrom, WWCD Radio
19. Andrew Marceline, WOSU, Columbus
20. Michael Randolph, WOSU, Columbus
21. Tom Wicker, *New York Times*
22. Arthur Tate, warden, SOCF
23. Peggy Vallandingham, widow of Officer Robert Vallandingham
24. Homer and Wanda Vallandingham, parents of Robert Vallandingham

25. Mr. and Mrs. John Kemper, former Lucasville hostage and his wife
26. Mr. and Mrs. Richard Buffington, former Lucasville hostage and his wife
27. Allen K. Tolen, special agent, FBI, Cincinnati
28. Ed Boldt, FBI, Cincinnati
29. Niki Schwartz, attorney, Cleveland
30. Tim Smith, Kent State University School of Journalism
31. Greg Trout, chief legal counsel, DRC
32. David Marburger, attorney, Cleveland
33. James Onder, U.S. Department of Transportation
34. Dave Michael, hostage negotiator, Dayton Police Department
35. Frank Navarre, hostage negotiator, Dayton Police Department

The task force met for six full-day sessions over the following six months. It reviewed:

- Thirteen government agency documents, reports, and letters;
- Fifteen Lucasville-related newspaper articles;
- Eight periodicals;
- *Lucasville Media-Radio Montage* audiotape, prepared by Stephen Dean, WCMH-TV, Columbus;
- *Video Synopsis of Lucasville Disturbance Media Issues*, prepared by the governor's press office; and
- "Bibliography for the Lucasville Prison Riots," prepared by the E.W. Scripps School of Journalism, Ohio University.

After six months, and after listening to the testimony of thirty-five witnesses and the review of thirty-nine documents, the task force centered around the following themes:

- Almost from the beginning there was distrust and conflict between media representatives and state officials on the scene. As the crisis continued, the atmosphere grew worse.

- Physical conditions at the scene and lack of equipment made it difficult for both media representatives and state public information officers to do their jobs.
- State agencies had comprehensive and generally progressive public information policies in place, but state officials did not follow them during the Lucasville emergency.
- PIOs on the scene were ill prepared for a lengthy hostage emergency. They lacked the equipment necessary to disseminate information efficiently and appeared unclear about their role. Briefings were not scheduled on a regular basis, making it difficult for the media to plan coverage.
- There was confusion and perhaps conflict between officials on the scene and officials in Columbus, and this impeded the flow of information to the media and public.
- Information often has to pass through several layers of command at Lucasville and Columbus, and this impeded the flow of information to the media and public.
- PIOs on the scene had uneven access to information about the status of negotiations and were afraid to release what they did know. DRC spokeswoman, Sharron Kornegay, told the task force that she asked prison officials not to tell her everything so she wouldn't have to lie. State officials were not in agreement about the role of the PIOs and the level of access they should have.
- Everyone agrees rumors were a major problem both for the media and state officials.
- Some state officials believe the publication and airing of reports later proven to be untrue complicated the negotiations process. State officials are critical of the media for reporting inaccurate information.

- Many in the media believe the lack of reliable, timely public information about the situation contributed to the growth and dissemination of unconfirmed reports and inaccurate information.
- Many in the media believe the state illegally suspended the state's public records laws during Lucasville. State officials acknowledge they were operating in a "gray area" of the law but deny knowingly breaking the law.
- Generally, there was a lack of access to high-level public officials during the crisis, and this may have contributed to distrust between the media and state officials.
- There is considerable divergence of opinion between state officials and the media about the appropriate role for the media in a hostage situation. Many in the media are uncomfortable with members of the media becoming "players" in hostage release and prisoner surrender situations, especially when this results in restrictions on the release of information. State officials felt the media were one of the "tools" they could use to arrange a successful outcome to the crisis.
- Defining and organizing "pool" coverage and deciding when it was necessary were sources of confusion and conflict. Competitive pressures on the media contributed to this conflict.
- Hostage families resented media intrusion into their privacy during the crisis but were grateful for the information provided by the media and felt it served a useful role in bringing about a peaceful solution.
- Inmates were very media-savvy and relied on the media to provide them with reliable information and to get their message out to the public.
- Several witnesses commented on the need for more regular contact between the media and state officials,

especially prison officials, "in peace time." Some recommended joint training sessions.

As a result of these themes, the Lucasville Media Task Force made the following sixteen recommendations outlined in an eighty-one-page report presented to the governor on March 17, 1994:

1. The overarching recommendation of this task force is that it is essential for state officials, starting with the governor, to send a strong message throughout state government that it is the policy of the state to release information in a complete and timely manner during an emergency. The task force found a strong predisposition on the part of state officials, including public information officers, not to release information during the Lucasville emergency even when there was no operational reason not to release it. The only way to change this mindset, which we believe would exist in another, similar emergency today, is for the strongest possible signal from the top of state government and from the directors of each state department and agency. This recommendation is the heart of this report and appears, in various forms, in most sections.
2. The state should not enlist the media as direct participants in resolving crises or make other requests of the media that would compromise the independence or credibility of their coverage. (Role of the Media)
3. The governor should direct that all state departments have policies for the release of information during an emergency and establish mechanisms to ensure that they are followed. The guiding premise of these policies should be the maximum release of information. (Policies)
4. The task force endorses many of the guidelines contained in existing state emergency news media contingency plans. (Policies)

5. The governor should create and enforce administrative sanctions for officials who delay or deny access to public records at any time, but especially during an emergency. (Policies)
6. It should be state policy that state employees never lie to the media. Use of "no comment" should be prohibited. (Policies)
7. The state should conduct comprehensive training of public information officers and other state officials responsible for the release of information in an agency. (Training and Release of Public Records)
8. The state should provide a regular opportunity for state officials and representatives of the media to discuss how they interact in a crisis. (Training)
9. Media briefers must have complete access to information about the emergency. Briefings should be held regularly on a set schedule with media deadlines in mind. Unscheduled briefings always can be held if events dictate. (Procedures and Facilities)
10. The on-site media center should be as close to the scene of the emergency as possible. It should be staffed and equipped in a way that both state officials and media can do their jobs effectively. (Procedures and Facilities)
11. Applicable public information policies should be posted at the site of emergencies and be available to reporters on the scene. (Procedures and Facilities, Release of Public Records)
12. The state should make every effort to make available to the media decision-makers and ranking state officials during an emergency. (Procedures and Facilities)
13. The state should actively seek to discourage rumors during an emergency. This can be done through briefings, the use of hotlines, and other means. (Rumor Control)
14. The state should have a standard policy for the creation of a media pool at the scene of an emergency

if open coverage is not possible. The policy should address minimum media representation in the pool and expectations of the pool members. Selection of the pool members, within the guidelines established, should be left up to the media on the scene. (Media Pools)

15. State departments and agencies should develop procedures for handling large volumes of media requests during an emergency. Some types of information should be prepared and pre-positioned in anticipation of emergencies. (Release of Public Records)

16. The governor should designate an ombudsman to quickly mediate public records disputes during an emergency. (Release of Public Records)

A review of the above information, as well as the full report, was not, as noted by Porter, a self-examination of how the media managed to get things so fouled up. However, not all of Ohio's big newspapers chose to participate. Among them were the Toledo *Blade* and the *Plain Dealer*.

Porter also writes:

The report also considered various ideas for better educating the state's public relations people—one suggestion was to inflict workshops on them where they would role-play with journalism professors. The task force also spent a lot of time discussing whether state agencies should do things like provide portable toilets at the site of riots and other disasters, along with "hot food and drink area, depending on the length of the emergency." This latter suggestion prompted one task force member, Frank Hinchey, state editor of the *Columbus Dispatch*, to testily remind his fellow task force members: "Look, it's not as if we're covering a golf tournament here!"

The task force also heard some candid advice from Cleveland lawyer Niki Schwartz, whom many believed that because of his background as a prisoners' rights advocate and his strong civil liberties approach to the law he would offer some support for more open press access to prison records in times of crisis.

What the task force got, however, was, "For instance, they'd wanted the files of inmate negotiators, so presumably they could publish that Joe Dokes was a rapist and murderer." Schwartz stated that, in his opinion, such stories would not have only increased public pressure to storm the prison but would have caused the inmates to reconsider their determination to surrender.

Schwartz, in commenting on his task force testimony, stated, "I told them that I started out wanting to be a journalist, and as a lawyer and citizen, I'm devoutly committed to the First Amendment. But if the media had gotten some of this stuff and used it the way I suspect they wanted to use it, it would have inflamed passions down there, increased the pressure to go in with an Attica-style solution. The inmates, if the press had dug the bad stuff out of the files, would have regarded it as a hostile act on the part of the state, and it could have queered the deal and prevented the development of a higher rapport, which you needed to end it peacefully."

In spite of the fact that the press got very little of the facts right in Lucasville, it would appear from the hearings and subsequent report, the common phrase, "They still don't get it," certainly applies. The underlying fact remains that the media was willing—even eager—to assert as fact things it did not know to be true. In doing so, they abdicated their obligation to report the news and attempted to create it and in doing so created their own list of innocent victims. It could very well be argued that the press inflicted as much emotional damage as the inmate rioters themselves by compromising the hostage negotiations and, as a result, the health, safety, and welfare of the staff and inmates inside the riot-torn prison.

Chapter 17:
Criminal Investigation & Post-Riot Prosecution and Litigation

The Crime Scene

The criminal investigation, like many of the other investigations, began long before the inmates' surrender ended the nation's longest prison riot. The eight-acre crime scene, requiring the wearing of biohazard suits, was turned over to criminal investigators on April 22, 1993, and remains the largest and most complex in Ohio's crime history. The sheer size, magnitude, and complexity of the crime scene had to be seen to be believed. Under the jurisdiction of the Office of Investigative Services of the Ohio State Highway Patrol, the investigation was the responsibility of Sgt. Howard H. Hudson III, who stated, "On April 22, 1993, as I walked, for the first time, through the rubble that was once L-block, I thought to myself, 'We'll just have to do the best we can.'"

The Investigation Team

The lengthy investigation resulted in over twenty Ohio State Highway Patrol investigators assigned to SOCF during the height of the investigation, and four investigators would remain throughout the three-year investigation. The investigation team worked out of a base located in the SOCF school. The investigation resulted in 5,750 photographs taken, 1,395 interviews conducted, 20,000 pieces of evidence resulting in 4,227 evidence submissions into trial, 591 "tunnel tapes," 122 videotapes, seventeen hostage negotiation tapes, and a specially created computer database to accommodate and track 5,248 entries.

Investigators received on-the-job training from FBI forensics experts—including some of the same agents who had searched the rubble of the first World Trade Center bombing. A special computer program was utilized to store and retrieve data on crime witnesses, locations, and events. The safety of prisoners who testified against others was ensured by the creation of special housing units in seventeen DRC prisons and computerized separation programs. William O. Kempton was assigned to coordinate the DRC response and participation in the criminal investigation.

An integral part of the criminal investigation was the information and subsequent testimony provided by the former hostages. While all of the hostages provided information to investigators, two former hostages were able to provide the greatest assistance—Michael Hensley and Larry Dotson. In 1993, criminal investigators lacked the sophisticated forensic DNA technology available today, and with most of the inmates presenting a unified front and essentially refusing to cooperate with investigators, investigators spent a considerable amount of time and effort in trying to "turn" an inmate who could provide substantial and credible evidence as to the initiation and management of not only the riot but the murder of Correction Officer Vallandingham.

Assembling the Prosecution Team

The sheer size and magnitude of the SOCF crime scene and the number of potential defendants in this case was instantly overwhelming for the very small office of the Scioto County Prosecutor's Office of Lynn Grimshaw. Recognizing both the resource and expertise limitations of his office, Grimshaw turned to his political ally and fellow member of the County Prosecutor's Association, Joseph Deters of Hamilton County. With the decision to actively pursue those responsible for the murder of Officer Vallandingham, it was clear that trials with death-penalty specifications were in order.

The Hamilton County Prosecutor's Office had Ohio's best record with such cases. Deters named Assistant Hamilton County

Prosecutor Mark Piepmeier as the SOCF special prosecutor. At that time, the assistant county prosecutor for twelve years had successfully prosecuted fifteen death-penalty cases. Piepmeier, through his professional and political contacts, began to assemble a large and extremely competent prosecution team of twenty prosecutors.

- Hamilton County: William Anderson, Steve Martin, William Breyer, Steve Tolbert, Claude Crowe, Seth Tieger, Rick Gibson, Garry Krumplebeck, and Tom Longano.
- Franklin County: Jim Canepa, Dennis Hogan, Doug Stead, Dan Hogan, and Robert Krapenc.
- Clark County: Darnell Carter and David Smith.
- Butler County: Robin Piper.
- Cleremont County: Daniel Breyer.
- Warren County: Jim Beaton.

Turning a Riot Leader

Investigators and prosecutors knew that the key to winning convictions was to somehow erode the fear and loyalty gang members had to their gang leaders. Thirteen months into the riot investigation, they were finally successful in turning not one but several inmates intimately involved in the riot. First was the leader of the Black Gangster Disciples, Anthony Lavelle. Lavelle agreed to a plea bargain and gave investigators and prosecutors information on Vallandingham's death, which turned the tide of the whole investigation. Lavelle provided key testimony in the subsequent convictions of fellow riot leaders Sanders, Skatzes, Robb, and Were. In return, Lavelle's plea bargain permitted him to plead guilty to conspiracy to commit murder and receive a sentence of seven to twenty-five years.

Second was Aryan leader Roger Snodgrass. Snodgrass, like Lavelle, provided significant, substantial, and credible "behind-the-scenes" eyewitness testimony of the riot. In exchange for his testimony and cooperation, Snodgrass received a letter of understanding from DRC Director Wilkinson dated March 13, 1995, which contained four specifics:

First, as long as your conduct and safety permit you will be housed in the Warren Correctional Institution merit protective control block for the remainder of your incarceration.

Second, under no circumstances will you be incarcerated at the Southern Ohio Correctional Facility at Lucasville.

Third, in the event your behavior requires that you be disciplined, any and all assignments made will maximize your safety by not placing you in any housing unit with other inmates who may reasonably pose a threat to your safety.

Fourth, at no time will your protective control status be removed without your written permission.

Prosecutors utilized the testimonies of Snodgrass and Lavelle to gain convictions of numerous riot-involved inmates, including the critically important convictions of Carlos Sanders, George Skatzes, James Were, and Jason Robb. The convictions of Sanders, Skatzes, Were, and Robb resulted in each receiving the death penalty, and each currently awaits lethal injection on Ohio's death row and are housed at the super-maximum-security Ohio State Penitentiary in Youngstown. Six counties, including Ohio's largest of Hamilton, Franklin, and Montgomery, hosted post-Lucasville riot-related trials. To coordinate such a massive undertaking, special partnerships were formed between the Ohio State Highway Patrol, DRC, county sheriffs, and the courts.

Criminal Versus Administrative

Using information gained as a result of the investigation, DRC divided riot-involved SOCF inmates into two groups—those who would be criminally charged and those who would receive an administrative disciplinary hearing through DRC's administrative Rules Infraction Board (RIB). The RIB is a three-member panel charged with the responsibility of ensuring internal due process. Those who were to be administratively charged were divided into two groups. Group A involved offenses against persons, and group B involved offenses against property. Those inmates in group B were released from lockdown status. Eighteen inmates were found guilty, and six were acquitted. The guilty findings resulted in assignments to segregation cells, classifications to a higher security facility, and reports to the Parole Board.

As a result of the multi-agency investigation, 550 inmates were cleared of involvement, and 152 indictments involving fifty inmates, with eleven of the cases relating to the death of Officer Vallandingham, were issued. Fifty trials in ten counties resulted in forty-seven guilty findings or guilty pleas, two not-guilty findings, and one hung jury. Five inmates received the death penalty for their involvement in either the death of Correction Officer Vallandingham or the murder of several inmates during the first day of the riot. Carlos Sanders, Jason Robb, George Skatzes, James Were, and Keith LaMar have become known as the "Lucasville 5."

Carlos Sanders

The Scioto County Grand Jury returned indictments charging Carlos Sanders with two aggravated murder counts with regard to Officer Vallandingham and one aggravated murder count with regard to inmate Bruce Harris. All three counts carried death-penalty specifications. Sanders was also charged with various counts against other officers.

After two changes of venue, Sanders was tried in the Hamilton County Common Pleas Court. The jury convicted Sanders of the aggravated murder of Officer Vallandingham, with three death-penalty specifications: murder while under detention in violation of ORC 2929.04(A)(4); course of conduct in violation of Ohio Revised Code (ORC) 2929.04(A)(5); and felony murder (kidnapping) in violation of ORC 2929.04(A)(7). He was acquitted of the aggravated murder charge of Harris and of one count of felonious assault against Officer Larry Dotson, and convicted of all other counts.

After a penalty hearing, the jury recommended and the trial judge imposed a death sentence for the aggravated murder of Officer Vallandingham. The court of appeals affirmed the judgment of the trial court in all respects. Sanders appealed to the Ohio Supreme Court, citing thirty-four propositions of law. The court independently reviewed the death sentence, as ORC 2929.05(A) required, by reweighing the felony-murder aggravating circumstance against the mitigating factors and measuring the sentence against sentences in similar cases. The court concluded that Sanders' convictions and death sentences should be affirmed and so ordered.

Interestingly, Sanders cited as one of his defenses that the state of Ohio failed to negotiate in good faith with him and the other riot leaders, and as a result of this failure, Officer Vallandingham died. Chief Justice Thomas Moyer wrote for the majority of the court:

> ... *the authorities in lawful charge of a prison have no duty to negotiate in good faith with inmates who have seized the prison and taken hostages, and the failure of those authorities to negotiate is not an available defense to inmates charged with the murder of a hostage.*

Jason Robb

In July 1994, a grand jury indicted Robb on four aggravated murder counts. Counts 1 and 3 charged him with prior calculation and design in the murder of Correction Officer Robert Vallandingham and inmate David Sommers. Counts 2 and 4 charged Robb with their murders in the course of kidnapping. Each count contained capital or death-penalty specifications in that the murders occurred (1) while Robb was a prisoner in a detention facility, a violation of ORC 2929.04 (A)(4); (2) as part of a course of conduct in violation of ORC 2929.04(A)(5); and (3) during a kidnapping in violation of ORC 2929.04(A)(7). Additionally, count 5 charged Robb with kidnapping Vallandingham. An earlier grand jury had indicted Robb on two counts of kidnapping Officer Darrold Clark, and those counts were tried as counts 6 and 7.

The jury convicted Robb on counts 1 and 3, the aggravated murders with prior calculation and design of Vallandingham and Sommers, and count 2, the aggravated felony-murder of Officer Vallandingham, together with all capital specifications except the ORC 2929.04(A)(7) kidnapping specification contained in count 3. On count 4, the jury convicted him of the lesser included offense of the murder of Sommers. The jury also found the defendant guilty as charged of kidnapping Vallandingham and Clark in counts 5, 6, and 7. At the conclusion of the penalty phase of trial, the jury recommended the death penalty on counts 1 and 3 and life imprisonment on count

2. The trial court sentenced Robb to death for the aggravated murders of Vallandingham and Sommers as contained in counts 1 and 3, and to consecutive prison terms for kidnapping Officers Clark and Vallandingham.

The Court of Appeals affirmed the trial court's judgment and the death-penalty sentence, and Robb subsequently appealed to the Ohio Supreme Court on October 19, 1999, as a matter of right. The Ohio Supreme Court decided the case on March 1, 2000, and upheld the trial court's ruling. Jason Robb now pursues his legal appeals through the federal courts as he sits on death row at the Ohio State Penitentiary in Youngstown. Ironically, the next time Jason Robb arrives at the Southern Ohio Correctional Facility will be for his lethal injection.

George Skatzes

The Scioto County Grand Jury indicted Skatzes on six counts of aggravated murder, two counts each for the murders of Officer Vallandingham and inmates Elder and Sommers. Each murder count carried for death specifications: murder in a detention facility in violation of ORC 2929.04(A)(4), a prior aggravated murder conviction in violation of ORC 2929.04(A)(5), murder as a course of conduct in violation of ORC 2929.04(A)(5), and murder during a kidnapping in violation of ORC 2929.04(A)(7). Skatzes was also indicted on three counts of kidnapping in violation of ORC 2905.01.

The trial court changed the venue to Montgomery County, and the case was tried before a jury. After the state presented its case, the defense called five witnesses, including Correction Officer Jeff Ratcliff. Skatzes testified on his own behalf. The defense claimed that Skatzes had been a peacemaker during the prison takeover and had opposed killing a CO. Skatzes denied involvement in the Elder and Sommers murders. The jury found Skatzes guilty on all counts and specifications. After a mitigation hearing, the jury recommended death for the murders of Elder and Sommers and a life sentence for the murder of Officer Vallandingham. The trial judge sentenced accordingly. In January 2003, the court of appeals affirmed Skatzes' convictions and death sentence with modifications.

The Ohio Supreme Court upheld the convictions and further found that the death penalty was both appropriate and proportionate when compared with the death sentences imposed in the other Lucasville cases also decided by the high court. The court also found the death penalty proportionate for aggravated murders committed in a detention facility and for aggravated murders with a prior murder conviction. The court also found the death penalty appropriate for aggravated murders committed during kidnappings and for aggravated murders as a course of conduct involving the purposeful killing or attempt to kill two or more persons.

James Were

On July 29, 1994, the Scioto County Grand Jury indicted Were for aggravated murder with specifications in violation of ORC 2903.01, kidnapping with specifications in violation of ORC 2905.01, felonious assault in violation of ORC 2903.11, and assault with specifications in violation of ORC 2903.13. On September 20, 1994, the case was transferred to the Hamilton County Common Pleas Court of Judge Fred J. Cartolano. On October 23, 1995, the jury found Were guilty of counts 1, 2, and 5 and not guilty of counts 3 and 4. The jury further found him guilty of specifications 1 and 3 on counts 1 and 2. The penalty phase was conducted on October 30-31, 1995, with the jury recommendation of death.

Were appealed to the First District Court of Appeals on June 24, 1996, with the court affirming the conviction and sentence on April 10, 1998. Were appealed as a matter of right to the Ohio Supreme Court on October 28, 1998. On February 25, 2002, the Ohio Supreme Court reversed the lower courts and remanded the case to the trial court for a new trial, citing that Were's constitutional rights were violated as no competency hearing was conducted prior to trial. The case was assigned to Judge Cartolano with a trial date of April 28, 2003. On May 13, 2003, the jury returned a guilty verdict of the aggravated murder of Officer Vallandingham during the kidnapping of Officer Vallandingham while a prisoner in a detention facility, and guilty of committing the murder of Officer Vallandingham with prior calculation and design. On May 19, 2003, the trial court found Were not to be mentally retarded, and on May 21, 2003, the jury reported:

We, the Jury, do find, beyond a reasonable doubt that the aggravating circumstances which the defendant, James Were, was found guilty of committing, that I: the aggravated murder of Robert Vallandingham was done purposely and with prior calculation and design during the kidnapping of Robert Vallandingham and done purposely and with prior calculation and design while the defendant was a prisoner in detention, outweigh any mitigating factor or factors present. We, therefore, recommend that the sentence of death be imposed on the defendant.

On June 6, 2003, Judge Cartolano imposed the following sentence: On count 1, aggravated murder, sentenced to death. In the event the penalty of death is not carried out for any reason, the defendant is to serve the rest of his life in prison with parole eligibility after thirty full years. On count 5, kidnapping, sentenced to not less than fifteen years' or more than twenty-five years' actual confinement in the Department of Corrections, consecutive to any sentence the defendant is presently serving. Were is pursuing his legal appeals while serving his sentence at the Ohio State Penitentiary.

Keith LaMar

The grand jury indicted LaMar on nine counts of aggravated murder for his role in the deaths of Depina, Vitale, Staiano, Svette, and Weaver. Five of the aggravated murder counts alleged that LaMar killed each of the victims with prior calculation and design in violation of ORC 2903.01(A). The remaining counts charged LaMar with murdering Depina, Vitale, Staiano, and Svette while committing or attempting to commit kidnapping in violation of ORC 2903.01(B). In addition, the grand jury charged LaMar with four death-penalty specifications attached to the first eight counts of the indictment: ORC 2929.04(A)(4)(murder committed in a detention facility); (A)(5) (prior murder conviction); (A)(5)(murdering two or more victims); and (A)(7) (murder committed while committing or attempting to commit kidnapping). The ninth count, charging Weaver's murder, alleged only three of these specifications; it did not charge LaMar with the kidnapping specification.

239

The trial jury returned guilty verdicts on all the charges and specifications alleged in the indictment. Following the penalty-phase proceedings, the jury recommended the death penalty for the murders of Depina, Vitale, Svette, and Weaver. For Staiano's murder, the jury found that LaMar should be sentenced to life imprisonment with parole eligibility after thirty years. The trial court issued a sentencing opinion in which it agreed with the jury's recommendation and sentenced LaMar to death for the murders of Depina, Vitale, Svette, and Weaver. LaMar appealed to the Fourth District Court of Appeals, asserting nineteen assignments of error. The court of appeals overruled each of the assignments and affirmed the convictions and death sentence. LaMar appealed to the Ohio Supreme Court as a matter of right.

The Ohio Supreme Court rightly affirmed LaMar's convictions, including the sentences of death for the murders of Vitale, Depina, Svette, and Weaver, stating, "We also find that the death sentence in this case is appropriate and proportionate when compared with similar capital cases in which the death penalty has been imposed. We have affirmed the imposition of the death penalty in other cases involving murders committed during the SOCF riot."

By the Numbers

Altogether, 550 inmates were cleared of involvement, and 152 indictments involving fifty inmates, eleven of those relating to Officer Vallandingham, were handed down. Fifty trials were conducted in ten counties. Forty-seven resulted in either guilty verdicts or pleas. There was also one hung jury and two not-guilty findings. A very impressive record and a historic first for post-prison-riot prosecutions.

Inmate Litigation

On January 21, 1997, the DRC announced that it had reached a settlement in a class action lawsuit filed by inmates following the riot. The agreement created a settlement fund for three groups of inmates: those who were killed, those who were injured, and those who lost property. Inmates convicted of riot-related crimes were excluded from the settlement. The State of Ohio agreed to pay $4.1 million into the fund.

Part 4:
Lessons Learned?

Chapter 18:
The SOCF Riot Legacy

There can be no doubt that the riot at the SOCF has forever changed the correctional landscape in Ohio and arguably throughout the country. On May 30, 1994, in the *Portsmouth Daily Times*, then DRC director Wilkinson said that the DRC has "systematically stepped up security at the Lucasville prison and all the other 25 prisons in the state." Wilkinson also touted the establishment of two regional STAR (Special Tactics and Response) Teams and the "establishment of SRT (Special Response Teams) at each prison to respond to incidents, conduct searches, assist in training and to perform other security-oriented tasks ... Hostage Negotiation Teams (HNT) now jointly train with STAR and SRT." In addition, a tougher approach to gangs and other security threat groups (STGs) has been undertaken in each prison and at Central Office.

In addition, DRC has built its "super-max" prison in Youngstown for the most violent and predatory of Ohio's inmates. However, the federal courts have already weakened the security of that facility by their rulings. Public information teams have been established at each facility and Central Office and conduct training quarterly with the news media. The Ohio legislature approved the hiring of 900 additional correctional officers.

In 1997, in *Corrections Management Review*, Director Wilkinson and Assistant Director Stickrath wrote:

The SOCF riot highlighted for the Department, lawmakers and the public, unresolved problems such as security versus non-security staff alienation; mass inmate movement; recreation and the use of force weights; the influence of gangs; use of force issues; inmate religious, educational, recovery services, and medical and mental health issues; racial enmity and the effects of prison crowding.

- *Policies and procedures have been reviewed and strengthened, and new policies implemented.*
- *Training has been considerably expanded and enhanced.*
- *Union and management are working toward common goals.*
- *A Strategic Threat Group (gang) management and intelligence gathering network has been expanded and become more consistent and sophisticated.*
- *Maximum security inmates are now single-celled.*
- *A new $60 million, 500-bed "super-max" facility to house predatory inmates is under construction.*
- *The Ohio legislature authorized the Department to hire 904 new corrections officers and funding is in place to hire an additional 1,500 staff, including two hundred C.O.'s.*
- *Ohio's inmate to staff ratio has dropped from 8.7-to-1 in 1993 to 6.7-to-1 today.*
- *Since 1993, eleven new prisons, work camps and dormitories have opened.*
- *Greater attention is focused on "special needs" inmates such as those with mental illnesses. Mentally ill inmates are now housed and treated in special facilities and treatment units.*
- *The legislature has provided more resources to the Department. Our biennium budget now exceeds one billion dollars.*
- *Individual prison riot plans have been replaced with a system-wide Critical Incident Management (CIM) plan to ensure a consistent, rapid and forceful response*

to prison disturbances and disasters. CIM training has cascaded to all DRC staff.

• *Special Response Teams have replaced individual Disturbance Control Teams. Regional Special Tactical and Response (STAR) teams are in place to assist institutions in quelling disturbances. STAR teams also conduct institutional "Operation Clearout" shakedowns.*

However, as in nearly all paradigm-shifting events, time has a way of erasing many of the lessons learned. Indeed, many of the legislators, Central Office staff, as well as prison staff have since left the department, and things have had a way of returning to "normal." The prison system's budget rose from $680 million in 1993 to more than $1.5 billion in 2001. However, the state's budget crisis hit home in 2002, and the prison budget was cut for the first time in twelve years. Not only did the DRC take a $10 million hit from its 2001 budget, it also lost more than $120 million in additional spending that department officials had hoped would sustain the reform effort.

Oversight Panel Dismantled
The Correctional Institution Inspection Committee, which inspected prisons and investigated 1,500 inmate complaints every month, fell victim to budget cuts in 2001.

Closing Prisons
In response to the budget crisis, DRC responded by closing the Orient Correctional Institution, made dramatic cuts at their training academy, and closed the Lima Correctional Institution (LCI). That resulted in boosting inmate populations at other DRC prisons. The Lorain Correctional Institution (LorCI) in northeast Ohio became the most overcrowded prison in Ohio, operating at 268 percent capacity. It was only one of four prisons that housed twice as many inmates as they were designed to hold. Lucasville Special Prosecutor Mark Piepmeier stated, "Anytime prisoners want to take over, they can. Not like before, but it could happen."

In an article appearing in the *Cincinnati Enquirer*, Sunday, April 6, 2003, it was noted that

... prison budgets are facing their second straight year of cuts. Two-thirds of the state's prisons now house more inmates than they were designed to hold. And correctional officers are once again complaining about long hours and unsafe conditions. Some legislators and activists say the state's commitment to improve Ohio's prisons is fading, along with the memory of how and why the riot took place. Some even suggest that the risk of violence at one of Ohio's 33 state-run prisons is now as great as any time since Easter Sunday 1993, the day hundreds of inmates in Cell Block L seized control in Lucasville.

Then state senator and now Cincinnati mayor Mark Mallory, who had long been active in prison issues, stated in the same article, "We were ahead of the curve and now we're sliding back. We're following a formula that could lead us down the path to another Lucasville."

Inmate Murder

In the first murder since the 1993 riot, suspected Aryan Brotherhood leader Rex Elam, thirty-two, of Hamilton County was murdered at approximately 12:00 p.m. on September 25, 2005, by a black inmate. Elam was serving a seventy-years-to-life sentence from Hamilton County for aggravated murder, aggravated robbery, rape and kidnapping, and escape out of Warren County. He had been transferred to SOCF in March of 1992.

Increased Violence Against Staff

In a recent article on January 27, 2006, the *Cincinnati Enquirer* reported that "assaults on staff are up in one of Ohio's toughest prisons this year, including a recent attack on a guard so severe that a surgeon has to remove skull fragments from her brain." The article also documents that at SOCF, "the state recorded 169 attacks on guards this year, a 42% increase over last year and the highest in five years."

One of the worst attacks occurred on December 5, 2005, on forty-three-year-old Corrections Officer Marda Abrams. Abrams was a second-shift officer in charge of monitoring inmates as they moved around various parts of the prison. She was attacked by inmate Gary Hicks, thirty-five, who was an inmate porter (janitor) in charge of serving food and clean-up in the J-block corridor. Hicks took Officer Abrams' PR-24 and beat her unconscious. Abrams remained hospitalized for weeks for multiple skull, jaw, and nasal fractures as well as numerous broken teeth. Her hospitalization was followed by weeks of intensive physical and occupational therapy in a rehabilitation facility. She still has not returned to work.

Hicks is serving an eight-year sentence out of Belmont County for selling drugs and assault. After beating Officer Abrams, Hicks ran from the scene carrying Abrams' PR-24 and encountered two corrections officers, Zachary Ayers, twenty-six, and Wesley Caldwell, twenty-seven. Hicks struck both officers with the PR-24 and attempted to take the nurse hostage but failed. On February 17, 2006, the Scioto County Grand Jury returned five felony charges against Hicks—attempted aggravated murder with a repeat violent offender specification, three counts of felony assault with a repeat violent offender specification, and one count of possession of a deadly weapon while under detention.

On April 19, 2006, Hicks pleaded guilty to five counts, including attempted murder, and was sentenced by Common Pleas Judge William Marshall to forty-five years to be served after his current sentence ends in 2009. He will be released in 2054.

Chapter 19: A Case Study

Introduction

In the pages that follow, we take a look at the public organization of the Ohio Department of Rehabilitation and Correction (DRC) and its facilitative role in the tragic and deadly prison riot at the Southern Ohio Correctional Facility in Lucasville, Ohio, in April 1993. We will look at DRC's role as it fits the template of administrative evil as outlined in the book *Unmaking Administrative Evil*, authored by Professors Guy B. Adams and Danny L. Balfour.

Adams and Balfour begin with the premise that evil is an essential concept for understanding the human condition. Even a cursory review of history demonstrates "century after century of mind-numbing, human initiated violence, betrayal, and tragedy. They name as evil the actions of human beings that unjustly or needlessly inflict pain and suffering and death on other human beings" (Adams and Balfour 2004). The modern age, especially the last century and a half, has had as its hallmark what they identify as technical rationality. Technical rationality is described as a way of thinking and living (a culture) that emphasizes the scientific-analytical mindset and the belief in technological progress. The culture of technical rationality has enabled a new and bewildering form of evil that they have called administrative evil (Adams and Balfour 2004).

What is different about administrative evil is that its appearance is *masked*. Administrative evil may be masked in many different ways, but the common characteristic is that people can engage in acts of evil without being aware that they are in fact doing anything at all wrong. Indeed, ordinary people may simply be acting appropriately in their organizational role—in essence, just doing what those around them would agree they should be doing—and at the same time, participating in what a critical and reasonable observer, usually well after the fact, would call evil (Adams and Balfour 2004).

Even worse, under conditions of what is called *moral inversion*, in which something evil has become redefined convincingly as good, ordinary people can all too easily engage in acts of administrative evil while believing that what they are doing is not only correct, but in fact, good. The basic difference between evil, as it appeared throughout human history, and administrative evil, which is a fundamentally modern phenomenon, is that the latter is less easily recognized as evil (Adams and Balfour 2004).

Adams and Balfour cite that their understanding of administrative evil is rooted in the genocide perpetrated by Nazi Germany during World War II. The pain and suffering, the evil, if you will, that was inflicted on millions of "others" in the Holocaust was so horrific that it defied human comprehension and therefore must clearly be an instance of administrative evil.

Adams and Balfour refer to administrative evil as unmasked (although much of it was masked at the time) and suggest that identifying such administrative evil is easier, because the Holocaust was perpetrated by the Nazis (and others complicit with them) and because it occurred well over a half-century ago. The Holocaust occurred in modern times in a culture suffused with technical rationality, and most of its activity was accomplished within organizational roles and within legitimated public policy. While the results of the Holocaust were horrific and arguably without precedent in human history, ordinary Germans fulfilling ordinary roles carried out extraordinary destruction in ways that had been successfully packaged as socially normal and appropriate—a classic moral inversion (Adams and Balfour 2004).

A central theme of the modern age is the emphasis on the value of technical rationality and the attendant narrowing of the concepts of reason, professionalism, ethics, and politics. When linked to bureaucracy and organization, the result can be an unintentional tendency toward compliance to authority and the elevation of technical progress and processes over human values and dignity. Compliance and technical rationality focuses on the social and organizational dynamics that lead individuals to comply with authority, even when the consequences of their actions are detrimental to other human beings (Adams and Balfour 2004).

In the interest of fairness, and as described by Adams and Balfour, it is certainly true that there are also many examples of cases in the private sector that could be included in any rational discussion of administrative evil—cases such as the Dalkon Shield, manufactured by the Robins Company, which caused severe health problems for hundreds of women; the American tobacco companies that jointly used distortion to minimize the serious health effects of tobacco; "as well as the Goodrich Corporation subcontract with the LTV Corporation to build a braking system for the A7D military aircraft in which the original design was hopelessly flawed but systematically covered up until in-flight testing revealed dysfunctional brakes during landing." In addition, there was Morton Thiokol's involvement as a private company contracting to build the solid rocket booster for the space shuttle resulting in the *Challenger* disaster.

The purpose here is to take a critical and reasonable look at the administrative actions of the DRC and its top administrators regarding the deadly 1993 riot, through the lens or template outlined in *Unmasking Administrative Evil*. Unfortunately, people have always been able to persuade themselves into thinking that their evil acts are not really so bad and that we have certainly had moral inversions in times past. As Adams and Balfour clearly identify, there are three very important differences in administrative evil. One is the modern inclination to un-name evil, an old concept that does not lend itself well to the scientific-analytical mindset. The second difference is found in the structure of the modern, complex organization, which diffuses individual responsibility and requires compartmentalized accomplishment of role expectations in order to perform work on a daily basis. The third difference is the way in which the culture of technical rationality has analytically narrowed the processes by which public policy is formulated and implemented, so that moral inversions are now more likely (Adams and Balfour 2004).

Armed with a basic overview of administrative evil, technical rationality, and moral inversion, let us turn our attention to a general discussion of correctional practice as it relates to our overview.

Correctional Practice and Administrative Evil

Adams and Balfour discuss a number of ideas that pertain to various correctional administrative practices, such as prison design and construction, paramilitary operation and structure, communication channels, inmate classification, and inmate rights. Here, we will explore how these correctional practices in some way pertain to each of these ideas.

Modernity, Technical Rationality, and Administrative Evil

Prison design has an important place in most correctional organizations. In most cases, prison design is indicative of their respective prison philosophy, and physical layout dictates the operational and management system of operation. Historically, there have been three basic stages in the evolution of correctional design and construction. These stages are referred to simply as first-, second-, and third-generation correctional designs and management styles.

In the classical view of criminology and penology, the assumption is made that people are rational and logical. According to the classical view of corrections, the penalty should be designed to fit the seriousness of the crime committed. Following this principle, **first-generation** correctional facilities were the original Pennsylvania and Auburn systems. The panopticon prison, a circular arrangement of cells around a central observation tower was first proposed and built in 1787 and represented the idealized institutional form. Radial or rectangular cellblocks and the telephone pole plan are all variations of the same first-generation design. The "hard" architecture resulting from the classical philosophy of punishment, retribution, and incarceration produced environments that institutionalized both staff and inmates. As such, these facilities were constructed with large secure walls, foreboding construction, and security watch towers with the primary emphasis on security (Dunham 1991).

While inmate classification, testing, and screening procedures improved in the 1950s through the 1970s, the positivist concept of determinism was represented in the second generation of correctional facility design, which emphasized modular design and remote surveillance.

Second-generation facilities have small, classified housing units to separate offenders by age, sex, crime, length of sentence, and propensity for violent behavior. All of the housing units are designed for maximum security because of the expectation of irrational behavior. Because inmates are viewed as dangerous and irrational, staff persons are positioned behind barriers to avoid direct contact with inmates (Dunham 1991). The basic assumption of second-generation facilities was that inmates would exhibit negative behavior simply because they were inmates. Subsequently, design was based on the premise that barriers should be placed between inmates and correctional staff. Daily activities, such as visitation, counseling, attorney consultation, dining, exercise, and recreation, occurred in locations removed from the inmate's living module. Single-occupancy cells were clustered around a common dayroom area and a secure control booth from which an officer observed inmate activity. The modular design was based on a restrictive management style, organized to respond to inmate problems rather than to prevent them. As a result, construction costs were high, due to the necessary security hardware (Dunham 1991).

Third-generation facilities embraced many of the theories and beliefs of the classical school regarding free will, choice, and rational behavior, in addition to many positivist concepts. Many third-generation correctional facilities have extensive classification and orientation programs to place inmates in a variety of programs. One of the benefits of the modular design with direct supervision concept is the highly individualized administration of incarceration through the use of single cells, direct contact with staff, and token economy, where the inmates determine their own level of program participation (Dunham 1991). If inmates act negatively or aggressively, they are isolated and given more direct supervision and fewer privileges. Third-generation facilities encourage the reformation and development of inmates by allowing them to earn their way from maximum-security to minimum-security units, and by providing many levels of housing, programs, and staff interaction and supervision. Inmate housing is divided into manageable-sized units of thirty-six to sixty persons with direct supervision. A correction officer works within the living module in a supervisory role (Dunham 1991).

The most significant single activity affecting prison operation and architecture during the first half of the 1980s was the development, refinement, and enforcement of standards for operation and construction. During this period, an awareness of the costs for staffing, operating, and constructing prisons as part of the overall system of justice, including law enforcement, adjudication, and detention, caused concern among elected public officials and the public in general (Dunham 1991).

This has led to a generation of more focused efforts in planning, developing, and operating existing and new facilities. The physical layout of correctional facilities has progressively evolved from the linear configurations that dominated the pre-1970s to the modular, from the barrier-intense to the more barrier-free, and from the remote control, indirect supervision to the direct control and direct supervision models of the present (Dunham 1991).

Compliance in the Context of Technical Rationality

The typical correctional managerial environment is the textbook example of classical management theory. It is a top-down paramilitary organization consisting of a very deep organizational structure and a politically appointed director with very strong central bureaucracies. Daily life inside a correctional facility is highly structured and regimented with one day a carbon copy of the day before. All activity for both staff and inmates is regulated by the clock and operates in a machine-like manner.

Organizations that are designed and operated like machines are called bureaucracies. Max Weber was one of the first organizational theorists to observe and document the parallels between the mechanization of industry and the bureaucratic form of organization (Morgan 1998). He cited that the bureaucratic form routinizes the process of administration exactly as the machine routinizes production. His comprehensive definition of bureaucracy as a form of organization emphasizes precision, speed, clarity, regularity, and efficiency. Each is achieved through the creation of a fixed division of tasks, hierarchical supervision, and detailed rules and regulations (Morgan 1998).

It is classical management theory at its best and worst that creates the managerial environment in most prison facilities. Many correctional systems of management are structured on the work of Henri Fayol, F. W. Mooney, and Colonel Lyndall Urwick, whose basic thrust was fostered in the belief that management is a process of planning, organization, command, coordination, and control (Morgan 1998). Many correctional systems indoctrinate new managers, supervisors, and administrators with the structures and beliefs of classical management theory. Weber saw that the bureaucratic approach had the potential to routinize and mechanize nearly every aspect of human life, thereby eroding the human spirit and decreasing the availability of workers to think creatively and initiate spontaneous action when required.

While the classical theorists detailed the work of Fredrick the Great's approach to the military organization, Fredrick Taylor expanded those same approaches to a logical extreme. Taylor, an American engineer, created the principles of scientific management that provided the bedrock for work design in the first half of the twentieth century and continues to this day (Morgan 1998). Many correctional organizations are disciples of Taylor, as they have mastered the five essential tenets of scientific management:

- Shift all responsibility for the organization of work from the worker to the manager,
- Use scientific methods,
- Select the best person to perform the job designed,
- Train the worker to perform efficiently,
- And monitor worker performance to ensure that appropriate work rules are followed.

While the incarceration of inmates may, because of legal ramifications involved, be reduced to a routine task, it must be remembered that inmates are highly volatile and unpredictable human beings. As such, they require a highly motivated and intelligent workforce that is both able to properly identify critical and non-routine situations with the ability, training, and authority to make the necessary modifications to ensure a safe environment for both inmates and staff alike.

Mechanistic organizations, like most correctional organizations, are designed to achieve predetermined goals and objectives. They are not designed for innovation, which would include decentralized decision-making and bottom-up communication. Because compliance stems in part from the human need for order, this fundamental need for social order helps in understanding just how strong the inclination to obey authority is for most people most of the time. The barriers inherent in mechanistic divisions between hierarchical levels, functions, and roles often block the flexibility and creative action that are so important in changing circumstances. As a result, (1) problems can be ignored because there are no ready-made responses, (2) communications can be ineffective because standardized procedures and channels of communication are often unable to deal with new circumstances, (3) paralysis and inaction can lead to a backlog of work, (4) senior management can become remote because they have no direct contact with front-line issues, (5) high degrees of specialization can create myopic views because there is no overall grasp of the situation facing the enterprise as a whole, and (6) mechanistic definitions of job responsibilities can encourage many organizational members to adopt mindless, unquestioning attitudes (Morgan 1998).

Bureaucratic organizations that are highly centralized are incapable of identifying and responding to critically important bottom-up communication. Being highly centralized allows the organization to hire front-line security positions, which make up two-thirds of the staff, with minimum qualifications. Because the DRC is a highly centralized top-down paramilitary organization, corrections officers are required only to have a high school diploma or a GED and be able to compute simple math.

Organizational Dynamics and the Pathway to Administrative Evil

The organizational and management style of classical management theory in a modern organization creates a target-rich environment for administrative evil. Modern bureaucratic organizations are characterized by the diffusion of information and the strict fragmentation of responsibility. With a highly centralized bureaucratic core that coerces and compels compliance of its workforce with top-down only communication, it is frequently incapable of evaluating the environment.

With classical management theory, too many times the focus is getting results, as in doing things right but not doing the right things. For an organization to be high-performance, as should be the overall goal of any organization, the growth and maturation of employees is critical. It is, however, easier to remain autocratic and authoritarian, but this does not create a high-performance organization. It fosters dependence rather than interdependence. In the autocratic or authoritarian system, most communication is downward in the form of mandates. Compliance is garnered through an atmosphere of fear and intimidation. As compliance increases, energy decreases. In this system, employees produce but they do not perform, a subtle but critical distinction. Staff who produce but do not perform typically produce to standards of minimums to avoid punishment. Activity is busy but mindless. Another critical disadvantage of this type of organization is that it doesn't build a competent second-tier management to function properly in critical situations where competent and knowledgeable leadership is most important.

Building a high-performance organization is a process of growth stages. The first stage of growth is referred to as the dependent stage. Here, employees are just learning the job and are very dependent on the direction of others. The role of the manager or administrator at this point is to use the authoritarian approach, to give specific directions; to set small, more immediate goals; and to give frequent feedback, both positive and negative. The authoritarian approach is usually appropriate at this level because the employees need direction and support as they learn a new job or set of responsibilities (Bucholz 1987).

As these same employees grow and learn, they become independent. At this stage, employees are able to think and function on their own. They have mastered the knowledge, skills, and abilities through repeated practice and performance. Here they are no longer dependent on the manager or administrator for knowledge, skills, or abilities; however, they do need guidance and influence regarding the more complex functions of organizational processes.

If the manager or administrator remains in the authoritarian mode with employees who have become independent and responsible, the atmosphere of a compliance environment is created where staff give time but they do not give energy. The critical element with independent staff is increased responsibility, mutual goal setting, and making feedback and communication a two-way process (Bucholz 1987).

Public Policy and Rational Problem Solving

Here, two major issues are relevant. First is classification, which lies at the heart of both correctional security and programming. Inmate classification is the way prisons allocate scarce resources and minimize the potential for escape and violence. It involves matching an offender's risks and needs with the available correctional resources. While there is no "perfect" or "best" method, a good system will avoid two common errors: over-classification, which is the unnecessary sending of low-risk inmates to maximum-security settings; and misclassification, making a mistake in diagnosing or classifying an inmate's risk or needs. In addition to the inmate classification, the prison system itself is also classified based on security level. The most common security levels are: super-max, maximum, medium, and minimum security. Each level is very specific. (See Table 1.)

While some of the principles of correctional classification date back to the 1870s reformatory era, it wasn't until the 1920s that prison administrators started talking about the critical need for diagnosis and diagnostic centers for prison systems. The need for diagnosis was the birth of the rehabilitation idea in criminal justice. Classification became the diagnostic method for assessing the treatment needs for offenders. Today, classification refers to the assessment of both "needs" and "risks."

A good and effective classification program will enhance prison security, enable better utilization of staff, and help with the inmate placement process. Placement is often part of what is called internal classification, which determines the security level of the inmate and subsequently which of the department's facilities is best able to house the inmate. All correctional systems have such reception and classification centers although they are known by several different names depending on the system.

An inmate's security score reflects his or her criminal propensity, or how likely he or she is to commit crime. This score is often based only on what we know about the inmate's past criminal record. Therefore, there is a need to know more about the inmate. In the process of determining this additional information, there is a propensity to discover the "needs," and therefore, a diagnosis is usually made. During the testing process of classification, the inmate will be interviewed extensively and given a number of psychometric, medical, educational, and intelligence tests. The testing and classification process will also identify the programming needs of the inmate. This process can take anywhere from six weeks to three months, depending on the number of inmates and the staff availability. Of all the variety of programming available to inmates during their incarceration, none is more interesting than the variety of counseling and psychotherapy programs that exist in theory and actual practice. Not all correctional institutions or facilities have psychotherapy programs, but all have one or more types of counseling.

The classification process is a critical initial process that affects the remainder of the inmate's incarceration, as well as the staff and inmates at the facility to which the inmate is sent to serve the remainder of his or her sentence. It is a process that is best conducted by experts in the areas of security, education, mental and medical health, counseling, and psychoanalysis.

Second is the control of communicable diseases like tuberculosis. Many prisons present optimal conditions for the spread of tuberculosis (TB), a disease that was resurgent in the United States in the 1980s and early 1990s. According to the National Institute of Justice (NIJ), correctional facilities house men and women who often come from those segments of the community with high rates and risk of TB because of such factors as poverty, poor living conditions, substance abuse, and HIV/AIDS. TB is a highly contagious airborne disease, transmitted via droplet nuclei from patients who have pulmonary or laryngeal TB and who cough, laugh, talk, or otherwise emit sputum containing the TB bacteria called *Mycobacterium tuberculosis* (NIJ 1996).

Overcrowding in a correctional facility increases the potential for close and repeated contact with an active case of TB (NIJ 1996). A survey conducted by the NIJ indicated that TB infection continues to be a frequently observed phenomenon among inmates in correctional facilities, but only a small percentage of infected persons ever develop active TB disease. The prevalence of infection serves as an indicator of how much disease activity is in a population and also identifies potential candidates for preventative therapy (NIJ 1996).

The Centers for Disease Control and Prevention (CDC) in Atlanta, Georgia, recognizes several types of screening for TB used in correctional facilities. The first is symptom screening, which involves checking for signs and symptoms of TB through a systematic interview that inquires about persistent, productive cough; chest pain; coughing up blood; fever; chills; night sweats; loss of appetite and weight loss; and tiring easily, especially during the preceding six weeks (emphasis added). A second screening procedure involves the PPD (purified protein derivative) or Mantoux tuberculin skin test. The PPD is injected under the skin and, after forty-eight to seventy-two hours, interpreted by an experienced reader, who measures the diameter of the swollen area, called an induration, which can be felt around the injection site, and records the result in millimeters. For all correctional facility types, the CDC recommends TB symptom screening of all incoming inmates. The CDC also recommends that while long-term facilities begin with symptom screening, they should also give a skin test to each asymptomatic inmate without a documented prior positive result. Screening for TB infection is more common than screening for TB disease.

Due to the litigious nature of much of the inmate populations, correctional officials may be concerned with the potential liability with respect to transmission and treatment of TB in their facilities. Recently adjudicated cases have centered on two issues:

- Failure to protect inmates from acquiring TB or provide adequate treatment or care.
- Failure to respect individuals' constitutional rights by instituting a mandatory TB testing program.

On these issues, courts seem to be split. In the cases cited by the NIJ report in 1996, many were dismissed citing that the complaints amounted to differences of opinion about proper medical treatment and not "the type of subjective indifference to the medical needs of prisoners that the controlling cases require." Two cases in Massachusetts dealt with the issue of violating inmates' civil rights through mandatory testing programs. The primary issue in one case was whether prison officials are authorized to compel inmates to submit to TB testing under state law. The appeals court ruled that the commissioner of correction has the responsibility to maintain security, safety, and order at all state correctional facilities. The court further ruled that, although an inmate's incarceration does not divest him or her of the right of privacy and interest in preserving his or her bodily integrity, it does limit those constitutional rights when the state's interest in prison security and inmate health are at issue (NIJ 1996).

However, on the other hand, a federal district court in New York ruled that the state correctional department must return to the general population a person who had been held in "medical keeplock" (solitary confinement) for three and a half years because he refused a PPD test. Skin testing is mandatory for New York State inmates, but this prisoner refused the test on the grounds that it violated the tenets of his Rastafarian religion. In an affidavit, the inmate stated that "accepting artificial substances into the body constitutes a sin and shows profound disrespect to our creator." The court held that the inmate, "in choosing to undergo the conditions of medical keeplock for a period of over 3-1/2 years, had shown remarkable conviction for what he stated are his religious beliefs" (NIJ 1996).

Public Policy as It Relates to Surplus Populations

R. L. Rubenstein writes, a surplus population can be defined as "one that for any reason can find no viable role in the society in which it is domiciled." It can be argued that many prison inmates are referred to as members of a surplus population. There have been numerous attempts to solve the problem of prison inmates. Rubenstein further states, "The history of the twentieth century has taught us that people who are rendered permanently superfluous are eventually condemned to segregated precincts of the living dead ..." (Rubenstein 1975). The twentieth century has been witness to the evolution of judicial thought and activism to the concerns of prison inmates.

The issue of inmates' rights is a relatively new philosophy in the field of criminal justice and corrections. Prior to the 1960s, it was generally accepted that upon criminal conviction, the individual forfeited all of his or her rights except those expressly granted by statute or the jurisdiction's corrections policy. As the National Advisory Commission on Criminal Justice Standards and Goals stated that the belief was common that virtually anything could be done with an offender in the name of "corrections" or in some instances "punishment," short of extreme physical abuse, he was protected only by the restraint and responsibility of correctional administrators and their staff. Whatever comforts, services, or privileges the offender received were a matter of grace—in the law's view a privilege to be granted or withheld by the state. Inhumane conditions and practices were permitted to develop and continue in many systems.

This judicial philosophy was referred to as the "hands off" doctrine, because courts were reluctant to interfere with the administrative management of prison management unless there was a clear and serious Eighth Amendment violation. The National Advisory Commission declared that the courts used three justifications for their "hands off" philosophy:

1. They believed that correctional administration was a technical matter to be left to experts rather than to courts ill equipped to make appropriate evaluations.
2. Society as a whole was apathetic to the area of corrections, and most individuals preferred not to associate or know about the offender.
3. Most judges believed that prisoners' complaints involved privileges rather than rights. There was no special necessity to confront correctional practices, even when they infringed on basic notions of human rights and dignity protected for other groups by constitutional doctrine.

As the civil rights movement began to develop momentum, public attention focused on many groups outside the mainstream of American culture, and efforts were made to improve the lot of these groups. As the civil rights of minorities became a central issue, it was only logical that inmates and their advocates would attempt to extend these same minority civil rights to those incarcerated in both federal and state correctional facilities by utilizing the Federal Civil Rights Act found in United States Code Title 42 §1983 which states, "Every person who, under color of any statute, ordinance, regulation, custom, or usage of any State or Territory subjects, or causes to be subjected, any citizen of the United States or other person within the jurisdiction thereof to be deprivation of any rights, privileges, or immunities secured by the Constitution and laws shall be liable to the party injured in any action at law, suit in equity or other proper proceeding for redress."

During and before the 1960s, enormous discretion was left to correctional administrators about how their facilities were run. While state law may have set some limits, relatively little control was imposed on the day-to-day operation of a prison or jail. In many cases, "the law" within the institution was set—and enforced—by the warden or individual officers in the cellblock. As long as the lid was kept on a prison, the public seemed to care little about what went on in the facility.

Southern Ohio Correctional Facility

There were two prison riots that every inmate had heard of; one was Attica, and the other was Sante Fe. Now we can add a third—Lucasville.

"Attention on the yard, attention on the yard. The yard is closed. I repeat, the yard is closed. All inmates return to your lock." The loudspeaker ordered recreation closed and all inmates off the yard. Inmates quickly began making their way toward the gymnasium door and the recreation metal detector. Stationed at the metal detector were two officers, one who carried keys to all of the L-corridor cellblocks. Coming in off the yard were more than 420 inmates. Muslim inmates led by Carlos Sanders brutally attacked the officers, taking their keys, handcuffs, and PR-24s. The special radios carried by all correctional staff were automatically set off by the attack.

The rioting inmates armed themselves with baseball bats, weight bars, mop wringers, broom handles, and anything else that could be used as a weapon. Staff responding to the alarm were beaten. Many were forced to withdraw, and several were taken hostage. The inmates

263

entered each of the eight cellblocks and freed all of the inmates, which sent staff running for their lives.

Many officers retreated, as they were trained to do, to the secure stairwells for safety. Upon entering the safe wells, they tried to call the Control Room 1 for help as they had been trained to do. Many found that either the telephones did not work or no one answered. Control Room officers tried repeatedly to activate the administrative pagers, which required a digital telephone, with their antiquated rotary telephone system.

Warden Tate, visiting family in London, Ohio, was notified by friends who telephoned him to inform him of the situation at SOCF after hearing of the trouble from radio news reports. Warden Tate tried unsuccessfully five times to contact the SOCF switchboard and was finally successful on his sixth attempt. It took Warden Tate nearly three hours to make the frantic drive to SOCF.

Inmates, seeing the staff retreat into the safe wells, tried to pound their way through the solid-steel doors to no avail. Then they turned their attention to the concrete wall that surrounded the safe well. Staff looked on with horror as they saw the inmates breaking through the wall of what they believed was their sanctuary. Within minutes, inmates had broken through the concrete wall using forty-five-pound weight bars and beat and took several staff hostage. After the hostages were secured, rioting inmates turned their attention to murdering other inmates that they believed were informants.

A "death squad" of rogue inmates was charged with the brutal responsibility of beating the informant inmates to death with baseball bats and other makeshift weapons. Thus began what was to become the longest and third bloodiest prison riot in our nation's history.

A full eleven days after the horror began, the last of the remaining five staff hostages was released on live television. Despite the progress made by Warden Tate, the previous twenty-two years of political and administrative apathy, abuse, and neglect could not save SOCF, the staff, or the inmates from the inevitable consequences. According to Warden Tate, the key factor was not the organization of the inmates, initially, but the disorganization of the department. Tate believed then and believes now that if a supervisor on site had made the command decision to lead a "shotgun team" into L-corridor within the first forty minutes, the riot would have been quelled. However, Tate is also well aware that the "political" climate within the department did not permit such decisive action on the part of anyone except Central Office.

The Result

The cost was then and continues to be incredible. Twelve officers were taken hostage, all beaten severely, and several with permanent disabling injuries. Four officers were released on the first night, having been left for dead wrapped in sheets and plastic trash bags. Two officers were released on days five and six due to negotiations. One officer was brutally murdered on day five. Five officers were held hostage throughout the full eleven days. Twenty-three million dollars was spent to conduct the post-riot investigations and prosecutions and to settle subsequent lawsuits from inmates and staff.

At the height of the investigation, over twenty Ohio Highway Patrol investigators were assigned to the riot aftermath. Nine grand jury sessions later, fifty inmates were indicted on 200 felony counts, forty-seven of those convicted on 110 felony counts, five of those sentenced to death for the murder of the corrections officer, automatically invoking decades of legal appeals, along with $45 million to rebuild the prison facility.

Discussion

To what extent, if any, do the problems connected with the riot at the Southern Ohio Correctional Facility coincide with administrative evil? To answer this question, we will apply the template of administrative evil through its four components. Adams and Balfour describe the first component of administrative evil as modernity and technical rationality. This portion of the template is described in the case study by prison design and construction. Previously, it was noted that prison design has an important place in most correctional organizations. In most cases, prison design is indicative of the respective prison philosophy, and physical layout dictates the operational and management system of operation. In our case study, the design and construction of the SOCF predated the actual creation of the DRC and therefore was not indicative of any particular operational or management system. It did, however, call for the construction of a revolutionary new concept in officer safety known as "safe havens," which were designed to be safe zones for staff in the event of a major disturbance.

The safe havens were to be located at the rear of each cellblock and accessed by heavy-duty steel doors that were secured with five-inch solid brass Folger-Adams keys. Having steel-reinforced concrete block walls and direct contact with the main Control Center 1, these safe havens were designed to provide outside access to facilitate evacuation of staff. For twenty-one years, the staff at SOCF had been trained on access and operation of the safe havens.

However, for some reason yet to be explained, the steel reinforcement was omitted during construction, and the walls of the safe havens were built just two hollow concrete blocks thick, which took rioting inmates approximately ten minutes of pounding with forty-five-pound universal weight bars to break through the walls.

One can only imagine the sheer horror on the officers' faces as they watched rioting inmates pound through the walls after being assured that upon successful access to the safe haven they would be safe and subsequently rescued. There are two ways to view this gross construction error. The first, of course, is that both the staff and administration quite properly relied on the technical building design standards and subsequently drafted policy and procedure to fully maximize the utilization of those standards. Conversely, however, not having a fully operational secondary escape plan for staff in a critical situation was an over-reliance of the technical design standards that in this case proved to be deadly.

Adams and Balfour argue that the fact that administrative evil is masked suggests that evil also occurs along another continuum: from acts that are committed in relative ignorance to those that are committed knowingly and deliberately, or what they would characterize as masked and unmasked evil respectively (Adams and Balfour 2004).

Whether a tragic human error or a deliberate act to hurry construction or save money, when coupled with the tragic failure to draft an operational secondary escape plan, this becomes unconscionable, and these failures needlessly inflicted pain and suffering and subsequent death on others (Adams and Balfour 2004).

When the word of the faulty construction causing the taking of five staff hostages came to light, the construction contractor dissolved his business; thereby, no one could be held legally liable for the faulty construction.

The second component of the template of administrative evil is in the context of technical rationality and is outlined by the top-down paramilitary mechanistic organizational structure defined by classical management theory. Compliance stems in part from the human need for order, which the organization created, fostered, and strictly and punitively enforced through a structure that all but eliminated meaningful bottom-up communication. It forced what is described by J. Patrick Dobel, author of *Public Integrity*, as an "agentic shift," in which individuals surrender their judgments and responsibilities to their superiors. This shift effectively eliminates them as checks on government abuse or as a source of initiative and new ideas (Dobel 1998). This shift created a climate permitting those at the DRC Central Office to elevate and isolate themselves in such a manner as to sever any real connection to problems or legitimate concerns being incurred by those at the institutional level. Such a shift begins to see the social and political dynamics that can result in eruptions of administrative evil. Adams and Balfour believe:

> ... that a culture of technical rationality has fostered a model of professionalism that exacerbates tendencies toward compliance—and administrative evil—in groups and organizations in our culture. Consider the Milgram experiments, in which legitimate authority is cloaked in the mantle of science and professionalism. In the mid-1960s, Professor Stanley Milgram of Yale University set up an experiment designed to show that Americans were less prone to obey the dictates of authority than their German counterparts who have given themselves over to a totalitarian regime and obeyed it to the extremes of mass murder and genocide. His initial intention was to conduct the experiment with psychology students in the United States and Germany as the test subjects, but he quickly abandoned the comparison after finding that American students were remarkably willing to obey legitimate authority, even when the consequences entailed harming other human

beings. In this culture, which so highly values individualism, our expectation is that the individual response will trump the social situation and nearly everyone will break off—and most assuredly not fully comply. However, in at least this context, and perhaps in others, American culture seems as well adapted as most for administrative evil (Adams and Balfour 2004).

Here, the Machiavellian notion of "dirty hands" is combined with hubris, a very old word, which means an inflated sense of pride or sense of self. Hubris might be compared to an accelerant, which when added to an existing fire (administrative evil), can easily escalate something seemingly small into a conflagration (Adams and Balfour 2004).

The third component of the template, organizational dynamics, is clearly demonstrated by two specific areas. The first is a departmental "political" structure in combination with the top-down-only communication pipeline that effectively voided any real "intelligence" on inmate activity from reaching decision makers, thus hindering any effective inmate-management efforts. The strong centralized organizational management system in place throughout the DRC did not allow SOCF Warden Arthur Tate to select an administrative team that was qualified to operate a maximum-security prison. Requests to Central Office for competent administrators fell on deaf ears.

Warden Tate was at odds with at least two of his deputy wardens and several of his unit managers and shift commanders. While on paper the deputy wardens reported to the warden, in reality, all deputy wardens were appointed by the director and in fact reported to him and provided Central Office with a direct "back channel communication pipeline," thereby circumventing the warden in many cases. Deputy wardens who were more interested in "making points" with the director than administering a maximum-security prison hampered legitimate administrative efforts. DRC Central Office prevented Warden Tate from replacing several of his administrative staff that he distrusted. These top-level prison administrators, whom Tate believed were unable to properly and effectively evaluate the unstable environment, were permitted to remain in position for internal political expediency, thus acting as a prescription pad for disaster. Warden Tate was recruited and selected for the position of warden because of his record of being an extraordinary leader. Placing him in this position without the ability to surround himself with other competent staff is bureaucratization at its best and public service at its worst.

Second was the flippant and reckless manner in which DRC Central Office chose to deal with the increasingly volatile situation regarding the testing of the SOCF inmate population for tuberculosis. Repeated requests by both the SOCF's warden and medical director for assistance from the DRC Central Office in dealing with an increasingly critical situation went essentially unanswered. With a large segment of the Muslim inmate population vehemently refusing to be tested on religious grounds, an openly hostile face-to-face meeting between inmate Muslim leaders and Warden Tate set the stage for inevitable confrontation. When no assistance came from the DRC Central Office, Warden Tate was forced to proceed on his own by drafting a tactical plan and requesting riot-equipped Ohio Highway Patrol Troopers as well as heavily armed SOCF Special Response Teams to be on ready alert to respond to what Warden Tate believed was inevitable aggressive action on the part the refusing inmates.

Here, we are able to identify destructive organizational dynamics within the DRC believed to represent a typical organizational pathway that led to administrative evil even if no evil was intended. Even in the absence of evil intention, organizational dynamics that escalate the chances of disastrous outcomes can be termed—albeit with considerable caution—administrative evil, if the members of the organization could have (and should have) reasonably been expected to do better (Adams and Balfour 2004). Clearly, repeated pleas for assistance and guidance from an institutional warden and medical director was worthy of a response from Regional Director Eric Dahlberg, who could have and reasonably should have been expected to have done better. It must be argued that he had a moral, ethical, and quite possibly a legal obligation to act affirmatively.

DRC's Bureau of Classification makes up the fourth component of administrative evil, specifically public policy and rational problem solving. As previously noted, classification lies at the heart of both correctional security and inmate programming. Inmate classification is the way competent and high-reliability prison systems allocate scarce resources and minimize the potential for escape and violence.

However, in the DRC's organization, the Bureau of Classification, located on the first floor of DRC Central Office, housed demonstrably incompetent high-ranking administrators who were relocated there to continue their employment. "Friendship and loyalty are central to political life and success, but the limits of friendship are exceeded when public officials use their office to benefit their friends or when, as often happens, loyalty blinds them to their friends' incompetence or impropriety" (Dobel 1998). When demonstrated organizational incompetent staff are deliberately placed in critical positions by top-level administrators causing harm and death to fellow staff, these actions can be described as nothing but evil, and no amount of plausible deniability can erase or mitigate their guilt. Again, we are able to identify destructive organizational dynamics within the DRC that represented a typical organizational pathway that led to administrative evil even if no evil was intended.

According to Dobel's personal-responsibility model, for public officials a focus on personal responsibility can compensate for some of the limits of the legal-institutional model. "The commitments, capacities, and character that individuals have prior to taking office form the heart of integrity ... maintaining personal integrity and responsibility in public office means that individuals cannot deny responsibility for their actions. They cannot place blame on institutional structures or on others. Under the rubric of public integrity, all commitments are personal commitments. No rules or strict orders totally exonerate people from responsibility for outcomes to which they contribute and that they judge immoral, illegal, or wasteful" (Dobel 1998).

Finally, let us return to the question, to what extent, if any, do the problems connected with the riot at the Southern Ohio Correctional Facility coincide with administrative evil? Do the actions of the DRC and its top-level administrators fit the template of administrative evil? Regarding the first component, prison design and construction, here the design and construction of the facility pre-dated the agency; however, trying to fit a management system into a facility that clearly was not designed for such a system raises serious questions.

Secondly, top-level administrators created, fostered, and propagated a top-down paramilitary system that all but eliminated meaningful bottom-up communication that alienated top-level administrators at the DRC Central Office from accurate intelligence at the institutional level. Thirdly, punitive organizational dynamics created by top-level administrators created "a culture of fear" within the agency that "froze" supervisors from acting in a riot situation for fear of retaliation and liability. Fourthly, it appears clear that in the case of the tragedy at SOCF, demonstrably incompetent administrators were provided continued employment by placing them in the critical area of classification. Here, the DRC top-level administrators through "moral inversion" lit the fuse that led to the explosive riot at SOCF, leading to permanent pain, suffering, and the death of their very own staff.

References

Chapter 1

April 15, 1993. Mechanical failure is cited in crash of patrol helicopter. News Briefs: *Columbus Dispatch.* Columbus, OH. P 07C.

Berens, M. April 1993. Inmates may have planned riot. *Columbus Dispatch.* Columbus, OH.

Brooks, S. and J. Woods. May 9, 1993. To the flash point: Tensions stem from a murder in 1990. *Columbus Dispatch.* Columbus, OH. P 06B.

Correctional Institution Inspection Committee. June 1994. *Interim report on the April 11, 1993 riot at the Southern Ohio Correctional Facility.*

Department of Rehabilitation and Correction, Southern Ohio Correctional Facility. March 3, 2003. *Factbook.*

Hilterbrand, G. April 12, 1993. Prison riot chronology. *Lima News.* Lima, OH. P 1.

Johnson, A. April 13, 1993. Demands reflect warden's tough approach. *Columbus Dispatch.* Columbus, OH. P 05B.

June 1993. *Disturbance Cause Committee findings report.*

March 1994. *Lucasville Media Task Force report.*

Ohio Civil Service Employees Association, AFSCME Local 11. August 1993. *Report and recommendations concerning the Ohio*

Department of Rehabilitation and Correction and the Southern Ohio Correctional Facility Lucasville, Ohio.

Rohrer, J. April 1993. Inmates riot, take hostages. *Cincinnati Enquirer*. Cincinnati, OH.

Snell, R. June 11, 1993. Warden's memo set riot in motion. *Akron Beacon-Journal*. Akron, OH. Pp A1, 17.

The State of Ohio, Appellee v. Grinnel, Appellant 95APA10-1314.

Valentine, B. 2000. *Gangs and their tattoos: Identifying gangbangers on the street and in prison*. Boulder, CO: Paladin Press.

Chapter 2

Correctional Institution Inspection Committee. 1994. *Initial report*.

June 1993. *Disturbance Cause Committee findings report*.

Lynd, S. Who killed Officer Vallandingham? Retrieved from http://www.ohiodeathrow.com on March 26, 2003.

Ohio Department of Rehabilitation and Correction. 2002. *Gang training manual*.

Snodgrass, Roger. January 7, 1995. Notes from interview of Roger Snodgrass at Warren Correctional Institution with Special Prosecutors Daniel T. Hogan and Douglas P. Stead.

Valentine, B. 1995. *Gang intelligence manual: Identifying and understanding modern-day violent gangs in the United States*. Boulder, CO: Paladin Press.

Chapter 3

Baker, D. April 1993. Week closes on Lucasville prison riot with no resolution. *Toledo Blade*. Toledo, OH.

Brown, T.C. and M. Kavanaugh. March 30, 2003. Sunday, bloody Sunday. *Plain Dealer*. Cleveland, OH.

Dotson, Larry. April 2003. Interview by G. Williams.

Inmate pleads guilty to role in guard's death. *Cincinnati Enquirer*. Cincinnati, OH.

June 1993. *Disturbance Cause Committee findings report*.

Liston, J.R. April 17, 2003. Conquering chaos. *Portsmouth Daily Times*. Portsmouth, OH.

March 1994. *Lucasville Media Task Force report.*

Ohio Civil Service Employees Association, AFSCME Local 11. August 1993. *Report and recommendations concerning the Ohio Department of Rehabilitation and Correction and the Southern Ohio Correctional Facility Lucasville, Ohio.*

Ohio Department of Rehabilitation and Correction, Offender Search. 2003. DRC Homepage, Offender Search, http://www.odrc.oh.us.gov.

Ohio State Highway Patrol. 1993. SOCF Command Center time log.

Popyk, L. April 1993. Freed prison guard recalls his ordeal. Scripps Howard News Service.

Riepenhoff, J. January 4, 1994. Five more prisoners face charges from Lucasville. *Columbus Dispatch.* Columbus, OH.

———. March 1995. Prison riot trials move to Columbus. *Columbus Dispatch.* Columbus, OH.

Snodgrass, Roger. January 7, 1995. Notes from interview of Roger Snodgrass at Warren Correctional Institution with Special Prosecutors Daniel T. Hogan and Douglas P. Stead.

Southern Ohio Correctional Facility. April 11, 1993. Second shift duty roster.

The 3:00 P.M. to 6:00 P.M. Chronology Committee. June 1993. *Preliminary investigative report.*

Chapter 4

Baker, D. April 1993. Week closes on Lucasville prison riot with no resolution. *Toledo Blade.* Toledo, OH.

State v. LaMar. 95 Ohio St. 3d 181, 2002-Ohio-2128.

State v. Robb. 2002. 88 Ohio St. 3d 59.

The Associated Press. April 25, 1993. Autopsies: 5 inmates were beaten to death. *Cincinnati Enquirer.* Cincinnati, OH.

Chapter 5

Baker, D. April 1993. Week closes on Lucasville prison riot with no resolution. *Toledo Blade.* Toledo, OH.

Dotson, Larry. April 2003. Interview by G. Williams.
Ohio State Highway Patrol. 1993. SOCF Command Center time
log.

Chapter 6

Baker, D. April 1993. Week closes on Lucasville prison riot with no
resolution. *Toledo Blade.* Toledo, OH.
Dotson, Larry. April 2003. Interview by G. Williams.
Ohio State Highway Patrol. 1993. SOCF Command Center time
log.

Chapter 7

Baker, D. April 1993. Week closes on Lucasville prison riot with no
resolution. *Toledo Blade.* Toledo, OH.
Dotson, Larry. April 2003. Interview by G. Williams.
Ohio State Highway Patrol. 1993. SOCF Command Center time
log.
Paul, S.M. April 15, 1993. Ohio looks for help from experts, history;
Georgia prison official a known trouble-shooter. *Cincinnati
Enquirer.* Cincinnati, OH.

Chapter 8

Dotson, Larry. April 2003. Interview by G. Williams.
Ohio State Highway Patrol. 1993. SOCF Command Center time
log.

Chapter 9

Dotson, Larry. April 2003. Interview by G. Williams.
Ohio State Highway Patrol. 1993. SOCF Command Center time
log.

Chapter 10

Dotson, Larry. April 2003. Interview by G. Williams.
Ohio State Highway Patrol. 1993. SOCF Command Center time
   log.

Chapter 11

Dotson, Larry. April 2003. Interview by G. Williams.
Ohio State Highway Patrol. 1993. SOCF Command Center time
   log.

Chapter 12

Dotson, Larry. April 2003. Interview by G. Williams.
Ohio State Highway Patrol. 1993. SOCF Command Center time
   log.

Chapter 13

Dotson, Larry. April–August 2003. Interviews by G. Williams.

Chapter 14

Dotson, Larry. April–August 2003. Interviews by G. Williams.

Chapter 15

Correctional Institution Inspection Committee. 1994. *Initial report.*
June 1993. *Disturbance Cause Committee findings report.*
Ohio Civil Service Employees Association, AFSCME Local 11.
   August 1993. *Report and recommendations concerning the Ohio
   Department of Rehabilitation and Correction and the Southern
   Ohio Correctional Facility Lucasville, Ohio.*

Chapter 16

March 1994. *Lucasville Media Task Force report.*
Porter, B. May/June 1994. The Lucasville follies: A prison riot brings out the worst in the press. *Columbia Journalism Review.*

Chapter 17

Kempton, William O. May 2006. Interview by G. Williams.
State v. LaMar. 95 Ohio St. 3d 181, 2002-Ohio-2128.
State v. Robb. 2000. 88 Ohio St. 3d 59.
State v. Sanders. 2001. 92 Ohio St. 3d 245.
State v. Skatzes. 104 Ohio St. 3d 195, 2004-Ohio-6391.
State v. Were. 94 Ohio St. 3d 173, 2002-Ohio-481, 761 N.E. 2d 591.

Chapter 18

Wilkinson, R. April 1993. Hostage situation ends in Ohio. Association of State Correctional Administrators newsletter.
———. May 1994. Corrections a year after Lucasville. *Portsmouth Daily Times.* Portsmouth, OH.
———. August 1994. Lucasville: The aftermath. *Corrections Today.* Landham, MD.
———. 1997. After the storm: Anatomy of a riot's aftermath. *Corrections Management Review.* Landham, MD.

Chapter 19

Adams, G. and D. Balfour. 2004. *Unmasking administrative evil* (Revised edition). New York: Sharpe.
Bucholz, G. and T. Roth. 1987. *Creating the high-performance team.* Vernon Hills: Wiley.
Dobel, J.P. 1998. *Public integrity.* Baltimore: Johns Hopkins University.
Dunham, G. 1991. *History of prisons.* Atlas Safety & Security Design, Inc.
Inmate classification and correctional programming. Retrieved

March 13, 2005, from http://faculty.ncwc.edu/toconnor/294/ 294lect08.htm.

Morgan, G. 1998. *Images of organization: The executive edition.* Thousand Oaks: Sage.

National Institute of Justice (NIJ). 1996. *TB in correctional facilities.*

Useem, B. and P. Kimball. 1991. *States of siege: U.S. prison riots 1971-1986.* New York: Oxford University.

Williams, G. 2003. *Siege in Lucasville.* Bloomington, IN: AuthorHouse.

About the Author

Gary Williams is a training officer at the Warren Correctional Institution for the Ohio Department of Rehabilitation and Correction in Lebanon, Ohio. He began his corrections career in 1985 at the Marion Correctional Institution as a licensed practical nurse. He was promoted and transferred to the Corrections Training Academy (CTA) in Orient, Ohio, in 1995, where he served as a training officer until 2002. There, he developed the mid-level leadership program that received recognition in the American Correctional Association publication *Best Practices.*

A professional member of the American Correctional Association, Williams is a paralegal and obtained his Bachelor of Science degree in human resource management and leadership from Franklin University in Columbus with honors.

He is married with six children and previously served as a member of the adjunct faculty of Marion Technical College in the areas of criminal justice and business. Holding a master's degree in public administration from the University of Dayton, he is a frequent lecturer at numerous colleges and universities and is currently a member of the faculty at Sinclair Community College in Dayton, Ohio.

Printed in the United States
59804LVS00003B/1-51

Wheat germ
Walnuts

Canned lentils